D1243025

FORENSIC EPIDEMIOLOGY

INTEGRATING PUBLIC HEALTH AND LAW ENFORCEMENT

Sana Loue, JD, PhD, MPH, MSSA

Professor and Director
Center for Minority Public Health
Case Western Reserve University School of Medicine
Cleveland, Ohio

JONES AND BARTLETT PUBLISHERS
Sudbury, Massachusetts
BOSTON   TORONTO   LONDON   SINGAPORE

World Headquarters

Jones and Bartlett Publishers
40 Tall Pine Drive
Sudbury, MA 01776
978-443-5000
info@jbpub.com
www.jbpub.com

Jones and Bartlett Publishers
Canada
6339 Ormindale Way
Mississauga, Ontario L5V 1J2
Canada

Jones and Bartlett Publishers
International
Barb House, Barb Mews
London W6 7PA
United Kingdom

Jones and Bartlett's books and products are available through most bookstores and online booksellers. To contact Jones and Bartlett Publishers directly, call 800-832-0034, fax 978-443-8000, or visit our website www.jbpub.com.

Substantial discounts on bulk quantities of Jones and Bartlett's publications are available to corporations, professional associations, and other qualified organizations. For details and specific discount information, contact the special sales department at Jones and Bartlett via the above contact information or send an email to specialsales@jbpub.com.

This publication is designed to provide accurate and authoritative information in regard to the Subject Matter covered. It is sold with the understanding that the publisher is not engaged in rendering legal, accounting, or other professional service. If legal advice or other expert assistance is required, the service of a competent professional person should be sought.

Production Credits
Publisher: Michael Brown
Production Director: Amy Rose
Acquisitions Editor: Katey Birtcher
Editorial Assistant: Catie Heverling
Senior Production Editor: Tracey Chapman
Associate Production Editor: Kate Stein
Marketing Manager: Sophie Fleck
Manufacturing and Inventory Control Supervisor: Amy Bacus
Composition: Achorn International
Photo Research Manager and Photographer: Kimberly Potvin
Cover Design: Scott Moden
Cover Image: © Loren Rodgers/ShutterStock, Inc.
Printing and Binding: Malloy, Inc.
Cover Printing: Malloy, Inc.

Library of Congress Cataloging-in-Publication Data
Loue, Sana.
  Forensic epidemiology : integrating public health and law enforcement / Sana Loue.
    p. ; cm.
  Includes bibliographical references and index.
  ISBN-13: 978-0-7637-3849-5 (casebound)
  ISBN-10: 0-7637-3849-2 (casebound)
  1. Forensic epidemiology. I. Title.
  [DNLM: 1. Epidemiology—legislation & jurisprudence—United States. 2. Forensic Medicine—legislation & jurisprudence—United States. 3. Law Enforcement—United States. 4. Public Health—legislation & jurisprudence—United States. WA 33 AA1 L886f 2010]
  RA1165.L683 2010
  614'.1—dc22

                                                                              2008041501

6048
Printed in the United States of America
13 12 11 10 09   10 9 8 7 6 5 4 3 2 1

Contents

Acknowledgments

The author gratefully acknowledges Richard Goodman, MD, JD, MPH, for sharing his perspectives on forensic epidemiology, some of which are reflected in the chapter "Epidemiology and the Law," authored by Richard A. Goodman, Sana Loue, and Frederic E. Shaw, in *Applied Epidemiology: Theory to Practice* (Ross C. Brownson & Diana B. Petitti, Eds., Oxford 2nd ed., 2006). Gary Edmunds also deserves acknowledgment and thanks for his research assistance.

About the Author

Dr. Sana Loue is a professor in the Department of Epidemiology and Biostatistics, and the director of the Center for Minority Public Health of the School of Medicine of Case Western Reserve University, Cleveland, Ohio. She has secondary appointments in the Departments of Bioethics, Psychiatry, and Global Health. Dr. Loue holds graduate degrees in law (JD), epidemiology (PhD), medical anthropology (PhD), public health (MPH), social work (MSSA), and secondary education (MA) and is an ordained interfaith minister. In addition to her research related to forensic epidemiology, Dr. Loue's research focuses on HIV risk and prevention, and family violence in marginalized communities such as non-English speakers, immigrants, sexual and ethnic/racial minorities, and persons with severe mental illness; as well as ethical issues in the conduct of research with vulnerable persons. She has authored over 70 peer-reviewed articles and 58 book chapters, and she has authored and/or edited 27 books.

Events on local, national, and international levels have accentuated the need for joint investigation and collaboration between public health and law enforcement functions and their reliance on forensic epidemiology. As an example, past investigations have focused on risk factors for family violence and partner and child homicide, deaths among residents of nursing homes and other healthcare facilities, and the intentional infection of individuals with HIV and/or other sexually transmitted infections by individuals who knew that they were infected with the disease in question. The anthrax attacks on high-profile individuals and seats of government further underscore the need for such collaborative efforts and the development of an appropriate knowledge base across the relevant disciplines.

This text focuses specifically on the integration of principles and methods of epidemiology with law enforcement functions in the administrative and criminal contexts. This integration is essential if we are to enhance our ability to address critical events such as those previously indicated. The text expands the scope of coverage of two previously published texts by this author that also focus on forensic epidemiology: *Forensic Epidemiology* (SIU Press), which focuses primarily on concepts of causation in the context of civil law, and *Case Studies in Forensic Epidemiology* (Kluwer Academic/Plenum Publishing), which both expands upon the concepts in *Forensic Epidemiology* and addresses the use of epidemiology in the context of regulatory and legislative activities, in addition to civil litigation.

The first portion of *Forensic Epidemiology: Integrating Public Health and Law Enforcement* provides the reader with an overview of public health, administrative, and criminal law and foundational concepts in the use of evidence in administrative and criminal proceedings. The second portion of the text is devoted to an examination of the intersecting issues through the use of case studies in the areas of communicable disease, mental health and substance use, partner violence, biological terrorism, and environmental concerns, such as environmental tobacco smoke and exposure to television violence. The final portion of the text concludes with a look toward the future and suggestions for the training of professionals.

The case studies presented here challenge us to examine various policy issues. These policy questions include how to reconcile the goals of science with those of the legal system; the extent to which society is willing to tolerate a lack of perfect synchronicity between the infliction of harm against others and the retribution to be exacted; and how to balance the public health against the personal freedoms and interests of individuals and corporations in developing and enforcing standards. These questions also prompt readers both to evaluate their own values as they relate to these larger questions and to contemplate how they, as scientists, legislators, policymakers, and individuals, will manifest those values in relating to the larger world.

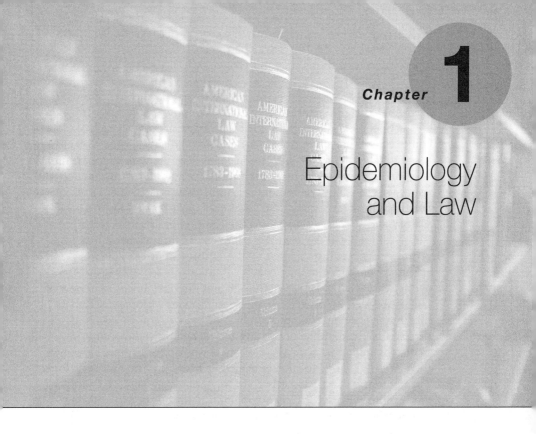

Chapter 1

Epidemiology and Law

Epidemiology in the Legal Context

Epidemiology is "the study of the distribution and determinants of health-related states or events in specified populations, and the application of this study to the control of health problems" (Last, 1988, p. 42). The word "forensic" has been defined as "(1) Relating to, used in, or appropriate for courts of law or for public discussion or augmentation . . . (3) Relating to the use of science or technology in the investigation and establishment of facts, or evidence in a court of law" (*American Heritage Dictionary*, 2000, p. 688).

These two concepts were first integrated into the term "forensic epidemiology" in 1999 to refer to the use of epidemiologic data in civil litigation and reliance on epidemiologists as expert witnesses in legal proceedings (Loue, 1999). Later, the term was used to refer to investigations of the source and the possible criminal nature of disease outbreaks (Alibek & Handelman, 1999; Altman & Kolata, 2002, quoting Dr. Julie Gerberding), in the formulation of legislative and regulatory provisions, as the basis for community organization and advocacy efforts, and as a process for the study of disease in the social context in which it is situated (Loue, 2002).

Previous texts have discussed forensic epidemiology in each of these contexts, with the exception of compliance and law enforcement. This text extends the inquiry into forensic epidemiology to focus specifically on its use in the context of law enforcement functions related to issues within the purview of public health. Law enforcement is viewed here broadly, to encompass the development and promulgation of regulatory and statutory provisions; the conduct of criminal and administrative investigations; and the conduct of administrative, civil, and criminal proceedings related to the enforcement of regulatory and statutory provisions.

The following section of this chapter provides a brief overview of our legal system to place the subsequent chapters in context. Chapters 2 through 4 provide an understanding of our systems of criminal, administrative, and public health law and related procedures and the relevance of epidemiology to each of these domains. Chapters 5 through 8 offer case studies to illustrate further how forensic epidemiology can be used in a variety of law enforcement contexts to enhance investigational efforts. Chapter 9 concludes with a discussion of the critical questions to be considered as we increasingly expand the scope of forensic epidemiology and its applications.

The US Legal System

THE US CONSTITUTION

The US Constitution has been called "the supreme law of the land." All state constitutions, statutes, administrative rules and regulations, and court decisions must be consistent with the provisions of the federal Constitution.

The federal Constitution defines the limits and functions of government and, additionally, indicates which powers fall within the purview of the federal government. These include, for example, the power to collect taxes, to regulate interstate commerce, and to declare war. Powers that are not specifically granted to the federal government are reserved to the states. This includes many functions related to public health, such as disease reporting, the regulation of housing conditions, and the enforcement of sanitation requirements, among others. State constitutions similarly define the powers, functions, and limitations of the state governments.

There are 27 Amendments to the Constitution; the first 10 are known as the Bill of Rights. It is beyond the scope of this chapter to review in detail all of the Amendments and provisions of the Constitution. A brief outline of these Amendments is provided in Table 1-1; those Amendments that are especially relevant to the later discussions in this volume have been bolded for ease of reference.

Table 1-1

Provisions of the Amendments to the Constitution

Amendment	Provisions
I	Freedom of religion; freedom of the press; freedom of assembly
II	Right to bear arms
III	Prohibition against quartering soldiers in homes
IV	**Right to be free from unreasonable searches and seizures; requirement that warrants be based on probable cause**
V	**Requirement of grand jury indictment for capital or "otherwise infamous crime"; prohibition against double jeopardy; right against self-incrimination; right to due process; requirement of just compensation for taking of private property**
VI	**Right to speedy and public trial in criminal prosecutions; right to be informed of charges, to confront witnesses, to present own witnesses, and to have the assistance of counsel**
VII	**Right to trial by jury**
VIII	Prohibition against excessive bail, excessive fines, and cruel and unusual punishment
IX	Provides that the enumeration of rights in the Constitution does not deny others
X	Powers not delegated to the federal government are reserved to the states
XI	Relates to judicial powers
XII	Relates to voting
XIII	Abolishes slavery
XIV	Relates to citizenship, eligibility to serve as member of Congress, public debt
XV	Prohibits denial or abridgement of rights based on race, color, or previous servitude
XVI	Allows Congress to impose and collect income tax
XVII	Relates to composition of Senate
XVIII	Relates to alcohol manufacture and sale; repealed by 21st Amendment
XIX	Prohibits denial or abridgement of rights on the basis of sex
XX	Relates to the terms of the president and vice president
XXI	Repeals the 18th Amendment
XXII	Prohibits election to office of president for more than two terms
XXIII	Relates to voting
XXIV	Prohibits imposition of poll tax
XXV	Provides that vice president to assume the duties of president if he or she is removed from office, dies, or resigns
XXVI	Provides that individuals 18 years of age may vote
XXVII	Relates to compensation for members of Congress

The federal Constitution also divides the government into three branches: the executive, the legislative, and the judicial. It has often been stated that the executive branch of government is responsible for the enforcement of laws that are promulgated by the legislature, while the judiciary is responsible for the interpretation of these laws and that a similar structure and similar function are created at the state level by state constitutions. However, this portrayal of the three branches of government, while accurate, greatly oversimplifies what actually occurs. A better understanding of the basic structure and function of each branch of government is critical to an understanding of how epidemiology relates to law enforcement within the context of our legal system.

THE STRUCTURE AND FUNCTIONS OF GOVERNMENT

The Executive Branch

The Constitution provides for the executive power to be vested in the President of the United States, who is to hold office for a 4-year term (Art. II). In the event that the president is removed from office due to death, resignation, or inability to perform his or her responsibilities, the vice president becomes responsible for the fulfillment of these responsibilities (Art. II).

The president serves as the commander-in-chief of the armed forces. He or she may enter into treaties with the advice and consent of the Senate and appoint ministers, consuls, and justices of the Supreme Court (Art. II). The Vice President of the United States serves as the president of the Senate. However, he or she may not vote unless there is a tie vote, in which case the vice president may vote to break the tie (Art. I).

The Legislative Branch

As indicated, the existence, structure, and function of the federal Congress derive from the federal Constitution. The Constitution provides that the legislature may provide for the common defense and general welfare, impose taxes, regulate the economy, create courts and military forces, declare war, and ratify treaties. According to the terms of the Constitution, it may not, however, tax state exports; pass bills of attainder, which is legislation that declares someone guilty of a crime without having had the benefit of a trial; or adopt ex post facto legislation, that is, legislation that modifies the legal standing of a past action or event (Art. I).

The federal legislature, known as Congress, consists of two chambers, the House of Representatives and the Senate (Art. I). The composition of the House of Representatives is dependent on the population of each state; the more populous a state is, the greater the number of representatives that it may elect to this House. Each such representative serves a 2-year term. The Senate consists of two senators elected from each state to serve a term of 6 years. In this way, there exists both a mechanism of direct representation through the House of Representatives and of indirect representation through the Senate (Art. 1).

Much of the work that is done in Congress initially passes through committees of the House and the Senate. Former President Woodrow Wilson observed:

> The House sits, not for serious discussion, but to sanction the conclusions of the Committees as rapidly as possible. It legislates in its committee-rooms; not by the determination of majorities, but by the resolution of specially-commissioned minorities; so it is not far from the truth to say that Congress in session is Congress on public exhibition, whilst Congress in its committee-rooms is Congress at work. (Wilson, 1885/1981, p. 69)

The number and focus of committees is determined by members of Congress; the number may vary across each chamber of Congress and over time. During the 103rd Congress, which spanned the time period 1993 to 1994, the House of Representatives had 22 standing committees, while the Senate had 17. During the 105th Congress (1997 to 1998), the House of Representatives had 19 committees compared to 17 in the Senate (Loomis, 1998).

Subcommittees of each committee may be limited in number. For example, during the 103rd Congress, committees were limited to six subcommittees. During the 105th Congress, the House of Representatives had 88 subcommittees, and the Senate had 68.

The committees and their subcommittees are characterized by specialized knowledge relevant to specific subjects, such as the Finance Committee and the Judiciary Committee. This specialized knowledge is to be shared with the relevant chamber at large to the benefit of the whole. Congresspersons try to obtain positions on particular committees based on the interests of the district that they represent, their own policy goals, and/or a desire for increased power within Congress (Loomis, 1998).

The laws that are promulgated by Congress, known as statutes, must be consistent with the US Constitution. Similar local governmental bodies may promulgate ordinances; these must be consistent with both the relevant state constitution and the federal Constitution. The legislative body may create administrative agencies through the promulgation of legislation; in doing so, the legislation must define the purpose of the agency and the scope of its authority. If granted the power to do so through legislation, these agencies may, in turn, promulgate rules and regulations, which serve to operationalize the purpose of the statute.

These rules and regulations and the processes by which they are for-mulated and enforced make up administrative law, which is the focus of Chapter 2. All rules and regulations must be consistent with the fed-eral Constitution and, in the case of a state rule or regulation, with the relevant state constitution.

The promulgation of legislation may come about in a variety of ways. First, a legislator in either the House of Representatives or the Senate may draft the legislation by him- or herself and seek to have it passed by both Houses of Congress. Or, a citizen or concerned group may draft the legislation and then approach their representative to have it introduced as proposed legislation (Sinclair, 1997). Alternatively, the ideas can be incorporated into legislation that is already being drafted by a legislative committee, or they can be offered as an amend-ment to someone else's proposed legislation. Congresspersons or their aides may consult experts outside of government on specific topics as they draft legislation and/or may rely on experts within governmen-tal agencies for information and guidance.

Regardless of what mechanism is used to draft the legislation, a member of Congress must introduce it into Congress. This can be ac-complished through either the House of Representatives or the Senate. The bill will be assigned a number, but it may also be known by a title or name (Smith, 1995). After the bill has been introduced into one of the chambers of Congress, the presiding officer of the chamber into which it was introduced will send it to the appropriate committee. In some cases, if the subject matter of the bill falls within the jurisdiction of several committees, it will be sent to multiple committees, a process known as multiple referral. The legislation is often sent to the sub-committee of a full committee. The committee and subcommittee may decide to conduct hearings on the bill, during which time they will receive testimony from interested parties and experts; such experts may include epidemiologists, depending upon the focus of the pro-posed legislation.

Committees may also mark up legislation, that is, consider legis-lation in detail and then amend it as they deem necessary. The com-mittee may report back on the bill to the full House of Representatives or Senate if a majority of the committee's members are present at the time. The committee is required to provide a report in reporting back the bill. These reports are frequently authored by a committee staff member and often include a minority viewpoint (Smith, 1995). Alternatively, committees may refuse to take any action on the proposed legislation (inaction). In this case, the proposed bill is said to have died in committee.

The general process of committee consideration, amendment, and mark up is followed by consideration of the proposed legislation on the floor of the chamber in which it is being considered. The procedure for the consideration of the legislation on the floor differs between the two chambers. In the House of Representatives, when major legislation is being considered, the sponsors of the legislation may request a special rule from the Committee on Rules. If granted, the special rule limits the general debate on the legislation to 1 hour. The order of voting on amendments to the legislation may be structured. Members may be permitted to vote on more than one version of the legislation.

There is no Rules Committee in the Senate. The scheduling of legislation that is to be heard on the floor is accomplished by making a motion to proceed to consider it. The motion to proceed can be debated, sometimes for so long that it is said that the legislation is "talked to death," a process known as a filibuster. A filibuster can be terminated through the process known as cloture, meaning that, if all of the senators are present, 60 of the 100 senators must support cloture to end the filibuster.

The final version of the bill as it is approved by one chamber of Congress is known as an engrossed bill (Smith, 1995). The bill, however, must be approved by both chambers of Congress before it can be sent to the President for executive action. To accomplish this, the second chamber may pass the legislation in the same form as it was passed in the chamber in which it was first considered. Alternatively, the two chambers may exchange amendments on the bill until they reach a version on which they can agree. Yet another approach consists of sending the proposed legislation to a conference committee that consists of representatives from both chambers of Congress, who have been appointed by committee leaders to attempt to resolve the differences that exist between the two chambers with respect to the proposed legislation.

The final version of the bill that has been approved by both chambers is known as an enrolled bill. This bill is printed on parchment and is certified by either the Clerk of the House or the Secretary of the Senate, depending on which chamber passed it first. It is then signed by the speakers of the House and the president pro tempore of the Senate, with space reserved for the President's signature (Smith, 1995).

Legislation relevant to agencies may be for authorization or appropriations. Authorizing legislation relates to an agency's organization, purpose, and ability to make rules, while appropriations legislations provides the funding necessary for the operation of the agency.

Lobbyists and special interest groups may also play a significant role in the legislative process by convincing a member of Congress to put a specific issue on the agenda or keep an issue off of the agenda. A lobbyist is "someone who is paid to communicate with Congress on behalf of others" (Smith, 1995, p. 326). Special interest groups may use one or more strategies in attempting to influence legislation, including testifying at hearings, contacting government officials directly, engaging in informal contacts with government officials, presenting research findings or technical information, sending letters to organization members to inform them about activities, entering into coalitions with other organizations, attempting to influence the implementation of policy, interacting with media representatives, consulting with government officials to plan legislative strategy, assisting with the drafting of legislation, participating in letter writing campaigns, organizing grassroots lobbying efforts, and prevailing upon local constituents to contact the local offices of their representatives (Schlozman & Tierney, 1986).

If Congress is still in session when the legislation is approved by both chambers of Congress and sent to the President, the President may sign the bill into law, veto the bill and send it back to Congress with a statement detailing his or her objections to the provisions of the legislation, or do nothing. A presidential veto can be overridden by a vote of two-thirds of both chambers. If the President chooses to do nothing, the bill will become law in 10 days (Smith, 1995).

If Congress is scheduled to adjourn within 10 days, the President has the same possible courses of action open to him or her. However, because Congress will not be in session and cannot override a veto, the bill will die if the President vetoes it or does nothing. The veto of a bill by doing nothing when the Congress is scheduled to adjourn within 10 days is known as a pocket veto. Not surprisingly, in view of this extensive process, relatively few bills—approximately 10%—ever become law, and most actually never make it out of committee to reach this point (Loomis, 1998).

There are mechanisms through which the President can exert influence on legislation in addition to the use of the veto. One of the most significant powers is the ability to set the national policy agenda through the proposed annual budget (Loomis, 1998). The President's agenda requires that Congress address the enumerated issues, and the President can engage in negotiations with key congresspersons. However, the ability of the president to accomplish his or her agenda may be limited by the partisan balance existing in Congress, the President's standing with the US public, and the President's political capital.

The Court System

Federal Courts

Although the federal Constitution provides for a judicial system, it does not specify the structure of that system other than to mandate the existence of a Supreme Court. The Constitution states, "The judicial Power of the United States, shall be vested in one Supreme Court, and in such inferior Courts as the Congress may from time to time ordain and establish" (Art. III). It was not until 1789 with the Judiciary Act that Congress created a system of lower federal courts.

The federal judicial system created by the Judiciary Act of 1789 established three levels of courts: the district courts, the courts of appeal, and the Supreme Court. The district courts hear criminal cases that arise under federal statutes and civil actions that arise under federal statutes or the US Constitution. The district courts will also entertain what are known as diversity actions, which involve a controversy between citizens of different states that involves a specified minimum sum. (The requisite amount in controversy has varied over time.)

Federal district courts have exclusive jurisdiction with regard to certain matters; these issues cannot be tried in state courts. In other matters, the federal courts may share jurisdiction with the state courts (concurrent jurisdiction).

Circuit courts of appeal hear appeals from the decisions of the federal district courts located within the relevant circuit. Appeals from the circuit courts of appeal to the US Supreme Court are not automatic. Rather, the party wishing to have the case heard by the Supreme Court must petition the Court to hear the case by filing a writ of certiorari.

The federal court system also includes various specialized courts whose jurisdiction is limited to specified matters, such as bankruptcy and tax. There are also administrative courts with limited jurisdiction, such as the Executive Office for Immigration Review and the National Labor Relations Board.

The scope of the US Supreme Court's authority was not established until 1803, with the decision in the case of *Marbury v. Madison* (1803). This case involved a refusal by Secretary of State Madison to deliver to two individuals their commissions as justices of the peace in the District of Columbia. Their appointments had been advised and consented by the US Senate as required by the Constitution, and the commissions had been signed by the past president. The court held that the appointment is complete and irrevocable after the commission is signed by the President and transmitted to the Secretary of State to be sealed and recorded. As a result of this decision, it became clear that it is the responsibility of the judiciary to say what the law is, that any law that conflicts with the Constitution is void, and that the courts and all other governmental branches and entities are bound by the provisions of the Constitution.

Judicial decisions are subordinate to statutes if the statutes are not in conflict with the relevant provisions of the applicable federal or state constitutions or with other statutes. Under our common law system of law, courts are guided in their decisions by the precedential decisions relating to similar issues that are entered by higher level courts within the same jurisdiction and by the court of last resort. For example, precedential decisions rendered by a federal circuit court of appeals are binding on federal district courts within that jurisdiction but not those district courts that are situated in a different circuit. All courts are bound by the decisions of the US Supreme Court. In essence, this is a body of law that is judicially made apart from statutory law. Every state has its own body of common law, and a federal body of common law exists as well. The judiciary is also charged with the interpretation of statutes and ordinances. The extent of courts' authority in this regard is discussed in greater detail in the chapters that follow.

State Courts

Although the structure of the state court system varies by state, there are generally three principal levels: courts of general jurisdiction that hear misdemeanor cases and civil cases involving a sum that is less than a specified maximum; an intermediate-level appellate court that hears appeals from these lower courts in addition to more serious criminal matters and civil cases involving sums above a threshold amount; and a state supreme court that hears appeals from the intermediate-level appellate courts. States also have specialized courts, which may include probate court, housing court, juvenile court, family court, mental health court, drug court, traffic court, and others.

At both the state and federal levels, depending upon the specific case, judges and juries may hear and weigh the opinions of expert witnesses in rendering a decision. Reliance on epidemiologists is becoming increasingly common, as the following chapters illustrate.

References

1. Alibek, K., & Handelman, S. (1999). *Biohazard*. New York: Random House.
2. Altman, L. K., & Kolata, G. (2002, January 6). A nation challenged: Anthrax—Anthrax missteps offer guide to fight next bioterror battle. *The New York Times*, p. A1.
3. *American heritage dictionary of the English language* (2nd ed.). (2000). Boston: Houghton Mifflin.
4. Last, J. M. (1988). *A dictionary of epidemiology* (2nd ed.). New York: Oxford University Press.
5. Loomis, B. A. (1998). *The contemporary Congress* (2nd ed.). New York: St. Martin's Press.
6. Loue, S. (1999). *Forensic epidemiology: A comprehensive guide for legal and epidemiology professionals*. Carbondale, IL: Southern Illinois University Press.
7. Loue, S. (2002). *Case studies in forensic epidemiology*. New York: Kluwer Academic/ Plenum Publishers.
8. Marbury v. Madison, 5 U.S. 137 (1803).
9. Schlozman, K. L., & Tierney, J. T. (1986). *Organized interest and American democracy*. New York: HarperCollins Publishers.
10. Sinclair, B. (1997). *Unorthodox lawmaking: New legislative processes in the U.S. Congress*. Washington, DC: Congressional Quarterly.
11. Smith, S. S. (1995). *The American Congress*. Boston: Houghton Mifflin Company.
12. Wilson, W. (1981). *Congressional government*. Baltimore: Johns Hopkins University Press. (Original work published 1885)

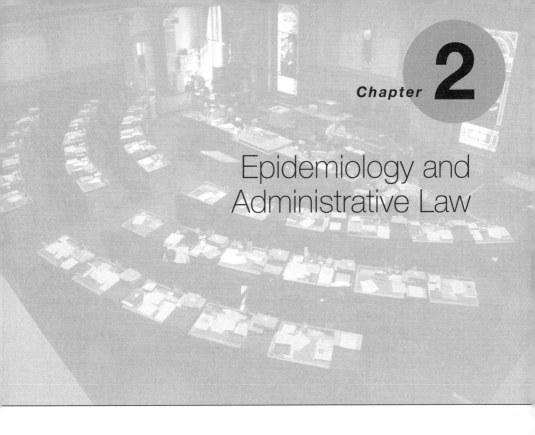

Chapter 2

Epidemiology and Administrative Law

L aw enforcement functions that necessitate the expertise of epidemiologists often derive from the activities of administrative agencies. Accordingly, it is important to have an understanding of the formation and responsibilities of such agencies and of the procedures that govern their performance.

An administrative agency is a governmental authority that affects the rights of private parties through either adjudication or rulemaking (Davis, 1972; Gellhorn, Byse, & Straus, 1979). This does not include courts or legislatures, but it does include commissions and boards that have been established as independent agencies.

There are several types of agencies. One type is an executive department, such as the United States Department of Health and Human Services, or a major division of an executive department, such as the United States Public Health Service. The head of an executive department is generally appointed by the executive branch, such as the President if it is a federal-level agency, or the governor if it is a state-level agency. A second type of administrative agency is one that is created to be independent of the executive branch of government. This type of agency is exemplified by the United States Food and Drug Administration.

Administrative agencies are responsible for the creation of administrative law through the promulgation of regulations, rules, order, procedures, and policies. This process occurs at various levels of government, including the municipal, state, and federal levels. Agencies themselves are created through legislative action; agency power and the scope of that power are defined in the enacting legislation. The legislation typically also gives the agency authority to make rules and regulations to effectuate its mandate.

Although created by the legislature and designed to implement the policies enunciated by the legislature, agencies are considered to be part of the executive branch of government. At the federal level, agencies generally operate more independently than at the local and state levels. However, even at the federal level, the legislature may attempt to influence agency action through informal means, such as informal contacts and deciding who should be appointed to the agencies, and through more formal channels, by controlling the level of agency funding and restricting or overruling agency actions through the promulgation of legislation.

Agency Rulemaking

THE PROCESS OF RULEMAKING

A rule is defined by the Administrative Procedure Act (APA) as "the whole or part of an agency statement of general or particular applicability and future effect designed to implement, interpret, or prescribe law or policy" (Administrative Procedure Act, 5 U.S.C.S. § 551). Accordingly, the rule (1) applies to situations that will occur in the future and (2) applies to a class of persons or entities. As indicated, rules can be formulated to implement particular statutory provisions, to interpret terms or provisions, or to provide for the effectuation of a goal contained in the statute. Regardless of the function of a specific rule, it must be consistent with both the statute that authorizes the rulemaking and with the Constitution (Administrative Procedure Act, 5 U.S.C.S. § 706(2), 2008).

Formal Rulemaking

Agencies may engage in both formal and informal rulemaking. Formal rulemaking to adopt a rule requires that a hearing be conducted on the record; the new rule results from the decision that the agency makes in the context of the particular case before it in this proceeding. These proceedings resemble adjudicatory proceedings. If a formal hearing is required, it will be indicated in the governing statute.

Frequently, one of the heads of an agency or an administrative law judge presides at the hearing (Administrative Procedure Act, 5 U.S.C.S. § 556). At the hearing, the parties involved are entitled to present evidence, to conduct cross-examination, and to present rebuttal evidence. The record of the hearing becomes the basis for rulemaking. Unlike informal rulemaking, discussed below, off-the-record communications with interested parties are not permitted.

Informal Rulemaking

At the federal level, informal rulemaking is governed by the Administrative Procedure Act. There is often a corollary to this Act at the state level. However, these statutory provisions do not apply unless the focus of the debate or discussion is a "rule" within the meaning of the APA. The term "rule" is synonymous with the term "regulation."

There are several advantages to making policy by rule as compared to making policy through adjudication. Decisions made through rulemaking are often clearer and more definitive than those made through the adjudication process. Rulemaking permits the agency to consider multiple perspectives through the notice and comment procedure, described later, and to impose comprehensive decisions on all interested parties at the same time. The process of rulemaking provides interested parties with advance knowledge of changes that are being considered and will occur. Finally, the rulemaking procedure is often more efficient than the adjudication procedure.

The APA provides for a notice and comment procedure so that interested parties will have an opportunity to review and comment on the various aspects of a rule before it is finalized, adopted, and implemented by the agency. The critical elements of the notice and comment procedure include (1) a statement of the time, place, and nature of the public rulemaking proceedings; (2) a reference to the legal authority under which the rule is being proposed; and (3) the terms or content of the proposed rule or a description of the subjects or issues that will be addressed. The agency must also publish or make available any critical data so that individuals who wish to review and comment on the rule may do so in a meaningful way.

The agency must consider the comments that it receives through the notice and comment procedure prior to the formulation and publication of the final rule. In issuing the subsequent rule, the agency must respond to the public comments that it received, indicate which of the suggestions were and were not followed and the reasons for such decisions, and explain the basis for adopting the rule that it does. A minimum of 30 days must elapse between the publication of the final rule and the date on which it is to become effective. The statutory section establishing these provisions is as follows:

(a) This section applies, according to the provisions thereof, except to the extent that there is involved—

(1) a military or foreign affairs function of the United States; or
(2) a matter relating to agency management or personnel or to public property, loans, grants, benefits, or contracts.

(b) General notice of proposed rule making shall be published in the Federal register, unless persons subject thereto are named and either personally served or otherwise have actual notice thereof in accordance with law. The notice shall include—

(1) a statement of the time, place, and nature of public rule making proceedings;
(2) reference to the legal authority under which the rule is proposed; and
(3) either the terms or substance of the proposed rule or a description of the subjects and issues involved.

Except when notice or hearing is required by statute, this section does not apply—

(a) to interpretative rules, general statements of policy, or rules of agency organization, procedure, or practice; or

(b) when the agency for good cause finds (and incorporates the finding and a brief statement of reasons therefore in the rules issued) that notice and public procedure thereon are impracticable, unnecessary, or contrary to the public interest.

(c) After notice required by this section, the agency shall give interested persons an opportunity to participate in the rule making through the submission of written data, views, or arguments with or without opportunity for oral presentation. After consideration of the relevant material presented, the agency shall incorporate in the rules adopted a concise general statement of their basis and purpose. When rules are required to be made on the record after opportunity for an agency hearing, sections 556 and 557 of this title shall apply instead of this subsection.

(d) The required publication or service of a substantive rule shall be made not less than 30 days before its effective date, except—

(1) a substantive rule which grants or recognizes an exemption or relieves a restriction;
(2) interpretative rules and statements of policy;

(3) as otherwise provided by the agency for good cause found and published with the rule.

(e) Each agency shall give an interested person the right to petition for the issuance, amendment, or repeal of a rule. (5 U.S.C.S. § 552)

The comments that the agency receives in response to a proposed rule are generally part of the public file. Off-the-record contacts, known as ex parte contacts, are permitted during the rulemaking process. Members of the legislative and/or executive branches may attempt to influence the rulemakers through ex parte communications. While there is no prohibition on such contacts, some agencies require that all written and oral ex parte communications be disclosed during the rulemaking process. A requirement that all such communications be disclosed helps to ensure to interested parties that the process will be fair and that they will have a meaningful opportunity to participate.

It is considered to be appropriate that the President of the United States meet with agency representatives regarding a specific issue during the rulemaking process because the President is constitutionally responsible for all executive decisions (*Sierra Club v. Costle*, 1981). Congressional contacts with agencies during rulemaking proceedings is also permitted.

Some agencies have utilized a procedure known as negotiated rulemaking, whereby individuals representing all affected interests are called together to reach a consensus on the relevant issues (Negotiated Rulemaking Act, 5 U.S.C.S. §§ 561–570). The rule that results from this consensus serves as the subject of the notice and comment procedure. Negotiated rulemaking is most successful in situations in which there are a limited number of identifiable interests and there are identifiable individuals to represent those interests. Agencies wishing to utilize this procedure must publish in the *Federal Register* a notice of the procedure, a list of the proposed committee members, the proposed agenda, and a timetable.

The *Code of Federal Regulations* (CFR) was developed in 1938 to provide a single authoritative compilation of the rules that have been promulgated by federal agencies. The CFR is organized by title, as is the title of the United States Code, which contains the statutes governing the agency that promulgated those rules.

The republication of specific titles of the CFR occurs only once every 1 or 2 years. During these time intervals, however, Congress may adopt legislation that requires that an agency promulgate regulations and the agency may adopt new rules to implement or interpret already-existing legislation. These new rules are published in the *Federal Register*, which serves as an interim resource until their incorporation into the republished CFR.

TYPES OF RULES

Rules are often classified by the function that they serve. "Legislative" or "substantive" rules are formulated through the notice and comment procedure by an agency pursuant to a congressional mandate or authorization. A legislative rule serves to effectuate a change in existing law and policy and has a legal effect in later agency and judicial proceedings. A rule that amends a legislative rule will be considered to be a legislative rule, not an interpretive rule (see *National Family Planning and Reproductive Health Association, Inc. v. Sullivan*, 1992).

Procedural rules are those that describe the processes that the agency utilizes. Rules of organization explain how the agency is organized and how authority is distributed within the agency.

Interpretive rules are utilized to explain how an agency is interpreting its legal obligations pursuant to specific legislative provisions. Unlike legislative rules, they do not change existing legal obligations, rights, or duties. These rules are considered to be advisory and, although they are often published in the *Federal Register*, they are not subject to the notice and comment procedure. Unlike other rules that are generally prospective in nature, interpretive rules may have retroactive application if the agency was authorized by Congress to promulgate rules having a retroactive effect.

Agencies may also issue general statements of policy that do not modify existing legal rules. The agency cannot rely on or apply these general statements of policy as law. As an example, the United States Food and Drug Administration (FDA) issued a rule that specified the action level that would serve as the basis for the FDA to initiate an action against a particular product as one that was adulterated (*Community Nutrition Institute v. Young*, 1987). The agency argued that this statement constituted a general statement of policy that was not subject to the notice and comment procedure because it was not a binding rule. The Court of Appeals held against the agency position, finding that the agency had actually treated the statement as binding when it required that food producers apply for an exception from the action level if they intended to ship food that contained levels of a toxin higher than the established action level.

Agencies may promulgate rules that provide for civil and/or criminal sanctions for their violation. However, they do not have the power to prosecute or imprison for their violation.

EXCEPTIONS TO RULEMAKING REQUIREMENTS

Various exceptions exist to the notice and comment requirement. These include categorical exceptions, procedure exceptions, good cause exceptions, interpretive rules, and policy statements. Categorical exceptions include military and foreign affairs and matters relating to personnel or to public property. Procedure exceptions relate to rules regarding agency organization, procedure, and practice. Such rules are also exempt from the requirement of a 30-day period between the publication of the final notice and the effective date of the rule.

Agencies are also excused from complying with the notice and comment procedure "when the agency for good cause finds [and incorporates the finding and a brief statement of the reasons therefore in the rules issued] that notice and public procedure thereon are impracticable, unnecessary, or contrary to the public interest" (Administrative Procedure Act , 5 U.S.C.S. § 553(b)(B)). A regulation will be considered to be unnecessary if it will have only a trivial impact or relieve regulated parties of a regulatory burden. The notice and comment procedure will be considered to be impracticable or contrary to the public interest in situations in which immediate action is required or in which the delay engendered by the notice and comment procedure would either result in harm to the public safety or undermine the legislative intent (*Union of Concerned Scientists v. Nuclear Regulatory Commission*, 1983).

As previously noted, interpretive rules are not subject to the notice and comment procedure. It may be difficult, however, to determine whether a particular rule is interpretive in nature or whether it is legislative. In making this determination, the courts will consider the intention of the agency in making the rule. A rule will be considered to be legislative if the agency had the power to make legislative rules and intended to use it. The rule will be considered to be interpretive if the agency either did not possess the power to make legislative rules or if the agency had such power but did not intend to use it. The agency's initial characterization of its rule will often be accorded great weight by the court in making this determination. However, the court may find a rule to be legislative in nature notwithstanding the agency's characterization of the rule as interpretive if the rule mandates specified behavior (*Chamber of Commerce v. OSHA*, 1980).

Neither the notice and comment nor the delayed effective date provision apply to agency policy statements. These are tentative statements that explain how an agency intends to perform a discretionary function, such as an investigation or adjudication. In contrast, a definitive pronouncement will be considered to be a legislative rule and will be subject to the notice and comment requirement.

FORMULATING STANDARDS

The statutes that authorize agencies to formulate rules frequently enumerate the nature of the concerns that the agency can consider in formulating the rules. For example, the agency may be mandated to focus its attention on health issues and/or the economic ramifications of its actions. Agencies that are delegated rulemaking authority under several statutes may be required to set rules according to the differing standards contained in the various statutes. As an example, the Occupational Safety and Health Act mandates that the Occupational Safety and Health Administration regulate occupational exposures to toxic substances and harmful physical agents to the extent "reasonable, necessary and appropriate" (Occupational Safety and Health Act, 29 U.S.C. § 652). The National Environmental Policy Act requires that an environmental impact statement be prepared if a major federal action over which the agency has control has significant environmental effects (*Department of Transportation v. Public Citizen*, 2004; 42 U.S.C.S. § 4332(c)).

The type of information that the agency can utilize as the basis for its rules may also be specified by statute. The Occupational Safety and Health Act provides for the nature of information that is to be utilized by the Occupational Safety and Health Administration in setting standards to be used in regulating exposures to toxic or other harmful materials:

> [The agency must] set the standard which most adequately assures, to the extent feasible, on the basis of the best available evidence, that no employee will suffer material impairment of health or functional capacity even if such employee has regular exposure to the hazard dealt with by such standard for the period of his working life. Development of standards under this subsection shall be based upon research, demonstrations, experiments, and such other information as may be appropriate. In addition to the attainment of the highest degree of health and safety protection for the employee, other considerations shall be the latest available scientific data in the field, the feasibility of the standards, and experience gained under this and other health and safety laws. Whenever practicable, the standard promulgated shall be expressed in terms of objective criteria and of the performance desired. (Occupational Safety and Health Act, 29 U.S.C.S. § 655(b)(5), 2008)

AGENCY ACTION IN THE FACE OF UNCERTAINTY

The authority to regulate a particular substance may be designated to multiple agencies simultaneously, although each agency may exercise its authority in a different context. Consider, for example, how vinyl chloride was regulated by each of the following agencies:

- Occupational Health and Safety Administration: Exposure to vinyl chloride in factories, pursuant to the Occupational Health and Safety Act of 1970

- Environmental Protection Agency: Vinyl chloride emissions from factories, under the Clean Air Act
- Consumer Product Safety Commission: Vinyl chloride in household aerosols under the Federal Hazardous Substances Act
- United States Food and Drug Administration: Cosmetic aerosols containing vinyl chloride pursuant to the Food, Drug, and Cosmetic Act; drug aerosols pursuant to the New Drug Amendments of 1962 (Doniger, 1978)

Agency Adjudications

An agency may initiate a complaint against a party that is believed to be in violation of the law. A hearing will be held to decide the facts of the matter that are in dispute, to determine the application of policy in the particular situation in question, and to seek compliance with specific regulations.

Depending upon the nature of the issues, the hearing may be required prior to government action, rather than following the action (*Tennessee Valley Authority v. Whitman*, 2003). A hearing prior to agency action is more likely to be required if there will be a deprivation of liberty or property as the result of the agency action. (See the discussion of the destruction of citrus trees due to a virus in Chapter 4 for an example of such a situation.) Exceptions to this basic premise are permitted in situations necessitating emergency action to protect the public's health and safety, such as the destruction of rotting food being held in cold storage (*North American Cold Storage Co. v. Chicago*, 1908). Advance notice of the issues and the time and place of the hearing must be provided. The individuals or company that is the focus of the agency adjudication generally has the right to counsel, albeit at their own expense, and the right to confront the evidence that will be introduced against them, including the right to cross-examine adverse witnesses.

A neutral hearing officer or decision maker will preside over the matter (Gellhorn, 1972). The decision of the hearing officer can be based on findings from physical inspections or tests, as long as they were conducted fairly. The decision maker may also rely on the opinions of expert witnesses that have been offered into evidence.

Although the decision resulting from the adjudication is applicable directly only to the party involved in the hearing, the ruling may have implications for other agencies involved in similar activities or that confront similar issues.

Oversight of Agency Activities and Administrative Action

MONITORING AND REVIEWING AGENCY ACTIVITIES

There are several mechanisms by which the federal government can monitor agency activities. (There are analogous mechanisms at the state level.) Standing committees of the House of Representatives and the Senate review agency activities in specified areas; they may propose legislation to address needed modifications. Other committees hold responsibility for the investigation of the agencies. As an example, Congress held numerous hearings to investigate the actions of the United States Food and Drug Administration with respect to its lack of oversight of silicone breast implants. The Administrative Conference of the United States may recommend legislative modifications to Congress based on its analysis of federal administrative agencies and administrative law. Some federal agencies utilize ombudsmen to investigate complaints from members of the public about administrative actions and to recommend appropriate corrections. Legislators may also seek to have input into administrative matters that impact on their constituents.

Despite Congress's ability to monitor agency activities, its control over the agencies is limited. As an example, Congress cannot remove officials who are engaged in executive functions regardless of its level of displeasure with their actions. Additionally, Congress cannot appoint the members of the agency who are engaged in rulemaking.

The executive branch also maintains some degree of control over agencies through the President's ability to appoint the heads of the agencies. However, these appointments remain subject to the approval of the Senate. As an example, the President is empowered to appoint the Secretary of the Department of Health and Human Services, but that appointment is subject to Senate approval. The President also holds authority to create, abolish, and reorganize agencies within the executive branch of government.

Courts are called upon to review agency action through the initiation of lawsuits and appeals of parties from administrative adjudications. Courts will review the actions of the agency to determine whether the agency has exceeded its authority under the Constitution or the statute under which the agency derives its powers; whether it has interpreted the law correctly; whether it conducted a fair hearing; whether it avoided actions that are deemed to be arbitrary, capricious, or unreasonable; and whether the agency's determination was supported by evidence that is part of the record. Courts have required that agency action be consistent, be premised on clear criteria, and be in accordance with the agency's own rules. However, agencies retain discretion with respect to the choice of issues to focus on and whether to bring an enforcement action against a particular party (known as prosecutorial discretion).

MONITORING AND REVIEWING AGENCY RULEMAKING

Agency rulemaking is subject to controls that exist through the judicial, legislative, and executive functions of government. Courts are charged with the responsibility of reviewing agency rules to ensure that they are within the scope of authority that was granted to the agency through controlling legislation, that they are consistent with the Constitution, and that the agency has followed the mandated procedures in its promulgation of the rules. The executive branch of government may communicate with agency staff to have input into the rulemaking process and may also require that the agency adhere to specified procedures when contemplating specific types of actions.

Epidemiology and Agency Action

CHALLENGING AGENCY RULES

Challenges to an agency rule may be made on various grounds. An entity may claim that the agency failed to follow mandated procedure prior to finalizing and/or implementing the rule, that the agency failed to consider all of the information provided to it, that the rule is outside of the agency's scope of authority, that the rule is inconsistent with the governing statute and/or Constitution, and/or that the application of a particular rule to a specific party is improper. In considering such challenges, the court must review the complete record, which, depending on the focus of the challenge, may include the proposed rule, the notice of the proposed rulemaking, the public comments that were received, the transcripts of any public hearings that were held, and the agency's statement of the basis and purpose of the rule. The court generally considers only that information and those materials that the agency had prior to its decision regarding the rule (*Camp v. Pitts*, 1973). In reviewing agency action, the court must examine the procedural fairness, reasonableness, and good faith of the agency decision, but it cannot substitute its judgment for that of the agency. One court stated:

> [T]he court must consider whether the decision was based on a consideration of the relevant factors and whether there has been a clear error of judgement. . . . Although this inquiry into the facts is to be searching and careful, the ultimate standard of review is

> a narrow one. The court is not empowered to substitute its judgement for that of the agency. (*Citizens to Preserve Overton Park, Inc. v. Volpe*, 1971, p. 153)

Yet another court noted:

> The more technical the case, the more intensive must be the court's effort to understand the evidence. . . . The immersion in the evidence is designed solely to enable the court to determine whether the agency decision was rational and based on consideration of the relevant factors. . . . It is settled that we must affirm decisions with which we disagree so long as this test is met. . . . (*Ethyl Corp. v. EPA*, 1976, p. 36)

To help it understand technical evidence that is part of the record, the court may permit the introduction of expert testimony (*Bunker Hill Co. v. Environmental Protection Agency*, 1977).

INFLUENCING AGENCY RULEMAKING

Epidemiologic analysis of existing data may prove critical in an agency's decision to act in a particular situation and the direction or manner of such action. Consider the following example relating to the United States Food and Drug Administration and an outbreak of *Escherichia coli* O157:H7 infections.

The Epidemiology of Escherichia coli O157:H7

E. coli commonly resides in the intestinal tract of humans and of warm-blooded animals. Although it was long regarded as being essentially harmless, this notion was dispelled in 1971 following an outbreak of foodborne illness that was traced back to the presence of E. coli in Camembert and Brie cheeses that had been imported to the United States from France (Department of Health, Education, and Welfare, 1971). E. coli contamination has been found to originate from water, dust, air, food, kitchen utensils, rodents, flies, and food handlers; outbreaks have been traced to undercooked beef (Bell, et al., 1994), raw milk, lettuce, apple cider, and potatoes (Armstrong, Hollingsworth, & Morris, 1996).

E. coli flourishes best at a temperature of 98.6°F, but the temperature can range from 50°F to 104°F. The bacteria can survive in a pH that ranges from 4 to 8, although a neutral pH is most conducive to it.

Serotypes of E. coli that cause foodborne gastroenteritis are known as enteropathogenic; there are four major subgroups of enteropathogenic E. coli. Classical serogroups are associated with diarrhea in young children and infants. A second serogroup is associated with sporadic diarrhea and normal flora in the intestinal tract. Enterotoxigenic E. coli, which has a mean incubation period of 26 hours, may produce symptoms that include diarrhea, vomiting, dehydration, and shock. This serogroup is associated with traveler's diarrhea. Enteroinvasive strains, in contrast, have a mean incubation period of 11 hours, produce symptoms that include abdominal cramps, watery stools, fever, chills, and headache, and cause invasive infection of the gastrointestinal tract (Kornacki & Marth, 1982). Infection with E. coli O157:H7 results in approximately 250 deaths in the United States each year (Boyce, Swerdlow, & Griffin, 1995).

One of the more serious potential consequences of an infection with E. coli O157:H7 is the development of hemolytic uremic syndrome. It has been estimated that the pathogen causes between 20,000 and 40,000 cases of this syndrome in the United States each year (Boyce, et al., 1995). The syndrome, which occurs in approximately 6% of the individuals infected with E. coli O157:H7 (Griffin, 1995), is generally diagnosed within 2 to 14 days after the onset of diarrhea (Karmali, et al., 1985). The syndrome most frequently affects young children and the elderly (Griffin & Tauxe, 1991) and may lead to renal failure (Pickering, Obrig, & Stapleton, 1994).

In the United States, outbreaks of infection with E. coli O157:H7 occur more frequently in northern states than in southern states and more often during warmer months of the year, with a peak during the months of June through September (Ostroff, Kobayashi, & Lewis, 1989; Pai, et al., 1988). The largest outbreak in North America, which was traced to undercooked hamburger meat at a fast food restaurant, occurred in four western states and affected 700 people, of whom 4 died (Bell, et al., 1994; Griffin, 1995).

The 1997 Escherichia coli O157:H7 Outbreak

An outbreak of Escherichia coli O157:H7 in 1997 resulted in 70 cases of illness in California, Colorado, Washington, and British Columbia, leading to 25 hospitalizations and 14 cases of hemolytic uremic syndrome, including one death (Cody, et al., 1999). The initial epidemiologic investigation conducted by state, local, and Centers for Disease Control and Prevention (CDC) strongly suggested that the source of infection was unpasteurized commercial apple juice.

Later analysis revealed that isolates from the cases were indistinguishable from isolates found in the recalled apple juice. The contamination appeared to be specific to apple juice that had been produced on one specific date. Two of the three lots of apples used to produce that juice were found to have originated from an orchard frequented by deer that carried E. coli, and one lot consisted of decayed apples that had been waxed. It was found that the state-of-the-art procedures that had been used to produce the apple juice were inadequate to eliminate this risk.

The investigators believed that the public would be best protected by issuing a warning and recalling the particular brand of apple juice and, to this end, presented their findings to staff members of the Food and Drug Administration at an emergency session.

The Role of the US Food and Drug Administration

The United States Food and Drug Administration was the focus of investigator efforts to control the outbreak because of the responsibility and authority that this agency has for the development of standards and regulations relating to the production and distribution of legal foods and drugs. The basic framework for these functions derives from the Food, Drug, and Cosmetic Act of 1938. Later legislation increased the agency's authority to regulate food products; these include the Food Additives Amendment of 1958 and the Color Additive Amendments of 1960. The agency has explained its statutory authority, in relevant part, as follows:

> The law is intended to assure the consumer that foods are pure and wholesome, safe to eat, and produced under sanitary conditions. . . .
>
> The Federal Food, Drug, and Cosmetic Act prohibits distribution in the United States, or importation, of articles that are adulterated or misbranded. The term "adulterated" includes products that are defective, unsafe, filthy, or produced under unsanitary conditions. . . . "Misbranded" includes statements, designs, or pictures that are false or misleading, and failure to provide required information in labeling . . . (United States Food and Drug Administration, 1979, p. 1)

Currently, the agency has authority to regulate the majority of processed foods, including food additives. The statute defines "food" as "(1) articles used for food or drink for man or other animals; (2) chewing gum; and (3) articles used for components of any such article" (Food, Drug, and Cosmetic Act, 21 U.S.C.S. § 321(f)). The agency attempts to effectuate its purpose through the development of standards, rather than the investigation of practices:

> FDA's regulatory strategy is anticipatory rather than reactionary: preventive rather than corrective. FDA will never have the physical or financial resources to continuously police every segment of the industrial community. The Agency's strategy, therefore, is to assure that safety is built into the products it regulates. (United States Food and Drug Administration, 1977, p. 3)

The Impact of Epidemiology: Revised Regulations

As a result of the epidemiologic investigation into the outbreak, the FDA proposed two new regulations. The first of these, implemented on November 5, 1998, required that the label of unpasteurized fruit and vegetable juices bear the language: "Warning: This product has not been pasteurized and therefore may contain harmful bacteria that can cause serious illness in children, the elderly, and persons with weakened immune systems" (United States Food and Drug Administration, 1998a). The second regulation mandated utilization of a system that would aid in the identification of key production points during which contamination could occur and the implementation of specific monitoring procedures and interventions at these critical production points (United States Food and Drug Administration, 1998b).

INFLUENCING AGENCY ACTION

Health Effects of Agent Orange

In some situations, epidemiologic data may inform agency decision making and action outside of the context of rulemaking. This was the case with the findings of the Institute of Medicine Committee on Agent Orange.

Nearly 20 million gallons of military herbicides were sprayed over Vietnam and Laos during the period from 1961 through 1971. Approximately 11.2 million gallons of these herbicides consisted of Agent Orange, a mixture of equal parts of 2,4-dichlorophenoxyacetic acid (2,4-D) and 2,4,5-trichlorophenoxyacetic acid (2,4,5,-T) (Institute of Medicine, 1994; Stellman, Stellman, Christian, Weber, & Tomasallo, 2003). The military used this preparation in an effort to defoliate the dense jungle, which concealed enemy forces. In the process, however, an estimated 3 million American soldiers may have had contact with the preparation. The spraying was ceased in 1970 following the release of a scientific report that indicated a causal association between the preparation and birth defects in laboratory animals and the discovery that Agent Orange was contaminated with the toxin 2,3,7,8-tetrachlorodibenzo-p-dioxin (2,3,7,8,-TCDD), known as dioxin.

Subsequent epidemiologic investigations have confirmed the suspected association between exposure to TCDD and various disorders. Investigators who conducted a study of individuals in an 87 hectare region in Italy that was exposed to TCDD as the result of an industrial accident observed an increased risk of chronic ischemic heart disease, hypertensive disease, and chronic rheumatic disease among those most heavily exposed (Pesatori, et al., 1998). A study comparing the immunological status of Agent Orange-exposed Korean veterans from the Vietnam War to healthy age-matched controls concluded that Agent Orange exposure disturbs immune homeostasis, resulting in dysregulation of B cell and T cell activities (Kim, et al., 2003).

The Agent Orange Act of 1991

Initially, the Department of Defense and administrative agencies, such as the Department of Veterans Affairs, denied any relationship between exposure to Agent Orange and the injuries that were alleged to have occurred as a result of such exposure. Following significant Congressional debate and the commencement of a lawsuit against the US Veterans Administration (*Nehmer v. U.S. Veterans Administration*, 1989), Congress adopted the Agent Orange Act of 1991. It was recognized during the Congressional debates that our understanding of the effects of the exposure were imperfect:

> The evidence is not perfect, but it will never be perfect. Our understanding of cause and effect is still incomplete but we will never have a complete understanding of disease and its causes. . . . Leadership is a willingness to take action in the face of incomplete and imperfect data rather than accepting the paralysis inherent in a never-ending wait for understanding. . . . The search for answers must continue; however, the constant desire for just one more study should not be an excuse for inaction. (Stout, 1988)

The Act established a presumption that, subject to evidence to the contrary, any veteran who had served in Vietnam during the Vietnam War had been exposed to herbicides and dioxin:

> For purposes of establishing service connection for a disability or death resulting from exposure to a herbicide agent, including a presumption of service-connection under this section, a veteran who, during active military, naval, or air service, served in the Republic of Vietnam during the period beginning January 9, 1962, and ending on May 7, 1975, shall be presumed to have been exposed during such service to an herbicide agent containing dioxin or 2,4-dichlorophenoxyacetic acid and may be presumed to have been exposed during such service to any other chemical compound in an herbicide agent, unless there is affirmative evidence to establish that the veteran was not exposed to any such agent during that service. (38 U.S.C.S. § 1116(f), 2005)

The Act further provided that the Veterans Administration enter into a contract with the National Academy of Sciences to review the scientific literature relating to herbicide exposure and disease. The Act set forth the function of the Academy:

> For each disease reviewed, the Academy shall determine (to the extent that available scientific data permits meaningful determinations), A) whether a statistical association with herbicide exposure exists taking into account the strength of the scientific evidence and the appropriateness of the statistical and epidemiologic methods used to detect the association; B) the increased risk of the disease among those exposed to herbicides during

service in the Republic of Vietnam during the Vietnam era; and C) whether there exists a plausible biological mechanism or other evidence of a causal relationship between herbicide and the disease. (Agent Orange Act of 1991, 38 U.S.C. § 1116)

The Epidemiologic Investigation

The Institute of Medicine established a multidisciplinary committee in 1992 to address this charge. In evaluating the epidemiologic and statistical data that were available from scientific reports, this Committee on Agent Orange ("Committee") established four categories of association: (1) sufficient evidence, indicating that there was adequate evidence by which to establish a positive association between exposure and the outcome; (2) limited/suggestive evidence, meaning that, although evidence suggested an association between exposure and outcome, the results may have been due to confounding, bias, or chance; (3) inadequate/insufficient evidence, signifying a relative lack of studies that were sufficiently rigorous so as to permit a conclusion regarding a possible association between exposure and the outcome of interest; and (4) limited/suggestive evidence of no association.

The Committee concluded that sufficient evidence of exposure existed with respect to non-Hodgkin lymphoma, Hodgkin disease, chloracne, and porphyria cutanea tarda. Evidence was found to be limited/suggestive with respect to respiratory cancers, prostate cancer, and multiple myeloma. There was limited or suggestive evidence of no association with respect to skin cancer, gastrointestinal tumors, bladder cancer, and brain tumors. The remaining diseases that were evaluated for a possible association with Agent Orange exposure were placed in the category of inadequate/insufficient evidence. These initial findings were supplemented by later reports (Institute of Medicine, 1996, 1999, 2001). The conclusions of the Committee on Agent Orange were directly relevant to determinations of compensation for related injuries by the Department of Veterans Affairs (VA).

The Impact of Epidemiologic Findings on Disability Determinations

The VA provides a wide range of federal benefits to US veterans and their families. These include health care, disability payments, home loans, burial benefits, training, and rehabilitation (United States Department of Veterans Affairs, 2007). The disability compensation award consists of monthly benefits to those veterans who suffer disability due to service-connected injury and/or disease that was incurred or aggravated during their active military service. The amount of such payments is directly proportional to the degree of their service-connected injury. Accordingly, the VA is authorized by statute to pay disability compensation to veterans who suffer a "disability resulting from personal injury suffered or disease contracted in line of duty, or for aggravation of a preexisting injury suffered or disease contracted in line of duty, in the active military, naval, or air service" (38 U.S.C. § 1110).

The nexus between a disease or injury and the claimed service-connected exposure must be established with evidence of a scientific association between the claimed exposure and disease, evidence that the exposure occurred during active military service, evidence of temporal plausibility, and evidence of the magnitude of exposure. Regulation provides that "reasonable doubt" should be resolved to the benefit of the veteran:

> It is the defined and consistently applied policy of the Department of Veterans Affairs to administer the law under a broad interpretation, consistent, however, with the facts shown in every case. When, after careful consideration of all procurable and assembled data, a reasonable doubt arises regarding service origin, the degree of disability, or any other point, such doubt will be resolved in favor of the claimant. By reasonable doubt is meant one which exists because of an approximate balance of positive and negative evidence which does not satisfactorily prove or disprove the claim. . . . The reasonable doubt doctrine is also applicable even in the absence of official records, particularly if the basic incident allegedly arose under combat, or similarly strenuous conditions, and is consistent with the probable results of such known hardships. (38 C.F.R. § 3.102, 2005)

Alternatively, the VA can establish a presumption that the disease or condition results from an exposure occurring during active military duty, even in the absence of evidence sufficient to establish a direct service connection. Conditions falling within this presumptive category must create at least a 10% disability and generally must occur within 1 year following the individual's separation from military service (38 C.F.R. §§ 3.307, 3.309, 2005). Diseases falling within this provision include arthritis, leukemia, and Type II diabetes.

In making disability compensation determinations, the VA relied on the findings of the Committee's epidemiologic investigation that related to the likelihood of a causal association between exposure to Agent Orange and the claimed outcome of the exposure. The Agent Orange Act specifically required that the VA consider epidemiologic findings in making such determinations:

> Whenever the Secretary determines, on the basis of sound medical and scientific evidence, that a positive association exists between (A) the exposure of humans to an herbicide agent, and (B) the occurrence of a disease in humans, the Secretary shall prescribe regulations providing that a presumption of service con-

nection is warranted for that disease or the purposes of this section. In making determinations for the purpose of this subsection, the Secretary shall take into account (A) reports received by the Secretary from the National Academy of Sciences under section 3 of the Agent Orange Act of 1991, and (B) all other sound medical and scientific information and analyses available to the Secretary. In evaluating any study for the purpose of making such determinations, the Secretary shall take into consideration whether the results are statistically significant, are capable of replication, and withstand peer review. (38 U.S.C. § 1116(b)(3))

References

1. Agent Orange Act of 1991, Pub. L. 102-4, 105 Stat. 11 (1991) (codified as amended at 38 U.S.C. § 1116).
2. Armstrong, G. L., Hollingsworth, J., & Morris, J. G., Jr. (1996). Emerging foodborne pathogens: *Escherichia coli* O157:H7 as a model of entry of a new pathogen into the food supply of the developed world. *Epidemiology Review, 18*, 29–51.
3. Bell, B. P., Goldoft, M., Griffin, P. M., Davis, M. A., Gordon, D. C., Tarr, P. I., et al. (1994). A multistate outbreak of *Escherichia coli* O157:H7–associated bloody diarrhea and hemolytic uremic syndrome from hamburgers. *Journal of the American Medical Association, 272*, 1349–1353.
4. Boyce, T. G., Swerdlow, D. L., & Griffin, P. M. (1995). *Escherichia coli* O157:H7 and the hemolytic-uremic syndrome. *New England Journal of Medicine, 333*, 364–368.
5. Bunker Hill Co. v. Environmental Protection Agency, 572 F.2d 1286 (9th Cir. 1977).
6. Camp v. Pitts, 411 U.S. 138 (1973).
7. Chamber of Commerce v. OSHA, 636 F.2d 464 (D.C. Cir. 1980).
8. Citizens to Preserve Overton Park, Inc. v. Volpe, 401 U.S. 402 (1971).
9. Cody, S., Glynn, K., Farrar, J. A., Cairns, K.L., Griffin, P.M., Kobayashi, J., et al. (1999). An outbreak of *Escherichia coli* O157:H7 infection from unpasteurized commercial apple juice. *Annals of Internal Medicine, 130*, 202–209.
10. Community Nutrition Institute v. Young, 818 F.2d 943 (D.C. Cir. 1987).
11. Davis, K. C. (1972). *Administrative law* (3rd ed.). St. Paul, MN: West.
12. Department of Transportation v. Public Citizen, 541 U.S. 752 (2004).
13. Doniger, D. D. (1978). *The law and policy of toxic substances control: A case study of vinyl chloride*. Baltimore: Johns Hopkins University Press.
14. Ethyl Corp. v. EPA, 541 F.2d 1 (D.C. Cir. 1976) (en banc), cert. denied, 426 U.S. 941 (1976).
15. Food, Drug, and Cosmetic Act, 21 U.S.C.S. §§ 301 et seq.
16. Gellhorn, E. (1972). *Administrative law and process in a nutshell*. St. Paul, MN: West.
17. Gellhorn, W., Byse, C., & Straus, P. L. (1979). *Administrative law* (7th ed.). Mineola, NY: Foundation Press.
18. Griffin, P. M. (1995). *Escherichia coli* O157:H7 and other enterohemorrhagic *Escherichia coli*. In M. J. Blaser, P. D. Smith, J. I. Ravdin, H. B. Greenberg, & R. L. Guerrant (Eds.), *Infections of the gastrointestinal tract* (pp. 739–761). New York: Raven Press.

19. Griffin, P. M., & Tauxe, R. V. (1991). The epidemiology of infections caused by *Escherichia coli* O157:H7, other enterohemorrhagic *E. coli*, and the associated hemolytic uremic syndrome. *Epidemiology Review, 13*, 60–98.

20. Institute of Medicine. (1994). *Veterans and Agent Orange: Health effects of herbicides used in Vietnam.* Washington, DC: National Academy Press.

21. Institute of Medicine. (1996). *Veterans and Agent Orange, update 1996.* Washington, DC: National Academy Press.

22. Institute of Medicine. (1999). *Veterans and Agent Orange, update 1998.* Washington, DC: National Academy Press.

23. Institute of Medicine. (2001). *Veterans and Agent Orange, update 2000.* Washington, DC: National Academy Press.

24. Karmali, M. A., Petric, M., Lim, C., Fleming, P. C., Arbus, G. S., & Lior, H. (1985). The association between idiopathic hemolytic uremic syndrome and infection by verotoxin-producing *Escherichia coli. Journal of Infectious Disease, 151*, 775–782.

25. Kim, H-A., Kim, E-M., Park, Y-C., Yu, J-Y., Hong, S-K., Jeon, S-H., et al. (2003). Immunotoxicological effects of Agent Orange exposure to the Vietnam War Korean Veterans. *Industrial Health, 41*, 158–166.

26. Kornacki, J. L., & Marth, E. H. (1982). Foodborne illness, caused by *Escherichia coli*: A review. *Journal of Food Protection, 45*, 1051–1067.

27. National Family Planning and Reproductive Health Association, Inc. v. Sullivan, 979 F.2d 227 (D.C. Cir. 1992).

28. Negotiated Rulemaking Act, 5 U.S.C.S. § § 561–570.

29. Nehmer v. United States Veterans Administration, 712 F. Supp. 1404 (N.D. Cal. 1989).

30. North American Cold Storage Co. v. Chicago, 211 U.S. 306 (1908).

31. Occupational Safety and Health Act, 29 U.S.C.S. § 651 et seq. (2008).

32. Ostroff, S. M., Kobayashi, J. M., & Lewis, J. H. (1989). Infections with *Escherichia coli* O157:H7 in Washington State: The first year of statewide disease surveillance. *Journal of the American Medical Association, 262*, 355–359.

33. Pai, C. H., Ahmed, N., Lior, H., Johnson, W. M., Sims, H. V., & Woods, D. E. (1988). Epidemiology of sporadic diarrhea due to verocytotoxin-producing *Escherichia coli*: A two-year prospective study. *Journal of Infectious Disease, 157*, 1054–1057.

34. Pesatori, A. C., Zucchetti, C., Guercilena, S., Consonni, D., Turrini, D., & Bertazzi, P. A. (1998). Dioxin exposed non-malignant health effects: A mortality study. *Occupational and Environmental Medicine, 55*(2), 126–131.

35. Pickering, L. K., Obrig, T. G., & Stapleton, F. B. (1994). Hemolytic-uremic syndrome and enterohemorrhagic *Escherichia coli. Pediatric Infectious Disease Journal, 13*, 459–476.

36. Sierra Club v. Costle, 657 F.2d 298 (D.C. Cir. 1981).

37. Stellman, J. M., Stellman, S. D., Christian, R., Weber, T., & Tomasallo, C. (2003). The extent and patterns of usage of Agent Orange and other herbicides in Vietnam. *Nature, 422*, 681–687.

38. Stout, S. (1988). Statement. *Agent Orange legislation and oversight. Hearing before the Senate Committee on Veterans Affairs,* 100th Cong., 2d Sess., May 12.

39. Tennessee Valley Authority v. Whitman, 336 F.3d 1236 (11th Cir. 2003), *cert. denied,* 124 S. Ct. 2096 (2004).

40. Union of Concerned Scientists v. Nuclear Regulatory Commission, 711 F.2d 370 (D.C. Cir. 1983).

41. United States Department of Health, Education, and Welfare. (1971). *Morbidity and Mortality Weekly Report, 20*, Dec. 11.
42. United States Department of Veterans Affairs, Office of Public Affairs Media Relations. (2007). *Facts about the Department of Veterans Affairs.* Retrieved May 22, 2008, from http://www.va.gov/OPA/fact/docs/vafacts.pdf
43. United States Food and Drug Administration. (1977). *FDA annual report, 1976.* Washington, DC: Department of Health, Education, and Welfare and Public Health Service.
44. United States Food and Drug Administration. (1979). *Requirements of laws and regulations enforced by the U.S. Food and Drug Administration* [HEW Pub. No. (FDA) 79-1042]. Rockville, MD: Department of Health, Education, and Welfare.
45. United States Food and Drug Administration. (1998a). Food labeling: Warning and notice statements; labeling of juice products. *Federal Register, 63*, 20486–29493.
46. United States Food and Drug Administration. (1998b). Hazard analysis and critical control point (HACCP): Procedures for the safe and sanitary processing and importing of juice. *Federal Register, 63*, 20449–20486.
47. 5 U.S.C.S. § 552 (2008).
48. 38 U.S.C.S. § 1110, 1116 (2005).
49. 42 U.S.C.S. § 4332 (2008).
50. 38 C.F.R. § § 3.102, 3.307, 3.309 (2005).

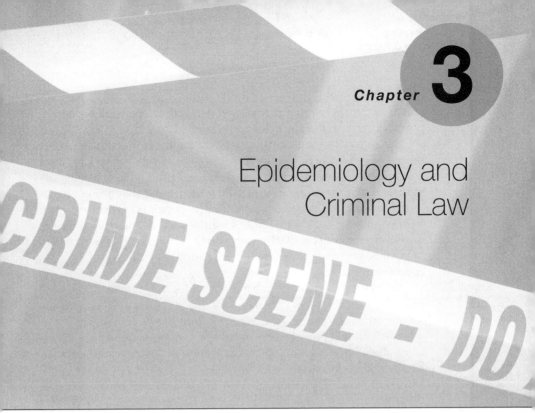

Chapter 3

Epidemiology and Criminal Law

U nlike civil law, which has as its principal aims the compensation of individuals who have been wronged and their restoration to the extent possible to a position prior to the experienced harm, criminal law seeks to reform those who have committed crimes, restrain individuals who have committed crimes, achieve retribution for the victims of crimes, and deter both individuals and society at large from committing crimes in the future (Zimring & Hawkins, 1973). A more recent perspective holds that criminal law also seeks to compensate society for the harm that has been inflicted on it through the commission of a crime by having the convicted individual repay the debt to society by contributing time or money to perform designated services to the community that has been harmed.

Other features distinguish civil law and procedure from law and procedure in the criminal context. In civil law, one party, the plaintiff, brings an action against the other, the defendant, based on a theory of the case. The plaintiff and the defendant may be persons, corporations, or governmental entities. Various mechanisms are utilized in an attempt to establish causation between the defendant's actions and the harm caused to the plaintiff. To prevail, the plaintiff must establish each element of the theory that is advanced and meet a specified burden of proof with respect to the evidence presented.

In contrast, an individual may not sue another individual, corporation, or governmental entity for a crime that is alleged to have been committed. Instead, the action is conceived of as a harm against the state, and it is the state, meaning the government, that prosecutes an individual for the crime committed. The person(s) who have been harmed may be called as witnesses for the state. In addition, the rules governing the process of discovery, that is, the seeking and exchange of evidence between the parties, are significantly different in the context of criminal law.

The first portion of this chapter provides an overview of the legal procedures involved in criminal cases. It then discusses the requirements for the establishment of guilt for the killing of one individual by another, which will provide the context for an examination of the advantages offered by epidemiologic investigation in the context of criminal law, as well as the barriers to its use. This is followed by a series of examples in which epidemiologic evidence was utilized by the prosecution to establish defendants' guilt for the killing of others. The chapter concludes with a general discussion of the difficulties inherent in the use of epidemiologic evidence in the criminal context.

Establishing Causation in Criminal Law

ESTABLISHING INTENT (*MENS REA*) AND ACTION (*ACTUS REUS*)

Mens rea refers to the state of mind that is required to establish a particular element of a crime. As an example, the crime of first degree murder is said to require a specific intent to kill. In contrast, an individual who kills someone while he is so intoxicated that he does not even realize he is shooting would not be able to form the specific intent required for first degree murder but could be found guilty of second degree murder, which requires only a general intent.

The Model Penal Code, promulgated in 1962 by the American Law Institute, has served as a model for criminal code reform. Many of its provisions have been adopted by the states. The Model Penal Code does not refer to specific and general intent but instead refers to four states of mind: purposeful, knowing, reckless, and negligent. The state of mind is purposeful when the defendant wants his action to bring about a certain outcome. It is knowing when the defendant is aware that his action is almost certainly going to bring about a specific outcome. In contrast, a defendant acts recklessly when he acts with the awareness that his conduct might bring about a specific outcome. Negligence occurs when the defendant should be aware, but is not, that his conduct will result in a certain outcome. Under the Model Penal Code, a defendant may have a state of mind known as "willful blindness," meaning that he is aware that there is a high probability that he is committing a crime, but he makes efforts to avoid knowing the relevant facts.

Intent is not an element of crimes for which there is strict liability. This means that the defendant will be found to be criminally liable if he or she committed acts that were prohibited by statute, regardless of his or her intent. Similarly, in some situations an individual may be found liable for the actions of another. As an example, if the employee of a bar sells liquor to a minor, or the salesperson at a small store sells cigarettes to a minor, the owner of each such establishment may be found culpable through the concept of vicarious liability.

The term *actus reus* refers literally to a guilty act. In general, this means that there must be some act done for there to be criminal culpability; a thought about committing a crime will not be sufficient. With few exceptions, the act must be performed voluntarily. Both the *mens rea* and the *actus reus* must occur concurrently

CAUSATION IN FACT AND PROXIMATE CAUSE

To successfully convict an individual for murder or a lesser offense, such as manslaughter, the state must establish both cause in fact and proximate cause. In such a case, to establish cause in fact, the state must demonstrate that "but for" the actions of the accused, the individual would not have died. This is relatively simple in cases in which the defendant held a gun to someone, pulled the trigger, and killed someone. However, in some circumstances, two forces may have acted together to bring about the death, but each could have caused it independently. In such cases, it will have to be demonstrated that the deceased individual would have lived longer but for the actions of the defendant.

Proximate cause is based on the foreseeability of the result and whether the defendant can fairly be found to be responsible for the death of the other individual. In some jurisdictions, the death of an individual must occur within a year and a day of the defendant's actions for proximate cause to be considered to exist. Consider the following classic hypothetical situations that deal with the intentional killing of another.

- The defendant shoots at an individual intending to kill him. The defendant does not know that his intended victim has a weak heart. Although the bullet misses the intended victim, the sound of the shot startles him to such an extent that he dies from a heart attack. If the victim would not have died "but for" the gun shot, even though it missed him, proximate cause will be deemed to exist and the defendant will be found culpable for the victim's murder.

- Defendant One attempts to kill his victim by strangulation. Believing that he has succeeded, he leaves his victim. Defendant Two encounters the unconscious victim and kills him. If the act of Defendant One can be shown to have shortened the victim's life, proximate cause will be deemed to exist, and Defendant One can be found guilty of the victim's murder. If the actions of Defendant Two were clearly responsible for the victim's death, Defendant One might still be found guilty of attempted murder, depending upon the circumstances surrounding the killing.

- The defendant attempts to kill an individual, but the individual survives long enough to be rushed to the emergency department of a local hospital. The ambulance is involved in a traffic accident while rushing to the hospital, and the victim dies following additional injuries suffered as a result of the accident. Alternatively, the victim arrives at the hospital safely, but the medical care that is administered is negligent, and the intended victim dies. In each such scenario, the defendant could be found guilty of murder because, even though his act did not cause the death of the victim immediately, the victim's death was foreseeable.

BURDEN OF PROOF

In general, the State must prove every element of the crime beyond a reasonable doubt to succeed with its prosecution. This is in contrast to the standard of proof of "a preponderance of the evidence" that is generally required in the context of civil litigation or the less frequently used standard of "clear and convincing." What constitutes "beyond a reasonable doubt" has not been quantified; however, whatever the extent of the doubt, it must be found to be reasonable.

An examination of cases involving appeals from convictions that relate to jury instructions provides some insight into the meaning of "beyond a reasonable doubt." The Nevada Supreme Court has held that the concept of "reasonable" is inherently qualitative and cannot be explained by a number (*McCullough v. State*, 1983). In so holding, the court reversed the ruling of the lower trial court because the judge had instructed the jury that "beyond a reasonable doubt" could be interpreted as "seven and a half" on a scale of 1 to 10 ($p > 0.75$). In *Victor v. Nebraska* (1994), the United States Supreme Court upheld the charge that was given to the jury in the California case *Sandoval v. California* (1994). That instruction defined "beyond a reasonable doubt" as follows:

> It is not a mere possible doubt; because everything relating to human affairs . . . is open to some possible or imaginary doubt. It is that state of the case which, after the entire comparison and consideration of all the evidence, leaves the minds of the jurors in that condition that they cannot say that they feel an abiding conviction to a moral certainty, of the truth of the charge. (*Sandoval v. California*, 1994, p. 7)

The Criminal Process

As indicated earlier, the individual(s) that have been harmed by the alleged perpetrator of the crime cannot bring a criminal action against the individual. Rather, the crime is considered to have occurred against the state or government. Accordingly, during all of the proceedings, an attorney will represent the interests of the government. The defendant has the option of being represented by an attorney but may choose to represent him- or herself.

During the entire proceedings, the criminal defendant is entitled to certain rights and protections that are derived from the United States Constitution. (See Chapter 1 for a brief review of the provisions of the US Constitution.) The 5th and 14th Amendments guarantee the defendant due process, meaning that he or she is entitled to clear notice of the charges brought; a presumption of innocence until guilt is established, usually beyond a reasonable doubt; a hearing; an opportunity to present evidence and to cross-examine witnesses at that hearing; the opportunity to appeal the decision of the original court; and appointment of an attorney in the event that he or she is unable to afford one. Additionally, the defendant is afforded by the Constitution the privilege against self-incrimination, meaning that he or she cannot be compelled to testify or to produce information that would assist the prosecution in the preparation of its case. No mention can be made at the trial of the defendant's refusal to testify, and no negative inference may be drawn by the judge or jury for the defendant's failure to do so.

The first step in the processing of a criminal case with an identified defendant is the investigation and, depending on the circumstances, possible arrest. The privilege against self-incrimination must be safeguarded from the time of these initial events throughout the process (*Miranda v. Arizona*, 1966). To protect this right, the individual must be informed of his or her right to remain silent. (The law relating to the point in time at which this right attaches and the requirements for a waiver of this privilege are quite complex and are beyond the scope of this chapter.) The investigation may involve a line-up, at which time the individual is presented to witnesses for identification. The conduct of a lineup requires notice to and the presence of the individual's attorney (*Gilbert v. California*, 1967; *United States v. Wade*, 1967).

In the case of a misdemeanor, the prosecution will be initiated through the issuance of an information, that is, a formal accusation, by the district attorney or other prosecuting authority. The information, which is filed with a lower-level court with criminal jurisdiction or a local magistrate, must be supported by sworn affidavits by the complainants, individuals who have knowledge of the facts that provide the basis for the charges. This information then becomes the basis for the court's issuance of a summons, which advises the defendant of the charges against him or her and orders the defendant to appear in court at a specified date and time to plead to the accusation. In some jurisdictions, the public health authority may be authorized to issue the summons instead of obtaining it from the court. In such cases, a duplicate copy of the summons, which contains notice of the charges, will be filed with the court and serve as the information. In felony cases, however, the case must be brought before a grand jury to assess whether there is sufficient evidence to indict the individual. This is a procedure that is required by the Fifth Amendment to the US Constitution.

The summons is generally served on the defendant personally but, in some cases, it may be mailed or left with a responsible adult in the same household as the defendant. In the case of a summons related to a traffic offense, the summons may be left on the defendant's car. The defendant's failure to appear in court on the date and time specified constitutes contempt of court, and the court may issue a warrant for the defendant's arrest.

A criminal defendant may encounter three types of proceedings before the trial: a Gerstein hearing to determine whether there is probable cause, the initial appearance, and the preliminary hearing. The Federal Rules of Criminal Procedure require both an initial appearance and a preliminary hearing. Each of these is discussed briefly in the following paragraphs.

A Gerstein hearing is a judicially created proceeding during which the court reviews the determination by the police that there is sufficient probable cause to support the detention of an arrestee (*Gerstein v. Pugh*, 1975). An individual is entitled to this type of hearing unless the arrest is supported by either a grand jury indictment or a warrant.

The initial appearance must occur without unnecessary delay (Federal Rules of Criminal Procedure 5(a)). At the initial appearance before the judge, the defendant will be apprised of the charges and will be informed of his or her rights, including the right to counsel, the right to remain silent, the right to a preliminary hearing, and the circumstances that would support the individual's release prior to trial (Federal

Rules of Criminal Procedure 5(d)(1)). The right to counsel begins at the stage of the initial appearance. Accordingly, depending on the circumstances, the court may adjourn the proceedings to allow the defendant sufficient time to obtain legal representation, or it may appoint counsel for the defendant. Bail will be established.

The right to a preliminary hearing is guaranteed only in federal court (*Lem Woon v. Oregon*, 1913), but this right can be waived by the defendant (Federal Rules of Criminal Procedure 5.1(a)). This hearing must occur no more than 10 days after the initial appearance of the defendant if the defendant is in custody and no more than 20 days after the initial appearance if he or she is not detained (Federal Rules of Criminal Procedure 5.1(c)). The hearing is required unless the defendant waives it or an indictment or information is filed before the date of the preliminary hearing (*United States v. Aranda-Hernandez*, 1996). This is because the preliminary hearing is intended to determine whether sufficient probable cause exists to bind the arrestee for trial, but that will have already been determined for the issuance of the indictment or information.

During the preliminary hearing, the defendant is entitled to be represented by an attorney, to cross-examine witnesses, and to introduce evidence (*Coleman v. Alabama*, 1970; *United States v. King*, 1973). If probable cause is not found, the complaint will be dismissed and the defendant released. However, this does not preclude the initiation of a subsequent prosecution for the same offense (*Stewart v. Abraham*, 2001).

At the time of the initial appearance, or subsequent appearance after counsel has been engaged, the defendant will be required to plead to the charges. The plea may be guilty, not guilty, or *nolo contendere* or *non vult contendere*, meaning that the defendant is not contesting the charges but is also not admitting them. In the case of either a guilty plea or a plea of *nolo contendere* or *non vult contendere*, sentencing may be imposed without the need for a trial. This may occur immediately or may be delayed pending the findings of a more detailed investigation by the appropriate authorities pursuant to an order of the court. Individuals may choose to plead guilty for any number of reasons, such as a wish to avoid the inconvenience, expense, and stress associated with a trial; the relatively low cost of the fine to be imposed; a desire to avoid unfavorable publicity; or a desire to avoid more severe consequences if a more egregious offense or worse conditions were to become known in the event of a more extensive investigation by the authorities.

Individuals who plead not guilty have the right to a trial. This may occur immediately following the plea if all witnesses are present and both the defense and the prosecution are prepared to proceed. Frequently, a later date and time will be set for the trial. In the case of more serious crimes, such as felonies, the defendant has the right to have the case heard by a jury; this right, however, may be waived by the defendant. Misdemeanor cases may frequently be tried by a judge without a jury.

A jury is selected through the process known as voir dire. Federal Rules of Criminal Procedure 24 provides for the examination of prospective jurors by the court (judge) or the attorneys, if the judge allows them to do so. If the court conducts the examination, the attorneys may either ask the jurors additional questions or request that the court do so. The questions are intended to test the competence and impartiality of the prospective jurors to assess their fitness to serve on the jury (State v. Berry, 1996); accordingly, voir dire is designed to expose bias on the part of the jurors (United States v. Bear Runner, 1974). Where bias exists, the defendant or government may challenge the juror for cause (United States v. Lampkin, 1946).

In felony cases, the defendant has 10 peremptory challenges, meaning that a prospective juror can be excused from serving on the jury without the challenger having to justify the excusal; the government has six such challenges. If the government chooses to seek the death penalty, however, each side is allowed 20 peremptory challenges. Peremptory challenges are also allowable in misdemeanor cases if the crime charged is punishable by fine, imprisonment of 1 year or less, or both. Peremptory challenges are also available with respect to alternate jurors.

The conduct of a trial follows a prescribed order that consists of the following steps:

1. Opening statements. The prosecution and then the defense has an opportunity to present an overview of its theory of the case and the evidence that will be presented to the court during the course of the trial.
2. Presentation of witnesses by the prosecution through direct examination, followed by cross-examination of each such witness by the defense attorney, followed by redirect examination by the prosecution and recross-examination by the defense.
3. Motion by the defense attorney to dismiss the case on the grounds that the prosecution has failed to present its case. Alternatively, the defense presents evidence and witnesses, with direct examination by the defense, followed by the cross-examination of the defense witnesses by the prosecution. This may be followed by redirect examination by the defense counsel and recross-examination by the prosecuting attorney.
4. Closing arguments to the jury by the defense attorney and the prosecution.
5. Jury deliberation and verdict.

If the jury finds that the defendant is not guilty, the case is dismissed. If the defendant is found to be guilty, the court may delay sentencing to allow adequate time for the preparation of a report by the probation department that will provide the court with additional information relating to the defendant's circumstances and past offenses and/or a further report from the investigative authorities related to the underlying condition or circumstances that gave rise to the original charges.

Whether epidemiologic evidence can be or is relied upon during the course of criminal proceedings depends on any number of issues, including the relevance and materiality of the evidence and the qualifications of the individual providing that evidence or testimony. Additional issues relate to the weight to be accorded to the epidemiologic evidence. These issues are best explained by way of illustration, using actual situations. The next section of this chapter provides an overview of the legal elements of crimes involving the killing of a person as a foundation for the examination of criminal cases in which epidemiologic evidence was utilized. This is followed in turn by a discussion of the difficulties that may be encountered in utilizing epidemiologic evidence in the context of a criminal trial.

The Epidemiologist as Sleuth: Investigating Murder

One does not ordinarily think of epidemiologists playing any role, let alone a prominent one, during the course of a murder investigation. Nevertheless, their skills may prove to be critical to the investigating authority and/or the prosecution. A review of the legal context relating specifically to murder and related crimes provides a foundation for understanding how and why this involvement may be essential.

DEFINING MURDER, HOMICIDE, AND MANSLAUGHTER

Although the killing of one person by another might be thought of by most people as constituting murder, the law makes a distinction between killings that are intentional and those that are not. Depending upon the circumstances, the killing may constitute murder or manslaughter; acts constituting murder and manslaughter are distinguished based on whether "malice aforethought" existed (murder) or did not exist (manslaughter).

The murder may be of a specified degree as defined by the relevant statute, and manslaughter may be voluntary or involuntary. A killing may be considered to constitute murder if it was intentional, if the individual intended to inflict severe bodily harm, if the behavior that led to the death was outrageously reckless, or if the killing occurred in the course of committing specified felonies, such as kidnapping, rape, or robbery. Killings that are classified as involuntary manslaughter, rather than murder, are those that occur in the heat of passion, such as when a man walks in on his wife having sex with another man, and those resulting from an individual's attempt to defend him- or herself from attack but the use of force in doing so is found to be excessive and causes the death. Those killings resulting from reckless or grossly negligent conduct and those occurring during the course of committing specified misdemeanor offenses are often classified as voluntary manslaughter.

Defining Murder

Each state defines the crime of murder and the degree of murder by statute. It is beyond the scope of this chapter to examine the statutes of all 50 states. Instead, the laws of California will be used as an example.

California Penal Code section 189 (2007) defines first degree murder as "[a]ll murder which is perpetrated by means of a destructive device or explosive, knowing use of ammunition designed primarily to penetrate armor, poison, lying in wait, torture, or by any other kind of willful, deliberate, and premeditated killing. . . . " As can be seen, specific means of killing, such as poisoning and lying in wait, may be deemed to constitute first degree murder even in the absence of premeditation (*State v. Johnson*, 1986).

The term "willful" refers to a specific intent to kill. This element must be met for an individual to be found guilty of first degree murder (California Penal Code § 189, 2007). However, the intent to kill can, in some circumstances, be inferred. Consider, for example, the situation in which an individual points a loaded gun at someone's head and pulls the trigger, causing a gunshot wound from which the individual dies. The individual can later claim that he intended only to injure the person and never intended to cause the individual's death. However, the judge or jury can infer the intent from the nature of the defendant's behavior: use of a loaded gun pointed at the individual's head.

A killing that is "deliberate" is one that the defendant commits essentially with a clear head. For example, a man who has lost his job, is facing bankruptcy and foreclosure, and is suffering from major depression might believe that he can no longer provide adequately for his family and that they will suffer as a result of his failures. He irrationally believes that it would be better for them if they were to die rather than having to endure the suffering that will confront them as a result of his failures. A killing while in this mental state could not be said to be "deliberate" because he is dominated by fear for his children; he cannot deliberate. The final element of premeditation requires that there be some evidence of the planning of the killing or the motive for the killing.

"Malice aforethought" is deemed to exist in situations in which the killing results from an individual's attempt to inflict serious bodily injury. "Malice aforethought" does not refer to whether the killing was done out of ill will or hatred, but it refers instead to the underlying intent with which the defendant acts. As an example, California law provides that:

> [s]uch malice may be express or implied. It is express when there is manifested a deliberate intention unlawfully to take away the life of a fellow creature. It is implied, when no considerable provocation appears, or when the circumstances attending the killing show an abandoned and malignant heart.
>
> When it is shown that the killing resulted from the intentional doing of an act with express or implied malice as defined above, no other mental state need be shown to establish the mental state of malice aforethought. Neither an awareness of the obligation to act within the general body of laws regulating society nor acting despite such awareness is included within the definition of malice. (California Penal Code § 188, 2007)

Accordingly, one California court has stated that a defendant will be considered to have acted with malice aforethought when he or she "with a wanton disregard for human life, does an act that involves a high degree of probability that it will result in death" (*People v. Conley*, 1966, p. 321). In some cases, the use of a deadly weapon will be sufficient to infer an intent to commit such serious bodily injury if the state's definition of "deadly weapon" encompasses that intent and a deadly weapon is used to commit the killing (*State v. Boyd*, 1971).

The definition of felony murder varies across states. California, for example, requires that the underlying felony be inherently dangerous (*People v. Phillips*, 1966). Felonies that fall into this category include, for example, rape and kidnapping. Other jurisdictions require that the act resulting in the death of another be both dangerous (*Jenkins v. State*, 1967) and intentional. An example of such a dangerous act would be slashing someone's jugular vein with a knife while attempting to rob a corner store. Finally, if the killing encompasses all of the elements of the underlying felony, the killing will not be considered to be murder within the felony murder rule. This is known as the "merger doctrine." As an example, all of the elements of assault and battery are encompassed within the definition of murder so that the killing will not be considered to be murder within the felony murder rule because it happened in the course of committing assault and battery. In determining whether a killing constitutes murder within the felony murder rule, states may also consider whether the killing was committed by one of the perpetrators of the crime or a third party, such as a police officer, during the commission of the underlying felony and the time that elapsed between the commission of the underlying felony and the killing.

Defining Manslaughter

A killing that might otherwise be considered murder may be voluntary manslaughter if (1) it is committed in the heat of passion, negating the ability to form a deliberate intent to take a life and (2) the circumstances that gave rise to this state of emotion are such that a reasonable person would be similarly governed. The classic example of such a situation is an individual who walks in on his or her spouse in bed with another individual and, in a blind rage, kills them both. To establish that this was sufficient provocation to engender such a state of rage, a defendant would have to show that the mythical "reasonable person" would be similarly enraged by such circumstances and that there existed an inadequate passage of time between the time of the provocation (the witnessing of this event) and the killing to allow him or her to cool off. Whether the provocation was sufficient to provoke the reasonable person is often a question for the jury to decide (*People v. Berry*, 1976).

> The Model Penal Code has adopted the following definition of manslaughter:
>
>> Criminal homicide constitutes manslaughter when . . . a homicide which would otherwise be murder is committed under the influence of extreme mental or emotional disturbance for which there is reasonable explanation or excuse. The reasonableness of such explanation or excuse shall be determined from the viewpoint of a person in the actor's situation under the circumstances as he believes them to be. (Model Penal Code, § 210.3)

This definition, however, raises additional issues, including how extreme the mental or emotional disturbance must be and what constitutes "reasonableness" of an explanation or excuse.

Involuntary manslaughter is said to occur when the killing results from an individual's recklessness or gross negligence. The concept of recklessness means that the individual proceeded with a specific action that resulted in the death of another, despite his awareness of the substantial and unjustifiable risk associated with his intended action. In contrast, gross negligence indicates that the individual proceeds with a course of action while unaware of the associated substantial and unjustifiable risk of which he should be aware. Some jurisdictions that are said to use an objective test for determining the level of negligence necessary to establish involuntary manslaughter utilize terms such as "criminal negligence," "gross negligence," or "culpable negligence."

Other jurisdictions that are said to utilize a subjective standard to assess the level of negligence necessary for involuntary manslaughter refer to "wanton" or "reckless" conduct. The Model Penal Code, which utilizes a subjective standard, requires recklessness for the killing to constitute involuntary manslaughter (Model Penal Code, § 210.4). It defines recklessness as a:

> conscious disregard [of] a substantial and unjustifiable risk. . . . The risk must be of such a nature and degree that, considering the nature and purpose of the actor's conduct and the circumstances known to him, its disregard involves a gross deviation from the standard of conduct that a law-abiding person would observe in the actor's situation. (Model Penal Code, § 2.02(2)(c))

Negligent and Reckless Homicide

Negligent homicide is a category of homicide or killing that is considered to be less serious than manslaughter and that requires a lesser level of negligence to be established. Some jurisdictions use this category of homicide to encompass homicide resulting from the operation of motor vehicles. The crime in such cases may be known as vehicular homicide. The Model Penal Code defines negligent homicide as criminal homicide that "is committed negligently." Negligence is said to occur when one:

> should be aware of a substantial and unjustifiable risk that [the death of another individual] will result from his conduct. The risk must be of such a nature and degree that the actor's failure to perceive it, considering the circumstances known to him, involves a gross deviation from the standard of care that a reasonable person would observe in the actor's situation. (Model Penal Code, § 2.02(2)(d)).

Misdemeanor Manslaughter

The misdemeanor manslaughter rule operates in much the same way as the felony murder rule, subject to some limitations. Some jurisdictions require that the underlying misdemeanor be one that is deemed to be wrong in itself (*malum in se*), such as a simple assault, and that it cannot be one that is prohibited because of legislative action (*malum prohibitum*). In Ohio, the Supreme Court upheld the conviction of a woman for involuntary manslaughter in connection with the death of three people who were killed when she suffered a heart attack while driving and negligently crossed the center line of traffic (*State v. Weitbrecht*, 1999).

Attempted Murder

The crime of attempted murder requires that someone have the specific intent to kill. This means that someone cannot be convicted of attempted murder if his intent was to cause serious bodily injury, if the killing resulted from recklessness, or if it occurred during the commission of a felony. Because the crime requires a specific intent—to bring about the death of another individual—this means that someone cannot be guilty of attempted murder if the facts of the situation indicate that the killing was involuntary, such as involuntary manslaughter.

A critical issue that requires resolution in determining whether someone is guilty of attempted murder is the extent to which the attempt has been effectuated and its proximity to completion for it to be considered an attempt. For example, someone cannot be convicted of attempted murder if his only action was to think about how he would like to kill someone, but he never takes any overt action. California, for example, allows an attempt conviction in circumstances in which the defendant has the necessary criminal intent and performs a substantial act toward the completed commission of the crime (*People v. Gibson*, 1949). The Model Penal Code indicates that an attempt occurs when an individual "purposely does or omits to do anything which, under the circumstances as he believes them to be, is an act or omission constituting a substantial step in a course of conduct planned to culminate in his commission of the crime" (Model Penal Code §§ 5.01(1)(c), 5.02(2)(a), (c), (g)).

In some circumstances, a defendant might change his or her mind in the course of carrying out a substantial act in furtherance of the intended crime. He or she might argue that a conviction for attempted murder is unjust because of the abandonment of the plan. This argument may be more successful if the defendant voluntarily abandoned his or her plan and the abandonment was not the result of an intervening factor, such as the unanticipated arrival of law enforcement.

CAUSATION IN EPIDEMIOLOGY REVIEWED

Causation in the context of epidemiology has been variously defined. Rothman (1976) conceived of a cause as "an act or event or a state of nature which initiates or permits, alone or in conjunction with other causes, a sequence of events resulting in an *effect*" (emphasis in original). Rothman and Greenland (1998, p. 2) view a cause as "an event, condition, or characteristic that preceded the disease event and without which the disease event either would not have occurred at all or would not have occurred until some later time." Susser (1991, p. 637) asserted that a cause is "something that makes a difference."

Causes may be necessary or sufficient. Rothman (1976) explained: "A cause which inevitably produces the effect is *sufficient*. . . . A specific effect may result from a variety of different sufficient causes. . . . If there exists a component cause which is a member of every sufficient cause, such a component cause is termed a *necessary* cause . . . " (emphasis in original).

This model of causation, known as modified determinism, recognizes that a cluster of factors, rather than a single agent, may produce an effect and that a specific effect may be the product of various causes. The strength of a particular causal factor necessarily depends upon the prevalence of component causes. For example, if the complementary causes are common, the strength of a particular factor may be strong even though that factor is rare (Rothman, 1986). Two component causes of a sufficient cause may also act synergistically if their joint effect exceeds the sum of their separate effects (Rothman, 1976).

This modified deterministic model of causation is limited in that we may be unable to identify all of the components of a sufficient cause that brings about a specific effect (Rothman, 1986). However, this formulation provides us with a better understanding of the etiology of disease than did the earlier model developed by Koch. That model, known as pure determinism, was formulated on the basis of Koch's work with tuberculosis and included five elements:

T1. An alien structure must be exhibited in all cases of the disease.

T2. The structure must be shown to be a living organism and must be distinguishable from all other living organisms.

T3. The distinction of micro-organisms must correlate with and explain the disease phenomena.

T4. The micro-organism must be cultivated outside the diseased animal and isolated from all disease products which could be causally significant.

T5. The pure isolated micro-organism must be inoculated into test animals and these animals must then display the same symptoms as the original diseased animal. (Carter, 1985)

This model, unlike the more recent model proposed by Rothman (1976) and Rothman and Greenland (1998), fails to recognize the multifactorial etiology of many diseases and syndromes, does not provide for the multiple effects that may be brought about by specific factors, does not consider the complexity of many causal factors, and fails to acknowledge both our incomplete understanding of many diseases and disease processes and the limitations in our ability to measure the causal process (Kleinbaum, Kupper, & Morgenstern, 1982).

Hill enunciated nine criteria to be utilized in evaluating the associations for causality: strength, consistency, specificity, temporality, biological gradient, plausibility, coherence, experimental evidence, and analogy (Morabia, 1991). Each is further discussed in the following paragraphs.

The *strength of an association* between a specific factor and the outcome of interest depends upon the relative prevalence of the other component causes. This, in turn, depends upon the frequency with which the factor of interest is found in cases of the disease or outcome of interest and the frequency with which it is found in the absence of the disease or outcome of interest (Sartwell, 1960). The criterion of *consistency* requires that the association between the suspected causal factor and the outcome of interest exist in various populations during varying time periods and circumstances (Susser, 1991). However, the absence of consistency does not negate the possibility that a causal association may actually exist because the occurrence of the outcome of interest depends on the existence of all causal components, some of which may be absent. Although Hill included *specificity*, that is, the association between a possible cause and a single effect (Rothman, 1986) as one of the criteria to be considered, he cautioned against the overemphasis of this criterion (Hill, 1965).

The criterion of temporality means that the cause must precede the occurrence of the outcome of interest (Rothman, 1986). *Biological gradient* refers to the dose-response; however, the extent to which cofounders are present or absent may impact this relationship. The hypothesized relationship between the factor of interest and the outcome of interest must be biologically plausible (*plausibility*) and consistent with our existing knowledge about the natural history and biology of the disease (*coherence*). Reference to other known examples may provide us with insights into other causes (*analogy*) (Rothman, 1986).

Hill's criteria for establishing a causal association have been compared to the prerequisites for the establishment of causality in the context of a murder investigation in the context of criminal law and procedure. One scholar explained:

> In criminal law, the presence of the criminal at the scene of the crime would be equivalent to the presence of an agent in a lesion of the disease. Premeditation would be similar to the requirement that the causal exposure should precede the onset of the disease. The presence of accessories at the scene of the crime might be compared to the presence of cofactors and/or multiple causes for human diseases. The severity of the crime or the consequences of death might be loosely equivalent to susceptibility and the host responses which determine the severity of the illness. The motivation involved in a crime should make sense in terms of reward to the criminal, just as the role of the causal agent should make biologic sense. The absence of other suspects and their elimination in a criminal trial would be similar to that of exclusion of other putative causes in human illness. Finally, need that the proof of guilt must be established beyond reasonable doubt would be true for both criminal justice and for disease causation. (Evans, 1978, pp. 254–255)

The strengths and limitations of this analogy should be identified and considered when reviewing the various elements constituting murder and related crimes and in evaluating our ability to utilize epidemiologic evidence in the criminal context. These issues are discussed in the next section.

EPIDEMIOLOGY AND CRIMINAL INVESTIGATION

The science of epidemiology and the skills of the epidemiologist have proven to be critical in the conduct of various criminal investigations. Recall the definition and elements of murder and the principles of establishing causation in epidemiology as the following examples are considered.

Death by Muscle Relaxants in Michigan

After patients at a Veterans Administration hospital in Ann Arbor, Michigan suffered a series of breathing failures, the FBI and the CDC were contacted to assist with the investigation (Stross, Shasby, & Harlan, 1976). It was found that the rate of cardiopulmonary arrests was four times the usual rate, and there was nothing in the patient population that could explain this sudden increase. As the result of an investigation by the hospital administrators and staff, it was discovered that the bodies of several of the patients contained pancuronium bromide, a muscle relaxant, although this had not been prescribed for them. The deaths were ultimately traced to intravenous injections that had been administered in the intensive care unit during the evening shift. Two nurses were indicted for murder and related offenses.

At trial, the government attempted to prove that the two nurses were the only individuals present at the time that the drug had been administered (United States v. Narciso, 1977). However, the testimony offered was found to be inconsistent. The epidemiological evidence was not introduced. Nevertheless, the jury found the two nurse-defendants guilty. This verdict was overturned on appeal.

Bolding and Potassium Deaths

In 1984, an unusually high number of cardiopulmonary resuscitation incidents occurred in patients who had been under the care of a Maryland nurse by the name of Jane Bolding. Some of these patients were found to have abnormally high levels of potassium in their blood. In 1985, following multiple episodes in one patient on Bolding's shift, the hospital suspended the nurse. Bolding subsequently confessed that she had killed two patients. Although she was charged with murder, the charge was later dismissed due to the lack of corroborating evidence and the questionable admissibility of her confession (Weaver, 1988).

A later epidemiological investigation conducted by an epidemiologist for the CDC found that Bolding had been the assigned care provider for 57 of the 88 patients who had experienced arrests during a particular shift (Sacks, Stroup, Will, Harris, & Israel, 1988b). It was found that patients in her care were 47.5 times more likely to suffer a cardiac arrest. The epidemic of arrests had ceased following her dismissal.

ICU Deaths in Georgia

Epidemiologic methods were utilized in a case in Georgia involving a series of cardiac arrests among patients in an intensive care unit (Franks, Sacks, Smith, & Sikes, 1987). It was believed that the patients had been administered unauthorized injections of potassium chloride. Controls were instituted on its use, and potassium blood levels were measured on all patients who suffered cardiopulmonary arrest. The nurse was found to have put potassium chloride in the intravenous tubing of a blood transfusion that she had just started. The epidemiologist who assisted with the investigation found that the deaths occurred during the 3:00 to 11:00 shift and that the patients who suffered the arrests were most often under the care of a particular surgical nurse, Terri Rachals, that same nurse (*Rachals v. State*, 1987). Rachals was charged with six counts of murder and 20 counts of aggravated assault. She was acquitted of all of the murder charges and all but one of the assault charges.

On appeal, Rachals argued that the epidemiological testimony should have been excluded. The Court of Appeals upheld her conviction for assault. Summarizing the epidemiological testimony that had been presented at trial, the court stated:

> In the month of November, five cardiac arrests had occurred in one day and one patient had a total of eight cardiac arrests in that one month. Dr. Franks listed all cardiac arrest patients for the period investigated and the primary nurse on duty with that patient. Rachals was the primary nurse for 11 cardiac arrest patients in the month of November. No other nurse was the primary care nurse for more than one cardiac arrest patient. Dr. Franks charted all 24 nurses for that month and the number of cardiac arrests that occurred when they were not on shift to calculate a "rate ratio." The "rate ratio" for most nurses was around one, while the "rate ratio" for Rachals was 26.6, which means that in 26.6 times, it was more likely that a cardiac arrest would occur while she was on duty than when she was not on duty. . . . [T]he rate ratio show infinitely large and unmeasurable [sic] because all of the cardiac arrests that occurred on the 3:00 o'clock to 11:00 o'clock shift occurred while she was on duty. (*Rachals v. State*, 1987, p. 674)

Pediatric Deaths in a San Antonio Hospital

In yet another case, the work of a CDC epidemiologist proved to be critical to the investigation of a series of deaths in a pediatric ICU in a San Antonio, Texas hospital (Istre, Gustafson, Baron, Martin, & Orlowski, 1985). Eighty-two patients had died during a period of 2.5 years. According to the appellate court, the epidemiologist had been:

able to eliminate a number of variables such as age, race, sex, medical history, severity of illness, procedures, surgery, surgeons and therapeutic intervention as an explanation. . . . The investigators determined that a child would have 10.7 times the risk of dying while appellant [Genene Jones] was working than at the times she was not working. (Jones v. State, 1988, pp. 683–684)

The court additionally noted that it had been found that "a CPR event was 25 times more likely to occur when appellant was working" and that "as to 8 of the 9 patients who had recurrent CPRs on different shifts in the epidemic period appellant was assigned to their care during each CPR episode" (Jones v. State, 1988, p. 684). Although Jones was indicted and later convicted, that conviction was overturned on appeal.

A separate case involving Jones occurred in Kerrville, Texas in August 1982 as the result of several respiratory arrests at a pediatric clinic. It was found that Jones had injected six infants with succinylcholine chloride, resulting in their deaths. Although Jones was charged with only a single murder, the court admitted evidence from the earlier cases. She was sentenced to prison for a term of 99 years (Lucy & Aitken, 2002).

Deaths in a Toronto Pediatric Hospital

The occurrence of 28 deaths over a 9-month period in the cardiac unit of a Toronto pediatric hospital prompted epidemiologic investigation (Buehler, et al., 1985). A postmortem examination revealed a high level of digoxin in a child's blood, although the drug had not been prescribed. Responsibility for the deaths was initially attributed to a nurse who was later acquitted. An epidemiologic investigation conducted by the Centers for Disease Control and the Ontario Ministry of Health revealed that, compared to children who died before or after the 9-month epidemic of deaths, children who died during the epidemic were more likely to have been 1 year old, to have had an intravenous line, and to have suffered unexpected deterioration in their health status. In addition, their deaths were more likely to have occurred between the hours of midnight and 6:00 a.m. when a particular nurse was more likely to have been on duty.

A Death Epidemic in Florida

The medical examiner in Florida requested the assistance of the Florida Department of Health and Rehabilitation Services and the Office of the State Epidemiologist in investigating the unexplained occurrence of 12 deaths in a 2-week period in a 54-bed, 25-patient Florida nursing home (Sacks, et al., 1988a). The deaths had been referred to the state's attorney and the medical examiner for possible criminal investigation.

The state epidemiologist obtained the monthly census and death data for all 69 nursing homes that functioned in the relevant county during a 9-year period and calculated the monthly death rates per 1000 patients for each nursing home. Based on analysis of the mortality data for the 2 years preceding the epidemic of deaths, the expected number of deaths for the nursing home was 2.5 for the month, compared to the 12 that had actually occurred. No association was found between the increased number of deaths and the age, sex, or race of the patients or the incidence of nosocomial infections. Investigators suspected that the administration of insulin may have been the death-causing agent in some of the cases. It was found that the presence of two specific staff members was consistently and strongly associated with the time of deaths. The epidemiologic investigators concluded with respect to this finding:

> These observations should be interpreted cautiously, since they do not establish cause nor do they prove exclusive access to patients. Although possible criminal activity was considered by local authorities before our investigation began, an epidemiologic study cannot determine whether intentional acts were committed against patients. (Sacks, et al., 1988a, p. 808)

Morphine-Induced Deaths in England

Dr. Harold Shipman was convicted in January 2000 in Manchester, England of the murder of 15 patients (Baker, 2001). He was apprehended following the investigation of the will of one of his patients, which appeared to have been forged. A toxicological examination of Shipman's patients who had been buried, rather than cremated, revealed that at least 15 of them had died due to the administration of a massive dose of morphine. Analysis of the deaths found that, compared to the practices of other nearby physicians, a greater proportion of the deaths than would be expected had occurred among those who were female and over the age of 65 years, those who died at home, and those who died during the week rather than on the weekends. It was estimated that Shipman had murdered up to 250 patients during the years of his career from 1974 to 1998 (Baker, 2001). Shipman was convicted on January 31, 2000, and was sentenced to a term of 15 concurrent life sentences.

Death by Thallium Poisoning

The case of *Trepal v. State* (2003) involved the prosecution and conviction of a chemist for the first degree murder of a neighbor's wife, six counts of attempted first degree murder of her other family members, seven counts of poisoning food or water, and one count of tampering with a consumer product, Coca-Cola. It was alleged that Trepal, a highly experienced chemist, had introduced thallium into Coca-Cola that was stored in the house of his neighbors, the Carrs. Thallium had been banned by the Food and Drug Administration in 1982 due to its toxicity. It is not available to the general public and can be accessed only by universities and research centers.

Law enforcement officers discovered a bottle of thallium in Trepal's garage, as well as a bottle-capping machine. Trepal indicated to an undercover agent that he had poisoned his neighbors to satisfy "a personal vendetta" (*Trepal v. State*, 2003, p. 407). On appeal from his conviction, Trepal challenged the testimony of the prosecution's expert witnesses. One of them, Dr. Karl Klontz, was the medical executive director of the Department of Health and Rehabilitative Services Epidemiology Program of the Disease Control office. He had authored a memorandum entitled "A Thallium Poisoning Cluster in a Single Family, Polk County, Florida, October–November, 1988." Using both clinical and epidemiologic information available to him, he had concluded:

> The clinical history of Mrs. P.C. [Peggy Carr], with an acute phase, followed by apparent improvement, and a secondary worsening phase suggest 2 successive exposures consistent with her history of Coke consumption. . . . The severity of illness and the concentrations of urinary thallium correspond to the amount of Coke ingested by each poisoned case. Furthermore the clinical history of Mrs. P.C. is consistent with her 2 successive exposures to the contaminated Coke. (*Trepal v. State*, 2003, p. 431)

The Supreme Court of Florida ultimately upheld Trepal's conviction, despite his various legal arguments.

EPIDEMIOLOGY AND THE PREVENTION OF CRIME

Epidemiologic methods can be used not only to help identify the cause of such unexplained deaths but also to prevent their occurrence. One research group found in their reviews of the serial murders of patients by nurses that an increase in patient risk of being killed by a nurse was associated with the administration of intravenous fluids, with evenings or nights, and with being in a bed that was out of sight of the nurses' station (Stark, Paterson, Henderson, Kidd, & Godwin, 1997; Stark, Paterson, & Kidd, 2001). A later review by Yorker and colleagues (2006) of 90 criminal prosecutions of healthcare providers who met inclusion criteria for serial killers revealed that injection was the preferred mode of killing, followed by suffocation, poisoning, and tampering with equipment. The majority of killings occurred in hospitals during the evening or night hours when there was reduced oversight. Patients at increased risk of being killed were those who were very old, very young, critically ill, and/or who had intravenous lines.

The recognition of these factors associated with an increased risk of becoming a murdered patient is a prerequisite to the prevention of such events. The identification of these particular factors suggests mechanisms that could be utilized to reduce the risk to patients, including reduced reliance on float nursing personnel, improved controls over drug storage, increased monitoring of the usage of potentially lethal medications and improved accountability procedures for that usage, and location of the most severely ill patients in the proximity of the nursing station whenever possible.

Issues in the Use of Epidemiological Evidence in the Criminal Context

THE ADMISSIBILITY OF EPIDEMIOLOGIC EVIDENCE

In each case previously noted, a determination was made that an excess number of deaths, or outbreaks of death, had occurred. This can be analogized to a situation requiring the investigation of a disease outbreak but, in these examples, the disease was death. Epidemiologic investigation of such an apparent outbreak necessitates (1) a determination as to whether the number of persons who died during a defined period of time is in excess of what would be expected; (2) the characterization of the cases, for example, by demographic features and exposures; (3) the development of various hypotheses that might explain the apparent outbreak; and (4) the testing of these hypotheses to determine which should be accepted or rejected in the face of newly available data from the progressing investigation (Roht, Selwyn, Holguin, & Christensen, 1982).

The development of an epidemic curve would help in such instances to identify periods of time, whether days or blocks of hours in days, during which the deaths were likely to occur and to focus attention on the circumstances that prevailed during such time periods. (For a review of how to construct an epidemic curve, readers are referred to Roht, et al., 1982.) The first death during the defined time period would constitute the primary case, while the first death brought to the attention of the epidemiologist would be the index case (Merrill & Timmreck, 2006). The primary and index cases of death may or may not be one and the same. Individuals who died during the defined period of time and whose deaths were suspected to be associated with the potential pathogen (perpetrator) would be considered suspect cases. This appears to have been the approach that was utilized by the state epidemiologist who investigated the Florida death epidemic, previously described.

Whether the findings from such an investigation would be admitted as evidence at all in the context of a criminal proceeding depends on several factors. In general, expert testimony is permitted if it involves scientific or technical knowledge and will help the "trier of fact to understand the evidence or to determine a fact in issue" (Federal Rule of Evidence 702). The individual who is to testify with respect to the findings of the death outbreak investigation must be qualified as an expert based on his or her knowledge, education, training, skill, or experience (Federal Rule of Evidence 702).

In addition, the findings to be presented must be considered reliable in the legal, as opposed to the scientific, context. To be considered reliable, the scientific testimony must be supported by appropriate validation (*Daubert v. Merrell-Dow Pharmaceuticals*, 1993; *United States v. Davis*, 1994). This requires a determination by the court as to (1) whether the theory or technique at issue could have been tested, (2) whether the methodology has been subjected to peer review, (3) the potential rate of error associated with the particular method or technique, and (4) the extent to which the methodology that was utilized has been accepted within the relevant scientific community (*Daubert v. Merrell-Dow Pharmaceuticals*, 1993).

In the context of civil trials, such as lawsuit by an individual against a corporation for injuries alleged to have resulted from a particular exposure, courts have demanded as a prerequisite to the *admissibility* of epidemiologic evidence that the plaintiff bringing the action demonstrate a relative risk of at least 1.5 (*In re Joint Eastern & Southern Asbestos Litigation*, 1993) or 2.0 (*Marder v. G.D. Searle & Co.*, 1986). Scholars have debated the merits of requiring a relative risk of 2.0 or greater (Black, Jacobson, Madeira, & See, 1997; Muscat & Huncharek, 1989). Given that the threshold for the *consideration* of epidemiologic evidence is a risk ratio of 1.5 or greater in the context of a civil trial in which the burden of proof is generally "more likely than not," one must ask how much greater it should be in the context of a criminal trial in which it is offered to establish an element of the crime for which the burden of proof is "beyond a reasonable doubt."

EPIDEMIOLOGY MEETS THE BURDEN OF PROOF

Even in situations in which the proffered epidemiologic evidence is found to be legally reliable and testimony from the individual offering the epidemiologic findings is permitted, the epidemiologic findings will be considered circumstantial only, that is, as one factor to be considered in conjunction with all others in assessing causation in fact. This can be explained as follows.

Recall the complexity involved in establishing causation in the legal context as a prerequisite to the establishment of an individual's guilt. This requires sufficient evidence of action, intent, causation in fact, and proximate cause. Further, each element of the alleged criminal act must be proven "beyond a reasonable doubt." Herein lies one of the primary difficulties inherent in the use of epidemiologic evidence in the criminal context.

Attempts to translate the standard for this burden of proof into the parlance of epidemiologists has met with failure. As noted earlier, one appellate court overturned a lower court's decision of guilt because the jury had been instructed that "beyond a reasonable doubt" could be analogized to a "seven and a half" on a scale ranging from 1 to 10, that is, where $p > 0.75$ (*McCullough v. State*, 1983). In the view of the appellate court, the concept of "reasonable" was inherently qualitative and could not be reduced to a quantitative value. Clearly, at least in some jurisdictions, the requisite burden of proof cannot be equated to a particular p value or confidence interval.

The quantification of risk as a measure against which the burden of proof may be calibrated would also be problematic. Recall the case of the pediatric deaths at a San Antonio hospital (*Jones v. State*, 1988). The court emphasized in its opinion the epidemiologist's finding that a child had 10.7 times the risk of dying while the accused was working compared to those times when she was not. Suppose, hypothetically, that the court established a threshold risk ratio of 10.0 because of the heightened burden of proof. Such a standard would have been sufficiently low to permit a finding of guilt in this particular case. However, such a high threshold could potentially result in a finding of not guilty in cases in which the individual had actually committed the acts of which he or she was accused.

This threshold requirement can be analogized to the concept of Type I and Type II errors. Let us assume that a risk ratio of less than 10.0 signifies that there is an insufficient (legal) association between exposure to the defendant and the resulting death to merit a determination of guilt (H_0) so that the defendant is innocent, while a risk ratio greater than 10.0 represents the alternative hypothesis (H_A), indicating that the exposure is (legally) sufficient to warrant a finding of culpability, such as in the cases of the San Antonio pediatric deaths and the Bolding potassium deaths. In any situation, one of the following must be true:

- The null hypothesis is rejected when it is true, resulting in the commission of a Type I error. As a result, the defendant is found to be responsible for the deaths when, in fact, he or she is innocent.
- The null hypothesis is rejected when the alternative hypothesis is correct. In this case, the decision that the defendant is guilty is the correct one.

- The null hypothesis is not rejected when the alternative hypothesis is actually true, resulting in a Type II error. This would result in a finding of innocence when, in fact, the defendant is responsible for the death outbreak.
- The null hypothesis is not rejected when the null hypothesis is true, resulting in a finding that the defendant is innocent of the death outbreak when, in fact, he or she actually is innocent.

As can be seen, a Type I error would result in a finding of guilt and conviction of an innocent individual, while a Type II error would result in a not guilty finding in situations in which the defendant was culpable for the outbreak of deaths.

Our criminal justice system rests on the premise that an individual is to be presumed to be innocent until proven guilty. The heightened burden of proof that is required in the context of criminal trials, as compared with that required in civil matters, reflects our policy determination that it is more unjust to wrongfully convict an innocent individual than to fail to convict one who is culpable. Just as reliance on a risk ratio without consideration of study design, confidence interval, sample size, confounding, effect modification, bias, and other methodological concerns would lead to erroneous causal inferences in the context of epidemiologic investigations, so too would reliance on the quantification of risk in the criminal context without consideration of intent, mitigating circumstances, and other factors likely to lead to miscarriages of justice.

References

1. Baker, R. (2001). *Harold Shipman's clinical practice 1974–1998*. UK: Her Majesty's Stationery Office.
2. Black, B., Jacobson, J. A., Madeira, E. W., Jr., & See, A. (1997). Guide to epidemiology. In B. Black & P. W. Lee (Eds.), *Expert evidence: A practitioner's guide to law, science, and the FJC manual* (pp. 73–115). St. Paul, MN: West Group.
3. Buehler, J. W., Smith, L. F., Wallace, E. M., Heath, C. W., Rusiak, R., & Herndon, J. L. (1985). Unexplained deaths in a children's hospital, an epidemiologic assessment. *New England Journal of Medicine, 313*, 211–216.
4. California Penal Code § § 188, 189 (2007).
5. Carter, K. C. (1985). Koch's postulates in relation to the work of Jacob Henle and Edwin Klebs. *Medical History, 29*(4), 353–374.
6. Coleman v. Alabama, 399 U.S. 1 (1970).
7. Daubert v. Merrell-Dow Pharmaceuticals, Inc., 509 U.S. 579 (1993).
8. Evans, A. S. (1978). Causation and disease: A chronological journey. *American Journal of Epidemiology, 108*(4), 249–258.
9. Federal Rule of Evidence 702.

10. Federal Rules of Criminal Procedure 5, 5.1.
11. Franks, A., Sacks, J. J., Smith, J. D., & Sikes, K. (1987). A cluster of unexplained cardiac arrests in a surgical intensive care unit. *Critical Care Medicine, 15*, 1075–1076.
12. Gerstein v. Pugh, 420 U.S. 103 (1975).
13. Gilbert v. California, 388 U.S. 263 (1967).
14. Hill, A. B. (1965). The environment and disease: Association or causation? *Proceedings of the Royal Society of Medicine, 58*, 295–300.
15. In re Joint Eastern & Southern Asbestos Litigation, 827 F. Supp. 1014 (S.D.N.Y. 1993), *reversed* 52 F.3d 1124 (2d Cir. 1995).
16. Istre, G. R., Gutafson, T. L., Baron, R. C., Martin, D. L., & Orlowski, J. P. (1985). A mysterious cluster of deaths and cardiopulmonary arrests in a pediatric intensive care unit. *New England Journal of Medicine, 313*, 205–211.
17. Jenkins v. State, 230 A.2d 262 (Del. 1967).
18. Jones v. State, 751 S.W.2d 682 (Tex. App. 1988).
19. Kleinbaum, D. G., Kupper, L. L., & Morgenstern, H. (1982). *Epidemiologic research: Principles and quantitative methods.* New York: Van Nostrand Reinhold.
20. Lem Woon v. Oregon, 229 U.S. 586 (1913).
21. Lucy, D., & Aitken, C. (2002). A review of the role of roster data and evidence of attendance in cases of suspected excess deaths in a medical context. *Law, Probability, and Risk, 1*, 141–160.
22. Marder v. G.D. Searle & Co., 630 F. Supp. 1087 (D. Md. 1986), *affirmed* 814 F.2d 655 (4th Cir. 1987).
23. McCullough v. State, 657 P.2d 1157 (Nev. 1983).
24. Merrill, R. M., & Timmreck, T.C. (2006). *Introduction to epidemiology* (4th ed.). Sudbury, MA: Jones and Bartlett.
25. Miranda v. Arizona, 384 U.S. 436 (1966).
26. Morabia, A. (1991). On the origin of Hill's causal criteria. *Epidemiology, 2*, 367–369.
27. Muscat, J. E., & Huncharek, M. S. (1989). Causation and disease: Biomedical science in toxic tort litigation. *Journal of Occupational Medicine, 31*, 997–1002.
28. People v. Berry, 556 P.2d 777 (Cal. 1976).
29. People v. Conley, 64 Cal. 2d 310 (1966).
30. People v. Gibson, 92 Cal. App. 2d 55 (1949).
31. People v. Phillips, 414 P.2d 353 (Cal. 1966).
32. Rachals v. State, 361 S.E.2d 671 (1987), *affirmed* 364 S.E.2d 671, *cert. denied* 108 S.Ct. 2909. [184 Ga. App. 420].
33. Roht, L. H., Selwyn, B. J., Holguin, A. H., & Christensen, B. L. (1982). *Principles of epidemiology: A self-teaching guide.* New York: Academic Press.
34. Rothman, K. J. (1976). Causes. *American Journal of Epidemiology, 104*, 587–592.
35. Rothman, K. J. (1986). *Modern epidemiology.* Boston: Little, Brown and Company.
36. Rothman, K. J., & Greenland, S. (1998). *Modern epidemiology* (2nd ed.). Philadelphia: Lippincott-Raven Publishers.
37. Sacks, J. J., Herndon, J. L., Lieb, S. H., Sorhage, F. E., McCaig, L. F., & Withum, D. G. (1988a). A cluster of unexplained deaths in a nursing home in Florida. *American Journal of Public Health, 78*(7), 806–808.
38. Sacks, J. J., Stroup, D. F., Will, M. L., Harris, E. L., & Israel, E. (1988b). A nurse-associated epidemic of cardiac arrests in an intensive care unit. *Journal of the American Medical Association, 259*, 689–695.

39. Sandoval v. California, 511 U.S. 1 (1994).

40. Sartwell, P. E. (1960). On the methodology of investigations of etiologic factors in chronic disease: Further comments. *Journal of Chronic Disease*, 11, 61–63.

41. Stark, C., Paterson, B., Henderson, T., Kidd, N., & Godwin, M. (1997). Counting the dead. *Nursing Times*, 93(46), 34–37.

42. Stark, C., Paterson, B., & Kidd, B. (2001). Opportunity may be more important than profession in serial homicide. *British Medical Journal*, 322, 993.

43. State v. Berry, 684 So. 2d 439 (La. App. 1996), *writ denied*, 703 So. 2d 603 (La. 1997).

44. State v. Boyd, 180 S.E.2d 794 (N.C. 1971).

45. State v. Johnson, 344 S.E.2d 775 (N.C. 1986).

46. State v. Weitbrecht, 715 N.E.2d 167 (1999).

47. Stewart v. Abraham, 275 F.3d 220 (3d Cir. 2001).

48. Stross, J. K., Shasby, M. D., & Harlan, W. R. (1976). An epidemic of mysterious cardiopulmonary arrests. *New England Journal of Medicine*, 295, 1107–1110.

49. Susser, M. (1991). What is a cause and how do we know one? A grammar for pragmatic epidemiology. *American Journal of Epidemiology*, 133, 635–648.

50. Trepal v. State, 846 So. 2d 405 (Fla. 2003), *cert. denied*, Trepal v. Florida, 540 U.S. 958.

51. United States v. Aranda-Hernandez, 95 F.3d 977 (10th Cir. 1996).

52. United States v. Bear Runner, 502 F.2d 908 (8th Cir. 1974).

53. United States v. Davis, 40 F.3d 1069 (10th Cir. 1994), *cert. denied*, 115 S.Ct. 1806 (1995).

54. United States v. King, 482 F.2d 768 (D.C. Cir. 1973).

55. United States v. Lampkin, 66 F. Supp. 821 (D.C. Fla. 1946).

56. United States v. Narciso, 446 F. Supp. 252 (D.C. Mich. 1977).

57. United States v. Wade, 388 U.S. 218 (1967).

58. Victor v. Nebraska, 511 U.S. 1 (1994).

59. Weaver, C. (1988). The chilling case of Nurse 14. *Regardies*, 8, 93–144.

60. Yorker, B. C., Kizer, K. W., Lampe, P., Forrest, A. R. W., Lannan, J. M., & Russell, D. A. (2006). Serial murder by healthcare professionals. *Journal of Forensic Science*, 51(6), 1362–1371.

61. Zimring, F. E., & Hawkins, G. J. (1973). *Deterrence: The legal threat in crime control*. Chicago: University of Chicago Press.

Chapter **4**

Epidemiology and Public Health Law

Public health law has been described as a branch of administrative law because many of the functions are carried out by government agencies (Grad, 1990). It has been defined as:

> the study of the legal powers and duties of the state, in collaboration with its partners (e.g., health care, business, the community, the media, and academe), to assure the conditions for people to be healthy (to identify, prevent, and ameliorate risks to health in the population) and the limitations on the power of the state to constrain the autonomy, privacy, liberty, proprietary, or other legally protected interests of the individual for the common good. The prime objective of public health law is to pursue the highest possible level of physical and mental health in the population, consistent with the values of social justice. (Gostin, 2007, p. 1)

Inherent in this definition is the tension between the interests of the individuals and those of the larger population. This theme is reflected in each of the case studies discussed in subsequent chapters.

In addition, some of the powers that are permitted to the government in the context of public health functions bear similarities to those that are familiar to us in the criminal context, such as the power to conduct a search and seize evidence and the power to impose sanctions. (For this reason, the discussion of public health law follows the chapters relating to administrative law and criminal law.) The responsibility of the government for the public health and the enforcement of public health laws has been stated as follows:

> One of the legitimate and most important functions of civil government is acknowledged to be that of providing for the general welfare of the people by making and enforcing laws to preserve and promote the public health and the public safety. Civil society cannot exist without such laws; they are, therefore, justified by necessity and sanctioned by the right of self preservation. The power to enact and enforce them is lodged by the people with the government of the State, qualified only by such conditions as to the manner of its exercise as are necessary to secure the individual citizen from unjust and arbitrary interference. But even under these restrictions, the power exists in ample measure to enable the government to make all needful regulations touching the well-being of society. (Parker & Worthington, 1892, Sec I, quoted in Tobey, 1947, p. 5)

The balance between the powers of the government and the rights of the individual is discussed in Chapter 9.

The issues that may arise in the context of public health law that may have implications for law enforcement are too extensive to review in a comprehensive manner in only one chapter. Examples of these issues and/or functions include:

- Abatement of public and private nuisances
- Availability and quality of contraceptive and abortion services
- Alcohol and tobacco manufacture, sale, and possession
- Civil commitment for mental illness and substance use
- Communicable disease control and reporting
- Disease and immigration
- Driving laws, such as seat belt use, motorcycle helmet requirements, cell phone use, and drunk driving
- Environmental tobacco smoke regulation
- Facilities inspection and licensure
- Family violence prevention
- Food inspection and labeling
- Health-related conditions of employment, such as the provision of adequate ventilation, means of ingress and egress, etc.

- Hospital and nursing home regulation
- Housing inspection
- Issuance of licenses and permits, such as for restaurants and beauty salons
- Legalization of medical marijuana
- Occupational licensing and licensing revocation
- Pharmaceutical manufacture, safety, and distribution
- Quarantine
- Sexually transmitted disease control and reporting
- Tuberculosis control and reporting

This chapter focuses on specific types of civil law enforcement functions conducted by public health agencies that may, at some point during the process, necessitate the input of epidemiologists. Law enforcement activities in the criminal context that may involve epidemiology were discussed in Chapter 3. Tuberculosis quarantine and isolation and HIV preventions provide the focus for Chapter 5 and will not be addressed here.

Searches and Inspections

THE NATURE OF ADMINISTRATIVE SEARCHES AND INSPECTIONS

Unlike a search that is conducted by law enforcement officers in the context of a criminal investigation, inspections that are conducted by a public health officer are done for the purpose of ensuring that the establishment or individual is complying with existing laws that were established to safeguard the public's health. Various federal and state statutes provide for the conduct of such inspections.

For a search or inspection to be valid, it must comport with constitutional requirements and with the relevant statutes. A search or inspection will not be considered valid unless it has been authorized by a specific statute, for a person encompassed within that statute, and by a person with the authority to conduct the search or inspection. In general, authorized individuals must be employees, officers, or agents of the agencies that are empowered by statute to carry out the inspection.

THE REQUIREMENT OF CONSENT OR A WARRANT

Although administrative in nature, these inspections are considered to be searches and, as such, are subject to the requirements of the Fourth Amendment of the US Constitution, which protects individuals from unreasonable searches and seizures, discussed briefly in Chapter 1. This includes the requirement of a warrant prior to effectuating the inspection or search. However, because they are administrative rather than criminal in nature, the standards for obtaining warrants are less stringent than they would be in the criminal context. Recall from Chapter 1 that the Fourth Amendment to the U.S. Constitution prohibits unreasonable searches and seizures and requires that a warrant be based on probable cause. Accordingly, in the criminal context, a search cannot be conducted without one of the following: the consent of the owner, the issuance of a warrant based on probable cause, or the existence of exigent circumstances. The case of *Florida Department of Agriculture and Consumer Services v. Haire* (2003) serves as an excellent illustration of the issues related to administrative search warrants, the nature of exigent circumstances in the administrative context, and reliance on epidemiology in the law enforcement context.

This case involved the search of private property to remove citrus trees located near trees that were infected with citrus canker. Citrus canker was first discovered in Florida in 1914. Eradication programs were initiated and continued throughout the 1930s. However, an Asian strain known as *Xanthomonas axonopodis* pv. *citri* was discovered in Manatee County during the 1980s. It was believed to have been eradicated in 1992, and the eradication program was terminated in 1994. However, an outbreak occurred yet again in 1995 near Miami's international airport, promoting renewed efforts to eradicate the disease.

Significant efforts to eradicate canker-infected trees were needed due to the nature of the infection. Citrus canker, a disease caused by a bacterial organism, attacks the fruits, leaves, and stems of citrus plants, resulting in defoliation, fruit drop, loss of yield, blemishes on the fruit, and reduced fruit quality. In severe cases, it can cause the death of a tree. Stem lesions can survive for years and produce bacterial inoculum up to 10 years later. And, although the tree may manifest symptoms within 7 to 14 days after infection, maximum visualization may not occur for 108 days, making it extremely difficult to control the disease, which can be spread by rain or through the use of equipment that has been inadvertently contaminated through use on trees not visibly displaying signs of canker infection. Infection of citrus crops would result in an immediate loss of revenue and possible federal quarantine of all fresh citrus products originating in the state of Florida.

A scientific study of the Miami canker epidemic concluded that control of the epidemic would require the destruction of all trees within a 1900-foot radius of an infected tree to create a buffer zone and effectuate the destruction of 95% of all infected trees. Based on these findings, the Florida Department of Agriculture adopted a rule on an emergency basis that would have allowed it to conduct warrantless countywide searches and destroy citrus trees within 1900 feet of an infected tree.

Following a series of lower court hearings, a Florida state court of appeals held that a warrantless search in these circumstances would be unconstitutional. A warrant would be required to conduct this administrative search. The appeals court found that the 1900-foot rule was valid, basing its conclusion on the testimony during the lower court trial of a nationally known expert in plant epidemiology. Although the court held that the Department of Agriculture was authorized by statute and the state Constitution to seize property to protect the public health, citrus canker did not, in the court's view, constitute an emergent circumstance that would justify the department's seizure of the property without providing the opportunity for a preseizure hearing and compensation for the destruction of healthy trees. (Notice here the need to balance the interests and rights of the tree owners against the interests of the government. The need for balance will be the focus of discussion in Chapter 9.)

It is important to note that a warrant would not have been required in the preceding case if the owners of the properties in question had consented to the search. As in the criminal context, the inspection or search in the context of health-related inspections may be conducted with the consent of the owner in lieu of a warrant. The individual who consents to a warrantless search must have the capacity and the authority to do so. For example, a tenant cannot provide valid consent to inspect areas of the building that are being leased by other tenants, but he or she can consent to a search of his or her own apartment. Similarly, the landlord of that building cannot give consent to an inspection of an apartment that is being rented by a tenant because that would infringe on the tenant's right to privacy.

The application of the heightened standard for the granting of a warrant in the criminal context to the conduct of public health inspections would seriously impede efforts to protect the public health. Accordingly, in a case involving the attempt of a housing inspector to enter a private dwelling without a warrant, the court ruled that warrants for such administrative inspections could be issued absent knowledge of a violation:

> [I]t is obvious that "probable cause" to issue a warrant to inspect must exist if reasonable legislative or administrative standards for conducting an area inspection are satisfied with respect to a particular dwelling. Such standards, which will vary with the municipal program being enforced, may be based upon the passage of time, the nature of the building (e.g., a multifamily apartment house), or the condition of the entire area, but they will not necessarily depend upon specific knowledge of the condition of the particular dwelling. . . . If a valid public interest justifies the

> intrusion contemplated, then there is probable cause to issue a
> suitably restricted search warrant. (*Camara v. Municipal Court*, 1967,
> pp. 538–539)

This decision, while recognizing the need for a warrant, made
clear that the basis for that warrant could be either specific knowledge
or the existence of a legislative or administrative standard that would
permit such an inspection. A later Supreme Court decision both reit-
erated this same standard and indicated that the issuance of a warrant
on the basis of a standard must be supported by evidence that both jus-
tifies the government interest in that particular type of industry or endeavor and that indicates that the premises to be inspected fall within
the scope of that government interest (*Marshall v. Barlow's Inc.*, 1978).

In general, warrants for health-related inspections must be signed
by a judge or a neutral magistrate, as required by the US Constitution.
In some cases, a clerk of the court may be able to determine if probable cause for the issuance of a warrant exists and sign the warrant.

In very limited circumstances, a search or inspection may be conducted without either a warrant or consent. For example, in industries
that are considered to be "pervasively regulated," such as the liquor industry, warrantless inspections are permitted. Industries that are considered to be "inherently dangerous," such as mining, are also subject
to warrantless inspections. Emergency situations will also justify a warrantless inspection or search, such as when the health of the public is
threatened by contaminated or unwholesome food (*North American Cold
Storage Co. v. Chicago*, 1908). However, the entry for the emergency is
valid only during the course of the emergency and for a short period
thereafter.

In the context of criminal procedure, an inspection or search that
is conducted without proper authority is subject to the exclusionary
rule, meaning that any evidence that results from that inspection or
search will not be admissible in court (*Mapp v. Ohio*, 1961). The exclusionary rule is intended to discourage law enforcement officers from
overzealous conduct that would violate the right of individuals to a reasonable expectation of privacy (*Terry v. Ohio*, 1968). The exclusionary
rule is not, however, consistently applied in the context of administrative searches and inspections. In deciding whether or not the rule
should apply, courts have looked to whether the violator would be
subject to criminal penalties, whether the admission of the "tainted"
evidence is justified by the public interest in the regulatory process,
whether the exclusion of the evidence will have a deterrent effect on
the agency that obtained it through the inspection or search, and
whether the officer(s) who obtained the evidence through the search
or inspection acted in "good faith," believing that the warrant that
was issued was valid (*Donovan v. Federal Clearing Die Casting Co.*, 1982).

Let us suppose that a health inspector has obtained a valid *administrative* warrant to conduct an inspection of an apartment complex following the receipt of numerous complaints from tenants relating to housing violations, such as a lack of heat and a rat infestation. During the course of the inspection, the inspector happens upon a cache of weapons in the basement that appears to be the property of the owner. Can the inspector seize the weapons to be used in a criminal proceeding against the building owner for violation of the gun laws?

The answer is . . . no. Because housing violations, not weapons, were the subject of the administrative warrant, the inspector cannot seize them. However, if the weapons were in "plain view" during the course of the inspection, the inspector can notify the police.

The Embargo, Seizure, and Destruction of Articles

An embargo is an order stating that an article cannot be moved because it is suspected of being in violation of law. When an embargo is placed on an item, it is usually done by placing a tag on it indicating that it cannot be moved.

Items that have been embargoed may be seized to protect the public health and prevent injury. Such seizures cannot be effectuated legally without first obtaining a warrant from a court. In general, the agency will not seize the articles until after it has made a request to the company to recall or destroy the offending items and that request has been denied or ignored. Unlike the federal agency, local and state agencies often have the authority to conduct a summary seizure, that is, a warrantless seizure without a prior court hearing, if it knows or suspects that there is a violation of law.

The seizure, confiscation, and destruction of goods by the state or federal government derives from the police power. Such proceedings are considered to be civil in nature, rather than criminal. The proceeding is against the thing (*in rem*), rather than against the person. Although the owner is entitled to a hearing, that hearing may or may not occur prior to the seizure or destruction of the thing. This is particularly true if it is believed that the article in question presents a threat to the health or safety of the public; in such cases, summary seizure and destruction of the article will be permitted, and a hearing will be held following this action. As an example, animals that are infected with a contagious disease may be seized and destroyed prior to a hearing to prevent infection of other animals (*Affonso Brothers v. Brock*, 1938).

Numerous federal agencies have been delegated authority under relevant statutes to embargo, seize, and destroy specific articles. The Department of Agriculture is authorized under the Federal Meat Inspection Act and the Poultry Products Inspection Act to inspect animals before and after they are slaughtered and to summarily seize and condemn products that do not conform to the existing standards. Similar authority to conduct inspections and seize particular products exists under the Egg Products Inspection Act, which seeks to protect consumers from harm associated with the ingestion of "unwholesome, otherwise adulterated, or improperly packaged-egg products" (Egg Products Inspection Act, 21 U.S.C.S. § 1031) and under the Consumer Product Safety Act, which attempts to assist consumers to evaluate the safety of consumer products.

The Federal Insecticide, Fungicide, and Rodenticide Act allows for the issuance of a "stop sale, use, or removal" order in the event that a pesticide or device that is found on the basis of inspections or testing is in violation of the statute's provisions or has been or is to be sold in violation of the statute. The Act also provides for the seizure of products under particular circumstances:

> Any pesticide or device that is being transported or, having been transported, remains unsold or in original unbroken packages, or that is sold or offered for sale in any State, or that is imported from a foreign country, shall be liable to be proceeded against in any district court in the district where it is found and seized for confiscation . . . if—
>
> (1) in the case of a pesticide—
>
>> (A) it is adulterated or misbranded;
>> (B) it is not registered [as required];
>> (C) its labeling fails to bear the information required by this Act . . . ;
>> (D) it is not colored or discolored and such coloring or discoloring is required under this Act . . . ;
>
> (2) in the case of a device, it is misbranded; or
> (3) in the case of a pesticide or device, when used in accordance with the requirements imposed under this Act . . . and as directed by the labeling, it nevertheless causes unreasonable adverse effects on the environment. (Federal Insecticide, Fungicide, and Rodenticide Act, 7 U.S.C.S. § 136k, 2008)

An authorized agent or employee of the Food and Drug Administration has the authority to detain a device that, upon inspection, is believed to be adulterated and misbranded and to detain food that is believed, on the basis of "inspection, examination, or investigation . . . if the officer or qualified employee has credible evidence or information indicating that such article presents a threat of serious adverse health consequences or death to humans or animals" (Food, Drug, and Cosmetic Act, 21 U.S.C.S. §§ 334(g), (h), 2008).

The FDA can initiate the seizure of adulterated or contaminated food, drugs, or cosmetics through the issuance of a libel of condemnation, which is an action against the goods, rather than the manufacturer or owner (Food, Drug, and Cosmetic Act, 21 U.S.C.S. § 334). Consider the following examples.

The Food and Drug Administration condemned as misbranded and adulterated an entire shipment of prophylactics to be used to prevent the transmission of sexually transmitted diseases where it was found during testing that a substantial percentage of the prophylactics were defective (*Gellman v. United States*, 1947). The agency seized as misbranded drugs bottles that contained liquid and capsules of crude petroleum that had been labeled as unrefined petroleum oil to be used for the treatment of psoriasis, eczema, athlete's foot, and leg ulcers (*United States v. 9 Bottles*, 1947). In yet another case, the agency proceeded against an over-the-counter medical device that was condemned as misbranded due to misleading labeling (*United States v. An Article ...ACU-DOT ...*, 1980). The device, sold in sheets of 10, consisted of a small, pin-sized magnet that was attached to a circular adhesive patch. The manufacturers had claimed in the pamphlet accompanying the device that it could relieve the minor aches and pains of muscles and joints. However, in reality the device only achieved its intended effect through a placebo effect and had no inherent effectiveness.

The owner of seized articles has several potential courses of action available. He or she can abandon the articles that were seized, contest the basis for the seizure, or ask the court for permission to bring the articles into compliance with the relevant legal provisions. This enforcement action initiated by the agency does not prevent the owner or manufacturer from distributing or producing more of the same item, although it would also be subject to a seizure action.

Criminal penalties, including fines and imprisonment, may be imposed. Publicity may also be utilized as a mechanism of enforcement. The publicity serves both to warn the general public of the possible health hazard associated with the product and to pressure the owner or manufacturer to effectuate the requested modifications.

Reporting Functions

Health agencies may compel the disclosure of specified information if authorized to do so by statute. Depending upon the particular statutory provisions, disclosure of this information may be effectuated through required reporting to the agency, agency inspection of records and premises, or the issuance of a subpoena for witnesses and documents by either the health agency itself or by request of the agency to a court for the issuance of the subpoena.

A subpoena duces tecum is an order to produce documents or records that are already in existence. For it to be valid, it can request only specified information that is relevant to the health agency's purpose. The purpose of the subpoena is to produce information, not to gather evidence for use in an action against the individual or entity. However, it is possible that facts will be discovered during the process of reviewing the information produced that provide the basis for the initiation of a complaint against the individual or entity.

In some cases, records are required to be open to inspection at all times. As an example, the federal Food, Drug, and Cosmetic Act provides that records must be maintained of all movements of food, drugs, and cosmetics in interstate commerce; a refusal to permit access to these records is deemed to be in violation of the law. In other circumstances, the reporting of specified events and activities to designated authorities may be required. For example, laboratories and physicians are required to report the occurrence of specified diseases to the relevant public health authorities. The failure to maintain and provide compulsory records as required is considered to be a violation of the law and may lead to criminal prosecution.

Remedies Available to the Public Health Agency

TEMPORARY RESTRAINING ORDERS AND INJUNCTIONS

An injunction is an order from a court that either mandates that a specific action be performed (mandatory injunction) or prohibits the performance of a specific act (prohibitory injunction). Unlike an award of damages, which is considered to be a legal remedy, an injunction is considered to be an equitable remedy and will be granted only when a legal remedy would be inadequate in the specific circumstances. Injunctions may be temporary or permanent. If the situation in question calls for immediate action, the court may issue a temporary restraining order (TRO) or preliminary injunction for a very limited period of time; this prohibits a party from engaging in a particular course of action until a hearing relating to the injunction can occur.

As an example of how an injunction might be used and why it is an important remedy, consider the following scenario. Suppose that the inspection of a food production company finds that there are unsanitary conditions that could threaten the health of the consumers of those products. The offending company could be issued a fine, be subjected to a cease and desist order, or suffer imprisonment. However, none of these approaches actually addresses the existence of the unhealthy conditions. In contrast, the issuance of an injunction by a court means that the individuals responsible for the unsanitary conditions must remedy the situation through removal or modification of the offending conditions. Injunctions have been used in a wide variety of circumstances, such as cases involving air and water pollution, unsanitary conditions, and the sale or distribution of contaminated drugs or medical devices.

A petition to a court by a public health agency for injunctive relief must be supported by a sworn affidavit that gives the court notice of the facts that are involved and explains the need for the injunction. As previously noted, if there is an emergent situation, the court may decide to issue a temporary restraining order, which will be in effect for a circumscribed period of time because it will have been issued without having heard from the party against whom it is to be enforced. The court will review the situation to determine whether the issuance of a longer-term order is merited. At this time, the opposing party must also file a sworn affidavit stating the facts as it sees them and reasons why the injunction should not be issued.

If the court decides that injunctive relief is warranted, it may issue a temporary injunction, which will prohibit or mandate the action for a longer period of time than did the TRO. Later, a full hearing will be held to determine whether a permanent injunction should be issued. In situations that do not involve an immediate threat to the public's health, the health agency may seek only a permanent injunction, which will eliminate the steps needed to obtain a TRO and a preliminary injunction.

A temporary or a permanent injunction will be issued only if the petitioning agency can demonstrate (1) that failure to issue an injunction may result in irreparable harm or imminent and substantial endangerment, (2) that the agency is likely to prevail at a hearing for a permanent injunction, and (3) that the public interest to be protected outweighs any private interests involved. (Issues to be considered in balancing private rights against the public interest are the focus of Chapter 9.)

If the party that is subject to the injunction refuses to comply, the court may punish the individual or company for being in contempt of its order if it can be shown that the party was aware of the order and the disobedience was willful. Depending on the particular circumstances, the contempt charge may be civil, requiring the payment of monetary sums, or criminal, resulting in a fine or imprisonment or both. The party charged with contempt may defend him- or herself with evidence of inability to comply with the order.

Injunctions may also be sought against an action of the agency by the individuals or companies that will be affected by a specified action. For example, in the case of *Florida Department of Agriculture and Consumer Services v. Haire* (2003) mentioned earlier, the growers of the citrus trees had sought an injunction from the court to halt the Department's intended warrantless search of property and destruction of healthy trees.

SANCTIONS

Civil Sanctions

A civil penalty may consist of a fine, the collection of sums to remedy a situation, or the imposition of liens against a property. Whereas the purpose of a criminal fine may be retribution, punishment, or deterrence, the purpose of a civil sanction is to a remedy a specific situation. The relevant statute may provide for the imposition of civil penalties, criminal sanctions, or both for violations of the law.

Civil penalties may be easier to obtain against a violating party than a criminal sanction. In a civil matter, the agency need only to prove that its case is a preponderance of the evidence, whereas in a trial to impose a criminal sanction, the agency must establish every element of its case beyond a reasonable doubt. However, it may be difficult to collect the civil monetary award and, because it is civil in nature rather than criminal, it may not have as much of a deterrent effect on the violating party.

Many federal laws contain provisions that specifically authorize the imposition of civil penalties. These include the Clean Air Act, the Clean Water Act, the Resource Conservation and Recovery Act (along with its Hazardous and Solid Waste Amendments), the Federal Insecticide, Fungicide, and Rodenticide Act, the Toxic Substances Control Act, and the Comprehensive Environmental Response, Compensation, and Liability Act (CERCLA), also known as Superfund.

Consider, for example, the spectrum of violations and corresponding penalties that exist under the Occupational Safety and Health Act, which is empowered to develop safety and health standards and perform workplace inspections to ensure compliance with the standards by employers who fall within the statutory provisions. The least serious violation will not result in either serious physical harm or injury but is directly related to job safety and health. Such violations may result in the imposition of a civil penalty that ultimately may be reduced depending upon the size of the business, the history of previous violations, and whether the employer has made a good faith attempt to comply with the relevant provisions of the Occupational Safety and Health Act (United States Department of Labor, 2007).

Violations that carry a substantial probability of leading to death or serious physical harm are considered to be serious if the employer knew or should have known of the hazard. The mandatory penalty may also be adjusted downward here, depending upon those same factors previously enumerated.

Willful violations are those that involve a hazardous condition that the employer knowingly or intentionally committed and has not tried to rectify. Downward adjustments of the penalty may be possible depending upon the size of the business and the history of previous violations. In addition to or instead of a fine, a prison sentence may be imposed if the willful violation led to the death of an employee.

Reinspections that result in a finding that previous violations have not been corrected can lead to the imposition of a fine for each violation. In addition, there can be a fine imposed for every day that the violation continues to exist (United States Department of Labor, 2007).

A civil penalty can also be imposed against a violating party by placing a lien on the property in question. For example, some states, such as Ohio, authorize the imposition of a lien against a property in the amount that would be required to clean up the hazardous waste that has been deposited there (Ohio Revised Code § 3734.20, 2008). To rely on this provision, it must be shown that there has been a failure to comply fully with a previously issued order of the director of environmental protection "to abate or prevent air or water pollution or soil contamination or to remedy a threat to public health or safety caused by conditions at such a facility" (Ohio Revised Code § 3734.20(B), 2008). The director of environmental protection must maintain an itemized list of all of the costs associated with the investigation and activities undertaken to remedy the situation, including the costs of labor, materials, and contract services. These costs are then recorded at the office of the county recorder in the county in which the facility is located; these costs then constitute a lien against the property. The director may request that the state attorney general initiate a civil action against the facility to recover the costs expended.

When a lien has been placed on a property, the owner cannot sell it without satisfying the lien. Ultimately, a lien against the property can be enforced through foreclosure. In cases in which multiple liens have been placed against a property by multiple parties for various purposes, state law must be consulted to determine which of the liens has priority for payment. In some cases, an agency may choose not to pursue an action to have a lien imposed on the offending property because of the expense that such action would entail and the relative unlikelihood of receiving payment should other liens against the property exist.

Criminal Sanctions

The violation of most public health laws and regulations is usually classified as a misdemeanor or a lesser level infraction or offense, rather than the more serious crime of a felony. The violation may be punishable by fine or imprisonment; in general, offenses are punishable by fine and do not often carry the threat of a jail sentence. The procedures involved in a criminal trial were described in Chapter 3 and will not be repeated here.

Criminal prosecutions have been initiated in a variety of cases, such as those involving the shipment of adulterated drugs (*United States v. Dotterweich*, 1943) and adulterated food (*United States v. Park*, 1975), and the disposal of hazardous waste (*United States v. Ward*, 1982). Each of these examples is discussed briefly in the following paragraphs.

In *United States v. Dotterweich* (1943), an information was filed against Buffalo Pharmacal Company, Inc. and Dotterweich, who was its president and general manager, charging them with violations of the Food, Drug, and Cosmetic Act. It was alleged that the company had purchased drugs from their manufacturers and then repacked them under its own label prior to shipping them in interstate commerce. In holding Dotterweich criminally liable for the misbranding of the drugs, the court emphasized that the legislation was intended "to keep impure and adulterated food and drugs out of the channels of commerce" to protect "the phases of the lives and health of people which, in the circumstances of modern industrialism, are largely beyond self-protection" (*United States v. Dotterweich*, 1943, p. 280).

United States v. Ward (1982) involved the prosecution of Ward, who was the chairman of the board of Ward Transformer Company. That company was engaged in the purchase, rebuilding, and resale of used voltage transformers. Many such transformers contained oil that was laced with polychlorinated biphenyls (PCBs), which have a high ignition temperature that reduces the likelihood of a fire in the event that a transformer ignites. However, PCBs were designated under the Toxic Substances Control Act as a toxic substance.

A friend approached Ward with a business scheme that would allow them both to profit from PCBs. According to the relevant regulations, further manufacture of PCB chemicals was prohibited, but the use of existing PCB-laced oil in electric transformers was permitted. Ward's friend purchased the oil from Ward Transformer Company with the intention of storing it and selling it back to dealers to be utilized to recondition used transformers.

However, Ward and his friend found that their scheme was unprofitable and sought to dispose of the unwanted product. They decided to dump the unwanted oil alongside the roads. The unlawful dumping was discovered by state and federal authorities. Ward was convicted of unlawful disposal of toxic substances and aiding and abetting the unlawful disposal of toxic substances.

United States v. Park (1975) involved an appeal from the court of appeals' reversal of the conviction of Park, the chief executive of Acme Markets, Inc., for the shipment in interstate commerce of adulterated food, in violation of the Federal Food, Drug, and Cosmetic Act. An FDA consumer safety officer had discovered during an inspection:

"Thirty mouse pellets on the floor along walls and on the ledge in the hanging meat room. There were at least twenty mouse pellets beside bales of lime Jello and one of the bales had a chewed rodent hole in the product . . . " (*United States v. Park*, 1975, p. 662).

The Food and Drug Administration issued a letter to Park advising him of the unsanitary conditions. A subsequent inspection revealed that the offensive conditions persisted despite the letter's admonition to correct the situation and comply with the law. At trial, Park was convicted of the sale of adulterated food. The Supreme Court found that Park was on notice of the violations and had the power and the responsibility to prevent them.

In some situations, the agency may seek both civil and criminal sanctions. This was the situation in a case involving Detroit Vital Foods, Inc. and two of its executives. The Food and Drug Administration initiated civil condemnation proceedings against Detroit Vital Foods, Inc. for the products "Korleen" and "Frutex," and a criminal action was commenced against the company's president, Kordel, and vice president, Feldten (*United States v. Kordel*, 1970; *United States v. Detroit Vital Foods, Inc.*, 1969). Kordel had consistently represented in lectures and advertising material that specified chemicals could improve health and that such "natural nutrients" were the constituent elements of the products Korleen and Frutex. It was claimed that Korleen could successfully treat cirrhosis of the liver and eliminate varicose veins. Frutex was claimed to be an effective preventive strategy and cure for bleeding gums, sore throat, earache, swollen neck glands, pneumonia, and acute rheumatism. In the criminal case, both Kordel and Feldten were convicted of having violated provisions of the federal Food, Drug, and Cosmetic Act and were fined and sentenced to prison. A fine was also imposed on the company.

References

1. Affonso Brothers v. Brock, 84 P.2d 515 (Cal. 1938).
2. Camara v. Municipal Court, 387 U.S. 523 (1967).
3. Clean Air Act, 42 U.S.C.S. § 7413(b).
4. Clean Water Act, 33 U.S.C.S. § 1319(d).
5. Comprehensive Environmental Response, Compensation, and Liability Act (CERCLA), 42 U.S.C.S. § 9601 et seq.
6. Donovan v. Federal Clearing Die Casting Co., 695 F.2d 1020 (7th Cir. 1982).
7. Egg Products Inspection Act, 21 U.S.C.S. § 1031 et seq.
8. Federal Insecticide, Fungicide, and Rodenticide Act, 7 U.S.C.S. §§ 136(k), (l).
9. Federal Meat Inspection Act, 21 U.S.C.S. § 601 et seq.
10. Florida Department of Agriculture and Consumer Services v. Haire, 836 So.2d 1040 (Fla. App. 2003).

11. Food, Drug, and Cosmetic Act, 21 U.S.C.S. §§ 301 et seq.

12. Gellman v. United States, 159 F.2d 881 (8th Cir. 1947).

13. Gostin, L. O. (2007). A theory and definition of public health law. *Journal of Health Care Law & Policy, 10,* 1–12.

14. Grad, F. P. (1990). *The public health law manual* (2nd ed.). Washington, DC: American Public Health Association.

15. Hazardous and Solid Waste Amendments, 15 U.S.C. § 2601 et seq.

16. Mapp v. Ohio, 367 U.S. 643 (1961).

17. Marshall v. Barlow's Inc., 436 U.S. 307 (1978).

18. North American Cold Storage Co. v. Chicago, 211 U.S. 306 (1908).

19. Occupational Safety and Health Act, 29 U.S.C.S. §§ 651–678.

20. Ohio Revised Code § 3734.20 (2008).

21. Poultry Products Inspection Act, 21 U.S.C.S. § 451 et seq.

22. Resource Conservation and Recovery Act, 42 U.S.C.S. §6901 et seq.

23. Terry v. Ohio, 392 U.S. 1 (1968).

24. Tobey, J. A. (1947). *Public health law* (3rd ed.). New York: Commonwealth Fund.

25. Toxic Substances Control Act, 15 U.S.C.S. § 2601 et seq.

26. United States v. 9 Bottles, 78 F. Supp. 721 (D.C. Iowa, 1947), *affirmed* 176 F.2d 554 (8th Cir. 1949), *cert. denied* 338 U.S. 911 (1950).

27. United States v. An Article . . . ACU-DOT . . . , 483 F. Supp. 1311 (N.D. Ohio, 1980).

28. United States v. Detroit Vital Foods, Inc., 407 F.2d 570 (1969), *reversed and remanded,* 397 U.S. 1 (1970).

29. United States v. Dotterweich, 320 U.S. 277 (1943).

30. United States v. Kordel, 397 U.S. 1 (1970).

31. United States v. Park, 421 U.S. 658 (1975).

32. United States v. Ward, 676 F.2d 94 (4th Cir. 1982).

33. United States Department of Labor. (2007, July). *Employment law guide: Occupational safety and health.* Retrieved August 10, 2008, from http://www.dol.gov/compliance/Guide/Osha.htm

Chapter 5

Law, Epidemiology, and Communicable Disease

Case Study 1: Criminal Prosecutions for HIV Exposure

An increasing number of states have promulgated legislation that requires HIV-infected individuals to disclose their serostatus to sexual partners and/or to use methods designed to decrease the risk of HIV transmission. Violation of these laws may, in some cases, result in criminal prosecution and conviction. This case study examines the nature of HIV and its transmission and the role of epidemiology and epidemiologists in related investigations.

THE EPIDEMIOLOGY OF HIV

The first reports of *Pneumocystis carinii* pneumonia (PCP) in homosexual men surfaced in 1981, when the disease was detected in five individuals (Centers for Disease Control, 1981b). Kaposi's sarcoma was detected in 26 others (Centers for Disease Control, 1981a). Both conditions were ultimately linked to an underlying immune deficiency (Gottlieb, et al.,

1981; Masur, et al., 1981) that was identified in 1983 to 1984 as human immunodeficiency virus (HIV), the causative agent of the acquired immunodeficiency syndrome (AIDS) (Barre-Sinoussi, et al., 1983; Popovic, Sarngadharan, Read, & Gallo, 1984).

HIV is transmitted by sexual intercourse, including vaginal (Laga, Taelman, Van der Stuyft, & Bonneux, 1989; Peterman, Stoneburner, Allen, Jaffe, & Curran, 1988), anal (Darrow, et al., 1987; Detels, et al., 1989; Moss, et al., 1987; Winkelstein, et al., 1987), and oral intercourse (Lifson, et al., 1990). It is also transmitted through injection drug use with contaminated injection equipment (Hoffman, Larkin, & Samuel, 1989; Sasse, Salmaso, Conti, & First Drug User Multicenter Study Group, 1989; Schoenbaum, et al., 1989); transfusion with virus-contaminated blood or blood products; and from mother to child before birth, during delivery, or through breastfeeding. Vehicles for transmission include semen (Chiasson, Stoneburner, & Joseph, 1990; Ho, Schooley, Rota, Kaplan, & Flynn, 1984; Levy, 1989), vaginal and cervical secretions (Vogt, et al., 1986; Wofsy, et al., 1986), blood and blood products (Donegan, et al., 1990), tissue and organs from HIV-infected donors (Centers for Disease Control, 1987, 1988; Kumar, et al., 1987), and breast milk (Colebunders, et al., 1988; Thiry, et al., 1985; Ziegler, Cooper, Johnson, & Gold, 1985). HIV is not transmissible through casual and household contact (Friedland, et al., 1990; Rogers, et al., 1990), despite its presence in tears (Fujikawa, et al., 1985) and saliva (Ho, et al., 1985).

Although HIV can be transmitted through a variety of sexual acts, the risk of transmission is not equivalent but differs depending upon the nature of the sexual act. The receptive individual is at higher risk of infection than is the insertive partner. Unprotected anal intercourse carries a 1 in 50 chance of HIV transmission from the insertive to the receptive partner (Vittinghoff, et al., 1999). In contrast, the risk of transmission associated with vaginal intercourse ranges from 1 in every 1000 or 2000 without a condom to 1 in 10,000 to 1 in 20,000 when a condom is used (Downs & De Vincenzi, 1996). Other activities, such as kissing and biting, that involve body fluids other than blood carry a negligible risk of transmission (Campo, et al., 2006; Royce, Seña, Cates, & Cohen, 1997). The presence or absence of other factors, such as a sexually transmitted infection, circumcision of the male partner, the health of the uninfected partner, and the viral load of the infected partner, may serve to increase or decrease the risk of transmission (Fowler, Melnick, & Mathieson, 1997; Royce, et al., 1997; Williams, et al., 2006).

The illness was initially referred to as gay-related immune deficiency (GRID) and attributed to lifestyle choices (Centers for Disease Control, 1986). Reports soon surfaced of its detection in nongay individuals, which prompted the identification of "risk groups": homosexuals, heroin users, Haitians, and hemophiliacs (Shilts, 1987; New

York City Commission on Human Rights, 1986, 1987). The resulting stereotyping of groups and emphasis on transmission through unprotected male–male sex and intravenous drug use severely hampered the detection of the illness in women and the prevention of the disease across populations (American Public Health Association, 1991; Mays & Cochran, 1987).

Worldwide, an estimated 33.2 million persons were infected with HIV as of December 2007; 2.5 million of them became newly infected that year (Joint United Nations Programme on HIV/AIDS & World Health Organization, 2007). It is estimated that, every day, more than 6800 individuals become infected with HIV, and over 5700 die from AIDS. A total of 2.1 million persons died in 2007 due to AIDS. AIDS is the leading cause of death in sub-Saharan Africa, while South Africa has the greatest number of HIV-infected persons of any country in the world. Increases of the incidence of HIV have been noted in Oceania and East Asia.

The profile of those infected with HIV at the beginning of the US epidemic differs significantly from the characteristics of those who are now infected. While the initial cases were detected in primarily white homosexual men, current data indicate a disproportionate impact of the epidemic on nonwhite populations and an increasing incidence and prevalence in heterosexuals and women (Osmond, 1999). As of 2005, the largest estimated proportion of HIV/AIDS diagnoses by transmission category was for men who have sex with men, followed by adults and adolescents who were infected through unprotected heterosexual contact (Centers for Disease Control and Prevention, 2007a).

In 2005, blacks accounted for 49% of all HIV/AIDS cases diagnosed that year (Centers for Disease Control and Prevention, 2007b), although they make up only 13% of the US population (Centers for Disease Control and Prevention, 2007a). AIDS was the fourth leading cause of death among African Americans ages 25 to 44 years in 2004 (Anderson, Mosher, & Chandra, 2006). In 2004, although Latinos accounted for 14% of the population, including Puerto Rico, they accounted for 18% of all new HIV diagnoses reported in the 35 areas with long-term confidential name-based HIV reporting and have accounted for 19% of all AIDS cases diagnosed since the beginning of the epidemic. In 2004, an estimated 20.4% of all deaths attributed to AIDS were among Hispanics (Centers for Disease Control and Prevention, 2006b). In 2002, HIV/AIDS became the fourth leading cause of death in the United States for Hispanics aged 35 to 44 years and the sixth leading cause of death among those aged 45 to 54 years (Anderson & Smith, 2005). HIV disease now ranks as the third leading cause of death among Hispanic men aged 35 to 44 years and the fourth leading cause of death among Hispanic women of the same age group

(Anderson & Smith, 2005). Puerto Ricans, in particular, have been disproportionately impacted (Centers for Disease Control and Prevention, 2006b). In 2005, rates of HIV/AIDS cases per 100,000 population were 71.3 among blacks, 27.8 among Hispanics, 10.4 among American Indians/Alaskan Natives, 8.8 among whites, and 7.4 among Asians/Pacific Islanders. From 2001 to 2005, the estimated numbers of AIDS cases increased among men who have sex with men, males exposed through heterosexual contact, and women exposed through heterosexual contact. The numbers of AIDS cases increased in all geographic regions of the country, with the exception of the West, where the number decreased (Centers for Disease Control and Prevention, 2007b).

Partner notification is a critical strategy in the prevention and control of infection. It was first used to control syphilis and was later applied to the control of HIV (Hogben & Kissinger, 2008). There are three types of partner notification procedures: public-health mediated, patient-based referral, and contract referral, which is an amalgam of the first two approaches. Partner notification permits the identification of exposed persons and affords an opportunity to conduct risk counseling and provide referrals for testing and treatment.

PROTECTING PUBLIC HEALTH THROUGH CRIMINAL PROSECUTION FOR HIV EXPOSURE

Media reports of the exposure by Nushawn Williams, a young African-American man recently released from prison, of dozens of young girls to HIV by trading sex for drugs prompted legislators in numerous states, as well as members of the general public, to reexamine existing laws related to the knowing exposure of one's sexual partners to HIV (Altman, 1997; Davis, 1997, 1998; Esmonde, Peradotto, & Michel, 1997; Palazetti, 1997b). Williams could not have foreseen the ultimate impact of his actions.

Williams came to the attention of public health officials in New York City in 1996 as the result of a referral for the treatment of a sexually transmitted infection. Williams agreed to be tested for HIV in accordance with their recommendation; that test revealed that Williams was HIV seropositive (Altman, 1997). The public health officials began contacting the women who Williams had named as having been his sexual partners. In addition, they advised Williams to disclose his HIV infection to his future partners and to use a condom during sexual relations (McCarthy, 1997).

A sharp increase in the numbers of women infected with HIV in Jamestown, New York ultimately led the public health authorities there to identify Williams as the probable source of infection (Galarneau, 1997; Palazetti, 1997a). In a highly unusual move, the Jamestown public health officials sought a court order authorizing them to release

Williams' identity to the general public, arguing that he posed an "imminent danger" to the public health and should not, therefore, be sheltered by the confidentiality laws that protected HIV test results (Galarneau, 1997). That court order was granted. (Note here the tension that exists in trying to balance the protection of the public against Williams' interest in maintaining the confidentiality of his HIV status and in safeguarding his privacy. This conflict is addressed in Chapter 9.)

It was later estimated that Williams had exposed 48 women in Jamestown and 50 to 75 women in New York City to HIV (Centers for Disease Control, 1999). It appears that Williams was suffering from schizophrenia and did not understand either his diagnosis or the need to use condoms (Cooper, 1999; Michel & Warner, 1997). He was charged by Jamestown prosecutors with assault and statutory rape and by prosecutors in New York City with reckless endangerment, sexual misconduct, attempted assault, and endangering the welfare of a minor with whom he had had sexual intercourse (Richardson, 1998; Waldman, 1999).

The public disclosure of these events brought about an immediate response by legislators. A 2004 survey of states reported that, at that time, 23 states had adopted HIV-specific statutes that created a separate crime for knowingly exposing another individual to HIV (Wolf & Vezina, 2004). The majority of these laws did not require a specific intent but only specified activity. Although some states limited the scope of their laws to address only those activities known to carry a risk of HIV transmission, such as unprotected vaginal or anal intercourse, others included behaviors that are deemed to carry minimal risk of transmission. New Jersey's statute, for example, criminalizes the "act of sexual penetration" in the absence of the partner's informed consent to engage in intercourse with the HIV-positive individual; sexual penetration is defined to include the "insertion of the hand, finger, or object into the anus or vagina" (New Jersey Statutes, 2007), acts that are believed to be the safest in terms of transmission. A minority of statutes address needle sharing or the donation of blood, plasma, organs, skin, or other tissue by someone with knowledge of his or her HIV seropositivity (Wolf & Vezina, 2004).

The promulgation of such laws rests on several premises. First, the laws seek to protect members of society from physical harm by others (LaFave & Scott, 1986). Second, it has been argued that the implementation of such measures will deter individuals from intentionally or recklessly exposing others to HIV transmission (Lazzarini, Bray, & Burris, 2002; Wolf & Vezina, 2004) and from engaging in behavior that is perceived as socially unacceptable (Wolf & Vezina, 2004), while encouraging conduct that conforms to social norms (Lazzarini, et al., 2002).

Several cases, albeit in the military context, have upheld criminal convictions of HIV seropositive individuals who exposed their sexual partners to HIV with the knowledge and consent of that partner (*United States v. Bygrave*, 1997; *United States v. Morris*, 1990). In upholding the defendant's assault conviction in *United States v. Bygrave*, the court explained why the partner's knowledge of the defendant's HIV status and her consent to intercourse could not negate the defendant's criminal liability:

> [B]y compromising her own health, she also risked compromising the health of others. The Government's interests in the present case are not limited to the health of [this woman], but also encompass the health of any sexual partners she may have in the future, any children she might bear, and anyone else to whom she may potentially transmit HIV through nonsexual contact. (*United States v. Bygrave*, 1997, p. 491)

In the civilian context, an HIV-positive man in Dallas who exposed a police officer to his saliva by spitting on him was convicted of harassment of a public servant (Ellis, 2008). The jury found that because the man was HIV positive, his saliva constituted a dangerous weapon. The defendant was sentenced to 35 years in prison. This verdict has promoted HIV-positive individuals to wonder if they must now disclose their HIV seropositivity even to individuals with whom they might share a drink, for fear that they will be prosecuted criminally, despite the unlikelihood of transmission through saliva.

Despite the promulgation of such laws and the ensuing prosecutions, there is little evidence to support the effectiveness of the legislation or the prosecutions in modifying behavior. Research findings suggest that as many as two-thirds of all cases of transmission occur when the HIV seropositive partner is unaware of his or her serostatus (Koopman, et al., 1997). It is believed that one-quarter of all individuals who are living with HIV in the United States do not know that they are infected with the virus, and it is these individuals who are most likely to transmit the infection to others (Holtgrave & Anderson, 2004; Marks, Crepaz, & Janssen, 2006). A study that evaluated the impact of criminal laws on HIV risk behavior found that, in general, the laws failed to distinguish clearly between permissible behavior and behavior that is deemed to be wrongful and dangerous and were rarely enforced (Lazzarini, et al., 2002). The authors of that study concluded, "With criminal law as a means of preventing HIV, we can say that the trial is not over, but the case looks weak" (Lazzarini, et al., 2002, p. 252).

THE ROLE OF THE EPIDEMIOLOGIST

The expertise of an epidemiologist may be sought by either or both the prosecution and the defense, depending upon the facts of a particular case and the controlling law. That expertise may be critical to the preparation of a case or to the presentation of testimony in court.

Recall the earlier discussion relating to Nushawn Williams and the cases of HIV transmission that were found to have resulted from his unprotected sexual activities. The efforts of the epidemiologists in the local health department and the Centers for Disease Control and Prevention were critical to the identification of sexual contacts of Williams who may have been infected as a result of their sexual relations with him (Coles, et al., 1999). The extent of his activity provided the impetus for the promulgation of legislation aimed at reducing the risk to prospective partners of HIV transmission as a result of a partner's undisclosed serostatus.

Consider the following hypothetical situation and the potential role that an epidemiologist might play:

> The defendant, who is HIV positive, engaged in sexual intercourse with a woman who later tested positive for HIV. The sexual act occurred in California, which criminalizes undisclosed exposure to HIV in the context of unprotected vaginal or anal sex only if the HIV-infected partner intends to infect the other. It is unclear whether the defendant actually used a condom. The newly HIV-infected woman tells prosecutors that the man told her that he was putting a condom on in the dark so that it would not ruin the romantic atmosphere, but she is unsure whether he actually did.

The prosecution might argue that the defendant actually never used the condom and that his insistence on putting it on in the dark when she could not see was indicative of his intent to refrain from using a condom and to cause HIV transmission. The defense could call on an epidemiologist to testify as to the relative difficulty of transmitting HIV even when the sexual intercourse is unprotected; the prosecution could reframe that same information to support its argument relating to the high degree of risk that the defendant caused to his sexual partner.

In fact, testimony by an epidemiologist relating to the risk of HIV transmission associated with various modes of transmission has been used in the context of criminal prosecutions. The case of United States v. Moore (1988) involved the prosecution of an HIV-infected inmate, James Vernell Moore, for assault with a deadly weapon after he bit two correctional officers with his mouth and teeth. It was alleged by the prosecution that Moore had told the nurse at the correctional facility after this incident that he had "wanted to hurt them bad, wanted to kill the bastards," and that he hoped "the wounds he inflicted on the officers when he bit them were bad enough that they get the disease that he [had]" (United States v. Moore, 1988, p. 1165). Although the epidemiologist testified that he knew of no "well-proven instances in which a human bite has resulted in the transmission of the [HIV] virus to the bitten person" (United States v. Moore, 1988, p. 1165), he could not rule out with complete certainty the possibility that transmission might occur via these means. He further testified that a human bite is "a very dangerous form of aggression" and "one of the most dangerous of all forms of bites" because it could cause serious infection apart from HIV (*United States v. Moore*, 1988, p. 1165–1166). Based on this testimony, the appellate court found:

> Although there is sufficient evidence in the record that the human mouth and teeth may be used as a dangerous and deadly weapon, we nevertheless wish to emphasize that the medical evidence in the record was insufficient to establish that AIDS may be transmitted by a bite. The evidence established that there are no well-proven cases of HIV transmission by way of a bite; that contact with saliva has never been shown to transmit the disease; and that in one case a person who had been deeply bitten by a person with AIDS tested negative several months later . . . While [the physician] testified "in medicine everything is conceivable," in a legal context the possibility of AIDS transmission by means of a bite is too remote to support a finding that the mouth and teeth may be considered a deadly and dangerous weapon in this respect.
>
> In short, we hold that the evidence was sufficient to support the finding that Moore's mouth and teeth were a dangerous and deadly weapon, regardless of the presence or absence of AIDS. (*United States v. Moore*, 1988, pp. 1167–1168)

Case Study 2: Quarantine

Increasingly, concerns have been voiced with respect to the transmission of multidrug-resistant tuberculosis by persons who are unwilling or unable to comply with medical advice to adhere to a prescribed drug regimen and avoid contact with others to prevent disease transmission. This case study provides a brief review of the epidemiology of tuberculosis and discusses the possible role of the epidemiologist in proceedings to involuntarily isolate a nonadherent individual as a means of preventing disease transmission and safeguarding the public's health.

THE EPIDEMIOLOGY OF TUBERCULOSIS

The Etiology and Diagnosis of Tuberculosis
Pulmonary tuberculosis results from exposure to the bacillus *Mycobacterium tuberculosis* in airborne droplet nuclei. Individuals are exposed to the bacillus through the coughing, sneezing, or singing of persons who have laryngeal or pulmonary tuberculosis.

Although individuals may be exposed, they may not become infected. Among those who do become infected, the infection may not manifest for some time. Approximately 5% of individuals with intact immune systems develop active disease, compared to approximately half of those with compromised immune systems. The risk of contracting tuberculosis increases with increasing frequency and duration of exposure to an individual with active disease (Murray, 1998).

Approximately 90% to 95% of individuals who become infected develop latent tuberculosis after the initial lesions heal. However, they may remain at risk of reactivation of the disease. Exogenous reinfection or endogenous reactivation of a latent focus may lead to progressive pulmonary tuberculosis which, if untreated, can result in death. Individuals with advanced disease may experience fatigue, fever, night sweats, cough, chest pain, hemoptysis, and hoarseness (Fox & George, 1992).

Extrapulmonary tuberculosis, which is less common than pulmonary tuberculosis, may occur in any organ or tissue, including the kidneys, bone, eyes, intestines, and lymph nodes. The infection results from exposure to tuberculous cattle through the ingestion of unpasteurized dairy products. Unlike pulmonary tuberculosis, extrapulmonary tuberculosis is not usually communicable (Fanning, 1999; Murray, 1998).

Diagnosis may be made by specified laboratory tests, clinical verification, or provider diagnosis (Centers for Disease Control and Prevention, 2007c). Laboratory case definition requires the isolation of *Mycobacterium tuberculosis* from a clinical specimen, the detection of *Mycobacterium tuberculosis* nucleic acid using approved detection and testing methods, or the demonstration of acid-fast bacilli in a clinical specimen when a culture is not obtained. Clinical verification may be accomplished by a positive tuberculin skin test, signs and symptoms compatible with tuberculosis, treatment with two or more antituberculosis medications, and a completed diagnostic evaluation (Centers for Disease Control and Prevention, 2007c).

Individuals who have not had a previous history of tuberculosis disease and display resistance to at least two drugs (isoniazid and rifampin) are said to have multidrug-resistant tuberculosis (MDR TB). Effective treatment of MDR TB requires the administration of four to six drugs to which the organism is susceptible for a period of time ranging from 18 to 24 months (Anonymous, 2007). Individuals who display resistance to isoniazid and rifampin, as well as resistance to any fluoroquinolone and at least one of the three injectable second-line drugs for tuberculosis (amikacin, kanamycin, or capreomycin) are said to have extensively drug-resistant tuberculosis (XDR TB) (Centers for Disease Control and Prevention, 2007c).

The Global Impact of Tuberculosis

On an annual basis, there are approximately nine million new cases of tuberculosis and two million deaths attributable to tuberculosis worldwide, despite the availability of affordable, effective treatment (Jong-wook, 2006). It has been estimated that over one-third of the world's population is currently infected with tuberculosis bacillus (World Health Organization, 2006); a single untreated person can infect between 10 and 15 people per year (World Health Organization, 2005c). The vast majority of incident cases occur in various parts of Africa, Asia, and newly formed states of the former Soviet Union, known as the Commonwealth of Independent States, with a 1% rise in tuberculosis cases worldwide each year and an increasing incidence worldwide of drug-resistant tuberculosis (Centers for Disease Control and Prevention, 2006a; Jong-wook, 2006; World Health Organization, 2002, 2006). It has been estimated that between 7% and 12% of all new tuberculosis cases in adults aged 15 to 49 years are attributable to HIV infection (Corbett, et al., 2003). The disease kills more people every year than any other infectious disease; in fact, someone dies of tuberculosis every 15 seconds (World Health Organization, 2005a, 2005b). These increasing rates of tuberculosis are associated with poverty, an increase in HIV prevalence, falling living standards, and failing public health systems (Almeida & Thomas, 1996; World Health Organization, 2002).

Tuberculosis in the United States

All states are required to report cases of tuberculosis to the Centers for Disease Control and Prevention (CDC). These reports are made by laboratories and healthcare providers to their health departments, which transmit the information to the relevant state health departments, which are responsible for transmitting the information to CDC. In 2006, the CDC received reports of 13,779 cases of tuberculosis from the 50 states and the District of Columbia; this represented a decrease of 2.1% in the number of cases from 2005 (Centers for Disease Control and Prevention, 2007c). California, Texas, New York, and Florida accounted for almost one-half of the total number of cases; 20 states reported increases in the number of cases from 2005. Hispanics were the ethnic group with the largest percentage of total cases. Less than 1% of the reported cases had primary multidrug resistance; three cases of extensively drug-resistant tuberculosis were reported.

Individuals who are seeking legal entry into the United States as refugees or are applying for an immigrant visa overseas are required to undergo a medical examination by US government-authorized physicians ("panel physicians") prior to the commencement of physical migration. That examination includes various tests to detect active tuberculosis infection. Individuals who are found to have active tuberculosis disease are required to be treated for the infection prior to the commencement of their physical journey to the United States (Public Health Service, n.d.a). Similar procedures apply for individuals who are already physically in the United States and are applying for permanent residence (their "green card" or "mica") from within the United States; these individuals must be examined by a US government-authorized physician known as a civil surgeon (Public Health Service, n.d.b). However, this tuberculosis screening requirement does not apply to the vast majority of foreign-born individuals seeking admission to the United States each year, such as tourists, students, and businesspersons who are here temporarily, and it does not apply to US citizens and to individuals who have already obtained permanent resident status in the United States.

Despite these screening procedures, reports consistently attribute a large proportion of newly diagnosed cases of tuberculosis to foreign-born persons. The Centers for Disease Control and Prevention (1998) reported that 39% of all cases of tuberculosis in the country in 1997 were detected in foreign-born persons. From 1985 to 1992, foreign-born persons in the United States accounted for 60% of the total increase in the number of incident cases of tuberculosis (Cantwell, Snider, Cauthen & Onorato, 1994). From 1998 to 2001, the annual number of tuberculosis cases among African immigrants and refugees in Seattle and King County, Washington increased almost threefold compared to the period from 1993 to 1997 (Nolan, Goldberg, & Wallace, 2002). Almost one-half of the individuals had extrapulmonary tuberculosis. From 1985 to 1994, of the 3364 cases of tuberculosis among Asians in Los Angeles County, California, 98% were immigrants (Makinodan, et al., 1999). The case rate per 100,000 foreign-born Asians living in that county was 162.1, compared to a case rate of 2.6 per 100,000 among US-born Asians living in the same county.

Various factors may play a role in the increased incidence and prevalence of tuberculosis among foreign-born residents of the United States. First, legislation that increases individuals' fear of detection by immigration authorities has been shown to exacerbate delays in seeking care (Asch, Leake, Abderson, & Gelberg, 1998; Asch, Leake, & Gelberg, 1994). Second, screening procedures required of individuals seeking entry into the country as refugees and those seeking permanent resident status may not be as effective as desired. In Minneapolis from 1992 to 1994, it was found that 51% of the chest radiographs of Tibetan immigrants were abnormal, despite initial screening for tuberculosis by US-authorized physicians in India prior to immigration to the United States (Truong, et al., 1997). A comparison with results from evaluations conducted in India indicated that 79% of the Tibetans had unchanged readings, and 21% showed evidence of potentially progressive disease.

Finally, misconceptions about the disease itself may play a role in the delay in seeking care. One study of individuals' understanding of the disease found that although the disease is viewed as highly contagious, it is believed to be caused by environmental exposures, such as cigarettes and alcohol, unsanitary conditions, wet clothing, and bacteria and viruses; by imbalances of the body occasioned by overwork, poor nutrition, respiratory illness, worrying, and family problems; by family inheritance; and by contagion from an infected person through touch, the sharing of utensils, or airborne spread (Yamada, Caballero, Matsunaga, Agustin, & Magaña, 1999). Respondents reported that tuberculosis could be treated through modern medical attention, traditional medicines, improved sanitation and air, smoking cessation, and the correction of imbalances in the body through proper rest, exercise, discipline, diet, and a positive outlook.

INTERNATIONAL DISEASE CONTROL EFFORTS

The objective of the International Health Regulations (IHR) of the World Health Organization is to "prevent, protect against, control and provide a public health response to the international spread of disease in ways that are commensurate with . . . contemporary public health risks, and which avoid unnecessary interference with international traffic and trade" (World Health Organization, 2005b, art.2). In the context of epidemic and pandemic alert and response, six core functions are listed:

1. Support Member States for the implementation of national capacities for epidemic preparedness and response in the context of IHR (2005), including laboratory capacities and early warning alert and response systems;
2. Support national and international training programmes for epidemic preparedness and response;
3. Coordinate and support Member States for pandemic and seasonal influenza preparedness and response;
4. Develop standardized approaches for readiness and response to major epidemic-prone diseases (e.g., meningitis, yellow fever, plague);
5. Strengthen biosafety, biosecurity and readiness for outbreaks of dangerous and emerging pathogen outbreaks (e.g., SARS, viral haemorrhagic fevers);
6. Maintain and further develop a global operational platform to support outbreak response and support regional offices in implementation at a regional level (World Health Organization, 2005b).

QUARANTINE AND ISOLATION: AN OVERVIEW OF PROCEDURES

The concepts of social distancing, isolation, and quarantine are often confused. Social distancing, the least restrictive of these measures, is comprised of "infection control strategies that reduce the duration and/or intimacy of social contacts and thereby limit the transmission" (Homeland Security Council, 2006, p. 209). Examples of social distancing include the use of face masks, teleconferencing, and school closures. According to the Centers for Disease Control and Prevention, isolation is "the separation of persons who have a specific infectious illness from those who are healthy and restriction of their movement to stop the spread of that illness" (Centers for Disease Control and Prevention, 2005).

In contrast, quarantine is "the separation and restriction of movement of persons who, while not yet ill, have been exposed to an infectious agent and therefore may become infectious" (Centers for Disease Control and Prevention, 2005). Quarantine may be imposed by a government, a governmental entity, a board of health, a police chief, or the National Guard (Page, 2007). The use of quarantine as a measure for disease prevention in the United States has become particularly contentious not only because of its infringement on individual liberties but also because of its historically racist and xenophobic application. As an example, the San Francisco Board of Health attempted in the early 20th century to quarantine only Chinese residents for bubonic plague (*Wong Wai v. Williamson*, 1900) and, in more recent years, the United States became known as the only country in the world to establish an internment camp for the quarantine of HIV-seropositive asylum seekers—all of whom were black and Haitian (*Haitian Centers Council Inc. v. Sale*, 1993).

Federal Quarantine Authority

Federal law authorizes the Secretary of the Department of Health and Human Services to control the movement of persons into and within the United States to prevent the spread of communicable disease (42 U.S.C.S. § 264 2008). That authority has been delegated to the Centers for Disease Control and Prevention (42 C.F.R. §§ 70.6, 71.32(a), 2008).

Federal authority for quarantine functions currently resides in the Division of Global Migration and Quarantine (DGMQ) of the Centers for Disease Control and Prevention in Atlanta, Georgia. Since 2003, there have been 18 quarantine stations at entry points around the country: Anchorage, Atlanta, Boston, Chicago, Detroit, El Paso, Honolulu, Houston, Los Angeles, Miami, Minneapolis, New York, Newark, San Diego, San Francisco, San Juan, Seattle, and Washington, DC. Additional quarantine stations were opened in 2007 in Philadelphia and Dallas.

The DGMQ is empowered to detain, medically examine, or conditionally release individuals and wildlife suspected of carrying a communicable disease. Personnel of the various quarantine stations respond to reports of ill travelers on ships, planes, and at land border crossings to assess the risk to the public health and to initiate an appropriate response. The DGMQ coordinates its activities with various other governmental agencies, transportation providers, health providers, foreign governments, the media, and the courts. Federal partner agencies include the Fish and Wildlife Service, the Department of Agriculture, the Food and Drug Administration, the Department of Homeland Security, the Department of Transportation, the Federal Bureau of Investigation, the Federal Aviation Administration, the Coast Guard, and the Department of State. International and overseas partners include the World Health Organization, the International Organization for Migration, the Public Health Agency of Canada, and Canadian and Mexican border authorities.

Currently, federal isolation and quarantine are permitted for individuals believed to have the following communicable diseases: cholera, diphtheria, infectious tuberculosis, plague, smallpox, yellow fever, viral hemorrhagic fevers, severe acute respiratory syndrome (SARS), and any flu that could cause a pandemic (Executive Order, 2005; Executive Order 13295, 2003). This listing can be amended by executive order of the President of the United States. The authority to carry out these functions has been delegated to the Centers for Disease Control and Prevention by the Secretary of the US Department of Health and Human Services. That agency is authorized by statute to take measures to prevent the entry and spread of communicable diseases from foreign countries into the United States and between states (42 U.S.C.S. § 264, 2008).

State Quarantine Authority

Each state has the authority to impose quarantine measures (*Gibbons v. Ogden*, 1824; *Ex parte Company*, 1922; *Ex parte Johnson*, 1919) but, in doing so, must balance the right of the individual to be free from government intrusion and the state's duty to protect the public health (Gostin, 2003). Quarantine may be imposed on public and private vehicles, and individuals may be ordered confined to their residence, to a state facility, or to another designated location (Mindes, 1996). Quarantine will continue until such time as the individual is no longer contagious to others (Barbera, et al., 2005). (Note the widespread use of "quarantine" to describe situations that others would characterize as necessitating isolation.)

As an example, in Ohio, departments of health are authorized:

> [i]n time of epidemic or threatened epidemic, or when a dangerous communicable disease is unusually prevalent . . . after a per-

sonal investigation by its members or an executive officer to establish the facts in the case, and not otherwise, [to] impose a
quarantine on vessels, railroads, or other public or private vehicles conveying persons, baggage, freight, or used for such purpose. (Ohio Revised Code Annotated, 2008)

The power to quarantine is subject to limitation, however. Quarantine
and isolation orders may be enforced by health authorities and police
and other law enforcement personnel (Ohio Revised Code Annotated,
2008).

THE ROLE OF THE EPIDEMIOLOGIST

Just as in the case of HIV, the efforts of an epidemiologist may be critical in locating the contacts of an individual who has active tuberculosis disease to which others may have been exposed. Their expertise
may also be critical in assisting legal personnel in their preparation of
court documents seeking the involuntary quarantine of an individual
who refuses to adhere to the recommended course of treatment and
who refuses to remain isolated in his or her own home to reduce the
risk to others. In a case involving the involuntary quarantine of an individual with multidrug-resistant tuberculosis, an epidemiologist could
assist with the drafting of a petition for the detention of the individual and/or provide an affidavit or testimony that addresses the key
points raised in the petition. Key points to be addressed in such a case
include:

- The risk of relapse for the patient as the result of interrup-
  tions in treatment
- The creation of more virulent, multidrug-resistant strains of
  tuberculosis due to interrupted treatment
- The risk presented to others of transmission of the disease by
  a relapsed patient
- The enhanced difficulty involved in the treatment of more
  virulent, multidrug-resistant strains of tuberculosis and the
  resulting increased threat to the health of the public
- The ease with which tuberculosis can be transmitted to others because the tuberculosis bacillus is airborne, so that any-
  one who might inhale what the infected person has exhaled
  would be at risk to acquire the infection
- The requirement either that the infected person wear a filtered mask or that all persons who breathe the same air as
  the infected person wear filtered, protective masks to prevent
  the transmission of tuberculosis from an infectious person to
  a noninfected person

- The inadequacy of physical separation as a means to prevent tuberculosis transmission because the airborne bacillus can travel through ventilated systems
- The difficulties involved in tracing possible hard-to-locate contacts of the infectious individual to provide them with treatment for their exposure, compared to the lesser difficulty involved in restraining the infectious individual

As an example, consider the situation involving Robert Daniels. Daniels held citizenship in both the United States and Russia (Wagner, 2007). He returned to Arizona in January 2006, following a visit to his wife and young son in Moscow. While in Moscow, he contracted multidrug-resistant tuberculosis. He became severely ill following his return to Arizona and was placed in a Maricopa County sanitarium for indigent tuberculosis patients. Daniels was later ordered by a court to be involuntarily quarantined due to his failure to adhere to the prescribed medication regimen. The court order was issued following testimony by the county physician that:

- Daniels had refused to adhere to his medication regimen
- Daniels' refusal was willful
- Daniels' refusal to take the prescribed medications had resulted in a decreased likelihood that the disease would be cured
- Members of the public were in danger of contracting the disease due to Daniels' failure to wear a mask during his excursions into public and his entertainment of visitors (Wagner, 2007)

The conditions under which Daniels was isolated became the focus of a lawsuit filed by the American Civil Liberties Union on his behalf. The details will be examined in Chapter 9 in conjunction with a discussion relating to the balancing of individual rights, government authority, and public health.

Exercise

The Illinois statute that criminalizes sexual behavior by an HIV-infected individual provides:

A person commits criminal transmission of HIV when he or she, knowing that he or she is infected with HIV;

(1) engages in intimate contact with another; . . . or

(3) dispenses, delivers, exchanges, sells or in any other way transfers any nonsterile intravenous or intramuscular drug paraphernalia (Illinois Compiled Statutes Annotated, 2008).

"Intimate contact with another" is defined as "the exposure of the body of one person to a bodily fluid of another person in a manner that could result in the transmission of HIV." Consent of the uninfected partner is an affirmative defense. The defendant accused under this statute must prove "that the person knew that the infected person was infected with HIV, knew that the action could result in infection with HIV, and consented to the action with that knowledge."

Assume that you have been retained as an expert by defense counsel. The defendant claims that he used a condom during intercourse. The attorney indicates that, according to his client, sexual intercourse did take place, the condom did not break, and the client and his sexual partner engaged in deep kissing. The attorney wants to argue that, in view of these circumstances, no "intimate contact with another" occurred within the meaning of the statute. How would you advise the attorney?

References

1. Almeida, M. D., & Thomas, J. E. (1996). Nutritional consequences of migration. *Scandinavian Journal of Nutrition, 40*(2, Suppl. 31), 119–121.
2. Altman, L. K. (1997, November 4). The doctor's world: Sex, privacy, and tracking H.I.V. infections. *The New York Times,* p. F1.
3. American Public Health Association. (1991). *Women and HIV disease: A report of the special initiative on AIDS of the American Public Health Association.* Washington, DC: Author.
4. Anderson, J. E., Mosher, W. D., & Chandra, A. (2006). Percentage of persons aged 22–44 years at increased risk for human immunodeficiency virus (HIV) infection by race/ethnicity and education—National Survey of Family Growth/United States, 2002. *Morbidity and Mortality Weekly Report, 55,* 1255.
5. Anderson, R. N., & Smith, B. L. (2005). Deaths: Leading causes for 2002. National Vital Statistics Report, 53, 17: 51 Table 2. Retrieved October 12, 2008 from http://www.cdc.gov/nchs/data/nvsr/nvsr53/nvsr53_17.pdf
6. Anonymous. (2007). Editorial note. *Morbidity and Mortality Weekly Report, 56,* 250–253.
7. Asch, S., Leake, B., Abderson, R., & Gelberg, L. (1998). Why do symptomatic patients delay obtaining care for tuberculosis? *American Journal of Respiratory and Critical Care Medicine, 157,* 1244–1248.
8. Asch, S., Leake, B., & Gelberg L. (1994). Does fear of immigration authorities deter tuberculosis patients from seeking care? *Western Journal of Medicine, 161,* 373–376.
9. Barbera, J., Macintyre, A., Gostin, L., Inglesby, T., O'Tolle, T., DeAtlry, C., et al. (2005). Large-scale quarantine following biological terrorism in the United States: Scientific examination, logistic and legal limits, and possible consequences. *Journal of the American Medical Association, 286,* 2711–2717.

10. Barre-Sinoussi, F., Cherman, J. C., Rey, F., Chamaret, S., Gruest, J., Dauguet, C., et al. (1983). Isolation of a T-lymphotropic retrovirus from a patient at risk for acquired immune deficiency syndrome (AIDS). *Science, 220,* 868–870.

11. Campo, J., Perea, M. A., de Romero, J., Cano, J., Hernando, V., & Bascones, A. (2006). Oral transmission of HIV, reality or fiction? *Oral Diseases, 12,* 219–228.

12. Cantwell, M. F., Snider, D. E., Jr., Cauthen, G. M., & Onorato, I. M. (1994). Epidemiology of tuberculosis in the United States, 1985 through 1992. *Journal of the American Medical Association, 272,* 535–539.

13. Centers for Disease Control. (1981a). Kaposi's sarcoma and Pneumocystis pneumonia among homosexual men—New York and California. *Morbidity and Mortality Weekly Report, 30,* 305–308.

14. Centers for Disease Control. (1981b). Pneumocystis pneumonia—Los Angeles. *Morbidity and Mortality Weekly Report, 30,* 250–252.

15. Centers for Disease Control. (1986). *Reports on AIDS published in the Morbidity and Mortality Weekly Report, June, 1981 through February, 1986.* Springfield, VA: National Technical Information Service.

16. Centers for Disease Control. (1987). Revision of the CDC surveillance case definition of acquired immunodeficiency syndrome. *Morbidity and Mortality Weekly Reports, 36* (Supp. 1S), 1S–3S.

17. Centers for Disease Control. (1988). Transmission of HIV through bone transplantation: Case report and public health recommendation. *Morbidity and Mortality Weekly Reports, 37,* 597–599.

18. Centers for Disease Control. (1999). Cluster of HIV-positive young women— New York 1997–1998. *Morbidity and Mortality Weekly Reports, 48,* 413–416.

19. Centers for Disease Control and Prevention. (1998). Recommendations for prevention and control of tuberculosis among foreign-born persons: Report of the Working Group on Tuberculosis among Foreign-Born Persons. *Morbidity and Mortality Weekly Report, 47,* 1–26.

20. Centers for Disease Control and Prevention. (2005, May 3). *Severe acute respiratory syndrome: Fact sheet on isolation and quarantine.* Retrieved January 28, 2008, from http://www.cdc.gov/nciDOD/sars/isolationquarantine.htm

21. Centers for Disease Control and Prevention. (2006a). Emergence of *Mycobacterium tuberculosis* with extensive resistance to second-line drugs—worldwide, 2002–2004. *Morbidity and Mortality Weekly Report, 55,* 301–305.

22. Centers for Disease Control and Prevention. (2006b, June). *HIV/AIDS among Hispanics.* Atlanta, GA: Author.

23. Centers for Disease Control and Prevention. (2007a). *A glance at the HIV/AIDS epidemic.* Atlanta, GA: Author.

24. Centers for Disease Control and Prevention. (2007b). *HIV/AIDS surveillance report: Cases of HIV infection and AIDS in the United States and dependent areas, 2005.* Atlanta, GA: Author.

25. Centers for Disease Control and Prevention. (2007c). *Reported tuberculosis in the United States, 2006.* Atlanta, GA: Author.

26. Chiasson, M. A., Stoneburner, R. L., & Joseph, S. C. (1990). Human immunodeficiency virus transmission through artificial insemination. *Journal of Acquired Immune Deficiency Syndromes, 3,* 69–72.

27. Colebunders, R., Kapita, B., Nekwei, W., Bahwe, Y., Lebughe, I., Oxtoby, M., et al. (1988). Breastfeeding and transmission of HIV. *Lancet, 2,* 1487.

28. Coles, F. B., Birkhead, G. S., Johnson, P., Smith, P. F., Berke, R., Clark, M., et al. (1999). Cluster of HIV-positive young women—New York, 1997-1998. *Morbidity and Mortality Weekly Report*, 48(20), 413–416.
29. Cooper, M. (1999, July 29). Drifter says he had sex with up to 300. *The New York Times*, p. B5.
30. Corbett, E. L., Watt, C. J., Walker, N., Maher, D., Williams, B. G., Raviglione, M. C., et al. (2003). The growing burden of tuberculosis: Global trends and interactions with the HIV epidemic. *Archives of Internal Medicine*, 163, 1009–1021.
31. Darrow, W. W., Echenberg, D. F., Jaffe, H. W., O'Malley, P. M., Byers, R. H., Getchell, J. P., et al. (1987). Risk factors for human immunodeficiency virus (HIV) infections in homosexual men. *American Journal of Public Health*, 77, 479–483.
32. Davis, H. L. (1997, December 10). Latest tests reveal Williams allegedly infected 13 women. *Buffalo News*, p. 4B.
33. Davis, H. L. (1998, January 29). Two births may bring Williams' HIV toll to 16. *Buffalo News*, p. 4B.
34. Detels, R., English, P., Visscher, B. R., Jacobson, L., Kingsley, L. A., Chmiel, J. S., et al. (1989). Seroconversion, sexual activity and condom use among 2915 HIV seronegative men followed up to 2 years. *Journal of Acquired Immune Deficiency Syndromes*, 2, 77–83.
35. Donegan, E., Stuart, M., Niland, J. C., Saks, H. S., Azen, S. P., Dietrich, S. L., et al. (1990). Infection with human immunodeficiency virus type I (HIV) among recipients of antibody-positive blood donations. *Annals of Internal Medicine*, 113, 733–739.
36. Downs, A. M., & De Vincenzi, I. (1996). Probability of heterosexual transmission of HIV, relationship to the number of unprotected sexual contacts. *Journal of AIDS*, 11, 388–395.
37. Ellis, T. M. (2008, May 17). 35-year sentence for HIV-positive spitter worries some. *Dallas Morning News*. Retrieved May 22, 2008, from http://www.dallasnews.com
38. Esmonde, D., Peradotto, N., & Michel, L. (1997, November 2). Drifter targeted crop of lost teens. *Buffalo News*, p. 1A.
39. Ex parte Company, 139 N.E. 204 (Ohio 1922).
40. Ex parte Johnson, 180 P. 644 (Cal. Dist. Ct. App. 1919).
41. Executive Order: Amendment to E.O. 13295 Relating to Certain Influenza Viruses and Quarantinable Communicable Diseases (April 1, 2005).
42. Executive Order 13295: Revised List of Quarantinable Communicable Diseases (April 4, 2003).
43. Fanning, A. (1999). Tuberculosis: 6. Extrapulmonary disease. *Canadian Medical Association Journal*, 160(11), 1597–1603.
44. Fowler, M. G., Melnick, S. L., & Mathieson, B. J. (1997). Women and HIV: Epidemiology and global overview. *Obstetrics and Gynecology Clinics*, 24, 705–729.
45. Fox, C. W., & George, R. B. (1992). Current concepts in the management and prevention of tuberculosis in adults. *Journal of the Louisiana Medical Association*, 144, 363–368.
46. Friedland, G., Kahl, P., Saltzman, B., Rogers, M., Feiner, C., Mayers, M., et al. (1990). Additional evidence for lack of transmission of HIV infection by close interpersonal (casual) contact. *AIDS*, 4, 639–644.
47. Fujikawa, L. S., Salahuddin, S. Z., Palestine, A. G., Masur, H., Nussenblatt, R. B., Gallo, R. C., et al. (1985). Isolation of human T-lymphotropic virus type III from

the tears of a patient with the acquired immunodeficiency syndrome. *Lancet, 2*, 529–530.

48.   Galarneau, A. Z. (1997, November 11). The doctor who dared. *Buffalo News*, p. 1C.

49.   Gibbons v. Ogden, 22 U.S. 1 (9 Wheat)(1824).

50.   Gostin, L. O. (2003). When terrorism threatens health: How far are limitations on human rights justified. *Journal of Law, Medicine, & Ethics, 31*, 524–528.

51.   Gottlieb, M. S., Schroff, R., Schanker, H. M., Weisman, J. D., Peng, T. F., Wolf, R. A., et al. (1981). *Pneumocystis carinii* pneumonia and muscosal candidiasis in previously healthy homosexual men: Evidence of a newly acquired immunodeficiency. *New England Journal of Medicine, 305*, 1425–1431.

52.   Haitian Centers Council Inc. v. Sale, 825 F. Supp. 1028, 1045 (E.D.NY. 1993).

53.   Ho, D. D., Byington, R. E., Schooley, R. T., Flynn, T., Rota, T. R., & Hirsh, M. S. (1985). Infrequency of isolation of HTLV-III virus from saliva in AIDS. *New England Journal of Medicine, 313*, 1606.

54.   Ho, D. D., Schooley, R. T., Rota, T. R., Kaplan, J. C., & Flynn, T. (1984). HTLV-III in the semen and blood of healthy homosexual men. *Science, 226*, 451–453.

55.   Hoffman, P. N., Larkin, D. P., & Samuel, D. (1989). Needlestick and needle-share—The difference. *Journal of Infectious Diseases, 160*, 545–546.

56.   Hogben, M., & Kissinger, P. (in press). A review of partner notification for sex partners of men infected with Chlamydia. *Sexually Transmitted Diseases.*

57.   Holtgrave, D. R., & Anderson, T. (2004). Utilizing HIV transmission rates to assist in prioritizing HIV prevention services. *International Journal of Sexually Transmitted Diseases and AIDS, 15*, 789–792.

58.   Homeland Security Council. (2006). *National strategy for pandemic influenza: Implementation plan.* Washington, DC: US Government Printing Office.

59.   Illinois Compiled Statutes Annotated § 5/12-16.2 (2008).

60.   Joint United Nations Programme on HIV/AIDS (UNAIDS) & World Health Organization (WHO). (2007). *AIDS epidemic update: December 2007.* Geneva, Switzerland: World Health Organization.

61.   Jong-wook, L. (2006). *Global plan to stop TB.* Geneva, Switzerland: World Health Organization.

62.   Koopman, J. S., Jacquez, J. A., Welch, G. W., Simon, C. P., Foxman, B., Pollock, S. M., et al. (1997). The role of early HIV infection in the spread of HIV through populations. *Journal of AIDS & Human Retrovirology, 14*, 249–258.

63.   Kumar, P., Pearson, J. E., Martin, D. H., Leech, S. H., Buisseret, P. D., Bezak, H. C., et al. (1987). Transmission of human immunodeficiency virus by transplantation of renal allograft, with development of acquired immunodeficiency syndrome. *Annals of Internal Medicine, 106*, 244–245.

64.   LaFave, W. R., & Scott, A. W., Jr. (1986). *Criminal law* (2nd ed.). St. Paul, MN: West.

65.   Laga, M., Taelman, H., Van der Stuyft, P., & Bonneux, L. (1989). Advanced immunodeficiency as a risk factor for heterosexual transmission of HIV. *AIDS, 3*, 361–366.

66.   Lazzarini, Z., Bray, S., & Burris, S. (2002). Evaluating the impact of criminal laws on HIV risk behavior. *Journal of Law, Medicine, & Ethics, 30*, 239–252.

67.   Levy, J. A. (1989). Human immunodeficiency viruses and the pathogenesis of AIDS. *Journal of the American Medical Association, 261*, 2997–3006.

68.   Lifson, A. R., O'Malley, P. M., Hessol, N. A., Buchbiner, S. P., Cannon, L., & Rutherford, G. W. (1990). HIV seroconversion in two homosexual men after re-

ceptive oral intercourse with ejaculation: Implications for counseling concerning safe sexual practices. *American Journal of Public Health, 80,* 1509–1511.

69. Makinodan, T., Liu, J., Yumo, E., Knowles, L. K., Davidson, P. T., & Harada, N. (1999). Profile of tuberculosis among foreign-born Asians residing in Los Angeles County, California, 1985–1994. *Asian American Pacific Islander Journal of Health, 7,* 38–46.

70. Marks, G., Crepaz, N., & Janssen, R. S. (2006). Estimating sexual transmission of HIV from persons aware and unaware that they are infected with the virus in the USA. *AIDS, 20,* 1447–1450.

71. Masur, H., Michelis, M. A., Greene, J. B., Onorato, I., Vande Stouwe, R. A., Holzman, R. S., et al. (1981). An outbreak of community-acquired *Pneumocystis carinii* pneumonia: Initial manifestations of cellular immune dysfunction. *New England Journal of Medicine, 305,* 1431–1438.

72. Mays, V. M., & Cochran, S. D. (1987). Acquired immunodeficiency syndrome and black Americans: Special psychosocial issues. *Public Health Reports, 102,* 224–231.

73. McCarthy, S. (1997, October 30). System worked, but public suffered anyway. *Newsday,* p. A54.

74. Michel, L., & Warner, G. (1997, November 4). Williams is found mentally ill. *Buffalo News,* p. 1A.

75. Mindes, P. (1996). Tuberculosis quarantine: A review of legal issues in Ohio and other states. *Journal of Law & Health, 10,* 403–428.

76. Moss, A. R., Osmond, D., Bacchetti, P., Chermann, J. C., Barre-Sinoussi, F., & Carlson, J. (1987). Risk factors for AIDS and HIV seropositivity in homosexual men. *American Journal of Epidemiology, 125,* 1035–1047.

77. Murray, J. F. (1998). Tuberculosis and HIV infection: A global perspective. *Respiration, 65,* 335–342.

78. New Jersey Statutes 2C:14-1, 2C:34-5 (2007).

79. New York City Commission on Human Rights. (1986, November). *AIDS and people of color: The discriminatory impact.* New York: Author.

80. New York City Commission on Human Rights. (1987, August). *AIDS discrimination and its implications for people of color and other minorities.* New York: Author.

81. Nolan, C., Goldberg, S., & Wallace, J. (2002). Increase in African immigrants and refugees with tuberculosis—Seattle-King County, Washington, 1998-2001. *Morbidity and Mortality Weekly Report, 51,* 882–883.

82. Ohio Revised Code Annotated §§ 3701.56, 3707.04, 3707.05 (2008).

83. Osmond, D. H. (1999). Epidemiology of HIV/AIDS in the United States. In P. T. Cohen, M. A. Sande, & P. A. Volberding (Eds.), *The AIDS knowledge base* (3rd ed., pp. 13–21). Philadelphia: Lippincott, Williams & Wilkins.

84. Page, E. M. (2007). Balancing individual rights and public health safety during quarantine: The U.S. and Canada. *Case Western Reserve Journal of International Law, 38,* 517–537.

85. Palazetti, A. (1997a, October 28). Chautauqua names HIV carrier accused of infecting at least 11. *Buffalo News,* p. 1A.

86. Palazetti, A. (1997b, October 29). Suspect kept score: Williams' records helped track infected women. *Buffalo News,* p. 1A.

87. Peterman, T. A., Stoneburner, R. L., Allen, J. R., Jaffe, H. W., & Curran, J. W. (1988). Risk of human immunodeficiency virus transmission from heterosexual adults with transfusion-associated infections. *Journal of the American Medical Association, 259,* 55–58.

88. Popovic, M., Sarngadharan, M. G., Read, E., & Gallo, R. C. (1984). Detection, isolation, and continuous production of cytopathic retroviruses (HTLV-III) from patients with AIDS and pre-AIDS. *Science, 224,* 497–500.

89. Public Health Service, Centers for Disease Control and Prevention. (n.d.a). *Technical instructions for medical examination of aliens.* Atlanta, GA: Author. Retrieved March 12, 2007, from www.cdc.gov/ncidod/dq/technica.htm

90. Public Health Service, Centers for Disease Control and Prevention. (n.d.b). *Technical instructions for medical examination of aliens in the United States.* Atlanta, GA: Author. Retrieved March 12, 2007, from www.cdc.gov/ncidod/dq/technica.htm

91. Richardson, L. (1998, August 20). Man faces felony charge of exposing girl to H.I.V. *The New York Times,* p. B3.

92. Rogers, M. F., White, C. R., Sanders, R., Schable, C., Ksell, T. E., Wasserman, R. L., et al. (1990). Lack of transmission of human immunodeficiency virus from infected children to their household contacts. *Pediatrics, 85,* 210–214.

93. Royce, R. A., Seña, A., Cates, W., & Cohen, M. S. (1997). Sexual transmission of HIV. *New England Journal of Medicine, 336,* 1072–1078.

94. Sasse, H., Salmaso, S., Conti, S., & First Drug User Multicenter Study Group. (1989). Risk behaviors for HIV-1 infection in Italian drug users: Report from a multicenter study. *Journal of Acquired Immune Deficiency Syndromes, 2,* 486–496.

95. Schoenbaum, E. E., Hartel, D., Selwyn, P. A., Klein, R. S., Darenny, K., Rogers, M., et al. (1989). Risk factors for human immunodeficiency virus in intravenous drug users. *New England Journal of Medicine, 321,* 874–879.

96. Shilts, R. (1987). *And the band played on: Politics, people, and the AIDS epidemic.* New York: St. Martin's Press.

97. Thiry, L., Sprecher-Goldberger, S., Jonckheer, T., Levy, J., Van de Perre, P., Henrivaux, P., et al. (1985). Isolation of AIDS virus from cell-free breast milk of three healthy virus carriers. *Lancet, 2,* 891–892.

98. Truong, D. H., Hedemark, L. L., Mickman, J. K., Mosher, L. B., Dietrich, S. E., & Lowry, P. W. (1997). Tuberculosis among Tibetan immigrants from India and Nepal in Minnesota, 1992–1995. *Journal of the American Medical Association, 277,* 735–738.

99. United States v. Bygrave, 46 M.J. 491 (Ct. App. Armed Forces 1997).

100. United States v. Moore, 846 F.2d 1163 (8th Cir. 1988).

101. United States v. Morris, 30 M.J. 1221 (Army Ct. Mil. Rev. 1990).

102. Vittinghoff, E., Douglas, J., Judon, F., McKiman, D., MacQueen, K., & Buchinder, S. P. (1999). Per-contact risk of human immunodeficiency virus transmission between sexual partners. *American Journal of Epidemiology, 150,* 306–311.

103. Vogt, M. W., Witt, D. J., Craven, D. E., Crawford, D. F., Witt, D. J., Byington, R., et al. (1986). Isolation of HTLV III/LAV from cervical secretions of women at risk for AIDS. *Lancet, 1,* 525–527.

104. Wagner, D. (2007, May 30). ACLU files lawsuit against county for treatment of TB patient. *Arizona Republic.* Retrieved August 10, 2008, from http://www.azcentral.com/news/articles/0530tbguy0530.html

105. Waldman, A. (1999, February 19). Guilty plea in an H.I.V. exposure case. *New York Times,* B3.

106. Williams, B. G., Lloyd-Smith, J. O., Gouws, E., Hankins, C., Getz, W. M., Hargrove, J., et al. (2006). The potential impact of male circumcision on HIV in sub-Saharan Africa. *PLoS Medicine, 3,* 1032–1040.

107. Winkelstein, W., Lyman, D. M., Padian, N., Grant, R., Sameul, M., Wiley, J. A., et al. (1987). Sexual practices and risk of infection by the human immunodeficiency virus: The San Francisco Men's Health Study. *Journal of the American Medical Association, 257,* 321–325.

108. Wofsy, C., Cohen, J., Hauer, L., Michaelis, B. A., Cohen, J. B., Padian, N. S., et al. (1986). Isolation of AIDS-associated retrovirus from genital secretions of women with antibodies to the virus. *Lancet, 1,* 527–529.

109. Wolf, L.E. & Vezina, R. (2004). Crime and punishment: Is there a role for criminal law in HIV prevention policy? *Whittier Law Review, 25,* 821-886.

110. Wong Wai v. Williamson, 103 F.1 (N.D. Cal. 1900).

111. World Health Organization. (2002). *WHO Report 2002: Global tuberculosis control: Surveillance, planning, financing.* Geneva, Switzerland: Author. Retrieved October 11, 2008 from http://www.who.int/tb/publications/2002/en/index.html

112. World Health Organization. (2005a). *Genes and human disease.* Geneva, Switzerland: Author. Retrieved June 14, 2006, from http://www.who.int/genomics/public/geneticdiseases/en/print.html

113. World Health Organization. (2005b). *International health regulations.* Retrieved June 14, 2006, from http://www.int/gb/ebwha/pdf_files/WHA58/A58_55-en.pdf

114. World Health Organization. (2005c). *Stop TB partnership: Annual report 2004.* Geneva, Switzerland: Author. Retrieved June 21, 2006, from http://www.who.int/hq/2005/WHO_HTM_STB_2005.33_eng.pdf

115. World Health Organization. (2006). *The world health report 2006:Working together for health.* Geneva, Switzerland: Author. Retrieved June 21, 2006, from http://www.who.int/whr/2006/en/index.html

116. Yamada, S., Caballero, J., Matsunaga, D. S., Agustin, G., & Magaña, M. (1999). Attitudes towards tuberculosis in immigrants from the Philippines to the United States. *Family Medicine, 31*(7), 477–482.

117. Ziegler, J. B., Cooper, D. A., Johnson, R. O., & Gold, J. (1985). Postnatal transmission of AIDS-associated retrovirus from mother to infant. *Lancet, 1,* 896–898.

118. 42 U.S.C.S. § 264 (2008).

119. 42 C.F.R. §§ 70.6, 71.32(a) (2008).

Chapter 6

Law, Epidemiology, and Mental Health

L
aw enforcement actions that relate to mental health and substance use may arise in the administrative, civil, or criminal contexts. For example, some jurisdictions have prosecuted women criminally for their ingestion of illicit substances during their pregnancies. Even more jurisdictions provide for the civil commitment of women who are believed to be endangering their unborn children through their use of illicit substances during the course of their pregnancies. In the context of immigration proceedings, which are administrative in nature, individuals seeking legal admission to the United States may be required to present evidence that they are not a threat to themselves or others because of their mental condition. In each such situation, the expertise of an epidemiologist may be critical to the preparation of the legal arguments on either side of the case. This chapter examines how epidemiological evidence may be important in these contexts. However, the complexity of each of these topics permits a relatively brief discussion of each, and interested readers are urged to consult additional resources for greater detail.

Case Study 1: Maternal Substance Use During Pregnancy

Widespread media attention has been focused on the use of both legal and illicit substances by women during the course of their pregnancies and the resumed adverse effects of such use on their unborn children. These alarming reports have spurred legislators to formulate a variety of proposed solutions to the perceived epidemic, which have included the amendment of civil child welfare laws to facilitate the removal of the newborn child from his or her mother and the promulgation of various criminal provisions that would permit the protective incarceration and/or criminal prosecution of the substance-using mother.

The first portion of this case study provides an overview of what is known about maternal substance use during pregnancy and its effects on the fetus. This is followed by a discussion of the laws that have been promulgated in the context of civil child welfare laws and criminal law. The final portion of the case study examines the role that an epidemiologist or other healthcare professional might be asked to play in such actions.

MATERNAL SUBSTANCE USE AND ITS EFFECTS

The Prevalence of Maternal Substance Use During Pregnancy

Findings from the National Household Survey on Drug Abuse (NHSDA) conducted by the Substance Abuse and Mental Health Services Agency (SAMHSA) indicate that, for the years 2002 and 2003, 4.3% of pregnant women aged 15 to 44 years ingested illicit drugs during the month prior to the study interview, compared to 10.4% of nonpregnant women in the same age range (Office of Applied Statistics, 2005). A substantially smaller proportion of the pregnant women consumed alcohol (9.8%) and engaged in binge drinking (4.1%) compared to their nonpregnant counterparts (53.0% and 23.2%, respectively). In addition, almost one-fifth of pregnant women (18.0%) smoked during the course of their pregnancies, compared to almost one-third of nonpregnant women (30.7%). Clearly, women's use of both legal and illicit substances is widespread and of concern for the health of the women themselves.

Data from the earlier NHSDA for 2000 and 2001 revealed that substance use among younger women, both pregnant and nonpregnant, is higher than among their older counterparts. Researchers who conducted the NHSDA study reported that 15.1% of pregnant women aged 15 to 17 years had used illicit substances during their pregnancy; only 14.1% of the nonpregnant women in the same age group reported illicit substance use. A study involving 241 unmarried pregnant adolescents aged 17 years and younger found that 4% of the respondents consumed alcohol on a regular basis during their pregnancy, compared with 55% prior to becoming pregnant (Gilchrist, Hussey, Gillmore, Lohr, & Morrison, 1996). Another study that involved an ethnically diverse sample of 145 first-time pregnant teens aged 15 to 18 years found that 52% of the teens had smoked prior to pregnancy, but only 27% smoked during pregnancy (Kaiser & Hays, 2005). The proportion of the teens who used alcohol and street drugs also decreased during pregnancy, from 44.8% prior to pregnancy to 0.7% during pregnancy, and from 35.9% prepregnancy to 6.2% during pregnancy, respectively. These reductions in the proportion of women who used substances during pregnancy suggest that pregnancy itself may provide a strong incentive to reduce or cease substance use (Gilchrist, et al., 1996).

The effects of maternal substance use on the fetus during its development and on the child after its birth vary significantly, depending on the substance used and the timing and extent of that use. It is also important to remember that the legality of use of a particular substance is a separate issue from the effects of its use.

Alcohol

The effects of alcohol ingestion on the fetus and the later development of the child have been widely studied. Research reports indicate that potential adverse effects resulting from the ingestion of alcohol during pregnancy include spontaneous abortion, stillbirth, low birth weight, fetal alcohol syndrome, fetal alcohol effects, certain congenital anomalies, and delayed or altered neurobehavioral development of the child (Krulewitch, 2001; Richardson, 1999). The brain is particularly vulnerable to the effects of alcohol ingestion; damage to the developing child's brain have been documented in the regions of the cerebellum, the hippocampus, basal ganglia, and corpus callosum (Mattson, Riley, Sowell, & Jernigan, 1996; Riley, Mattson, Sowell, & Jernigan, 1995; Swayze, Johnson, Hanson, & Piven, 1997).

A significant body of research has focused on the developmental impact of parental alcohol use. Research findings indicate that the offspring of middle-class women who drank more heavily during pregnancy experience higher levels of negative affect and insecure attachments (Olson, O'Connor, & Fitzgerald, 2001). As preschoolers, these same children evidenced signs of depression, which was associated with their prenatal alcohol exposure and maternal depression, suggesting that problems may be exacerbated by cumulative risk and that the quality and nature of mother-child interactions may help to maintain or reduce the adverse effects of prenatal exposure. An increase in tantrums and eating problems has also been observed in children who were born to mothers who used alcohol during pregnancy (Faden & Graubard, 2000).

Tobacco

Smoking may affect the developing fetus through several mechanisms. First, as the metabolites of the cigarette smoke pass from the mother to the fetus through the placenta, they may act as a vasoconstrictor, causing a reduction of blood flow and resulting in fetal deprivation of nutrients and oxygen, leading to episodic fetal hypoxia-ischemia and malnutrition (Ganapathy, Prasad, Ganapathy, & Leibach, 1999; Suzuki, Minei, & Johnson, 1980). This is the basis for the fetal intrauterine growth retardation.

Smoking during pregnancy may also interfere with the developing nervous system of the fetus, specifically the development of synaptic activity, ultimately resulting in neuronal damage (Levin & Slotkin, 1998; Slotkin, 1998). This injury may result even if the levels of smoking have not resulted in low birth weight of the newborn. Other potential adverse effects include spontaneous abortion, the delivery of a low birth weight or premature infant, sudden infant death syndrome (Lewis & Bosque, 1995; Mitchell, Ford, Stewart, & Taylor, 1993; Schoendorf & Kiely, 1992), later learning and behavior problems (Button, Maughan, & McGuffin, 2007), and respiratory difficulties, including asthma (Floyd, Zahniser, Gunter, & Kendrick, 1991; Kilby, 1997; Richardson, 1999).

Marijuana

Findings relating to the fetal and neonatal consequences of in utero exposure to marijuana have been inconsistent. Studies have reported an association and no association between cannabis use and lower birth weight (Fried & O'Connell, 1987; Zuckerman, et al., 1989). One study of over 12,000 women who were expecting singletons found that 5% of the women smoked cannabis before and/or during pregnancy (Fergusson, Horwood, Northstone, & ALSPAC Study Team, 2002). These women were found to be of lower parity and had higher levels of education. No statistically significant association was found between the prenatal marijuana use and either perinatal morbidity or mortality. Other studies, however, have reported an association between cannabis use during pregnancy and lower gestational age at delivery, an increased risk of prematurity, and a reduction in birth weight (Sherwood, Keating, Kavvadia, Greenough, & Peters, 1999).

Cocaine

Early research reports portrayed children who had been exposed to cocaine in utero as irreparably injured. More recent research suggests that

these earlier reports grossly exaggerated the effects of maternal ingestion of cocaine during pregnancy (Bauer, Shankaran, Bada, & Lester,
2002; Lester, LaGasse, Freier, & Brunner, 1996; Lester & Tronick,
1994). These more recent findings indicate that neurobehavioral effects in the infant may be determined by low birth weight and in
utero cocaine exposure (Lester, et al., 2002). Cocaine-exposed children may display small deficits in intelligence, moderate deficits in language, poor organizational skills, and difficulties with abstract thinking
and maintaining attention (Delaney-Black, Covington, Templin, &
Ager, 1998; Leech, Richardson, Goldschmidt, & Day, 1999; Lester,
LaGasse, & Seifer, 1998).

Methamphetamine

The prenatal use of methamphetamine and its consequent effects on
the fetus and newborn have not been studied extensively. One study of
1632 women found that 5.2% had used methamphetamine at some
point during their pregnancies (Arria, et al., 2006). Reports from animal studies indicate that prenatal methamphetamine use may result in
increased mortality among both the parent and the offspring, retinal
defects, cleft palate, rib malformations, decreased physical growth,
and delayed motor development (Acuff-Smith, George, Lorens, &
Vorhees, 1992; Cho, Lyu, Lee, Kim, & Chin, 1991; Weissman &
Caldecott-Hazard, 1995). The few studies that have been conducted in
human populations reflect numerous methodological problems, but
their findings are suggestive of possible cardiac anomalies, behavioral
problems, fetal growth retardation, and cranial abnormalities as a consequence of prenatal methamphetamine exposure (Billing, Eriksson,
Steneroth, & Zetterstrom, 1985, 1988; Plessinger, 1998).

Opiates

Opiate use has been linked to depressed breathing movements in the
newborn, preterm delivery, preterm rupture of the membranes, fetal
growth restriction, perinatal mortality, and sudden infant death syndrome (Rayburn, 2007). There are no known teratogenic effects on the
fetus. Because opiates can be used by smoking or injecting the drug,
the potential for adverse effects on the fetus depends to some degree
on how the drug is administered. Injection using shared, unclean injection paraphernalia, for example, carries a risk of contracting HIV infection, hepatitis B or C, and bacterial infection (Büttner, Mall, Penning,
& Weis, 2000; Finn, Leen, English, & O'Briain, 2003; Wood, et al.,
2004), while contaminants in the drug itself may result in venous foreign body reactions (Finn, et al., 2003).

LEGISLATIVE AND JUDICIAL RESPONSES

Responses in the Criminal Context

During the past several decades, numerous legislatures promulgated statutes in response to media reports of horrific consequences to offspring resulting from the maternal ingestion of both illicit and legal substances during pregnancy. These statutory provisions were often punitive in nature, providing for the characterization of substance use during pregnancy as child abuse, with its attendant consequences and/or proscribing criminal penalties. The Idaho legislature, for example, promulgated a statute that allows for the incarceration of violators for up to 5 years and additionally permits a fine of up to $50,000 to be levied (Senate Bill 1337, 2006). Approximately 240 women in 30 states have been criminally prosecuted for their substance use during pregnancy (Lester, Andreozzi, & Appiah, 2004). These prosecutions have been premised on statutes that prohibit the delivery of a controlled substance to a minor, child abuse or endangerment, and fetal murder/manslaughter (Harris & Paltrow, 2003; Schueller, 1999).

Prosecutions for the delivery of a controlled substance to a minor focus on the moments following birth that precede the cutting of the umbilical cord. During these moments, the infant is fully born and is therefore considered to be a person under the 14th Amendment. At the same time, however, the child is attached to his or her mother by the umbilical cord and may continue to receive drugs through the umbilical cord until it is cut (Linden, 1995; Schueller, 1999). As an example, in Seminole County, Florida, Jennifer Johnson was convicted and sentenced to 15 years of probation for having delivered a controlled substance to her baby through the umbilical cord following birth. She admitted to having smoked crack cocaine approximately three or four times every other day throughout the course of her pregnancy. The child's birth, however, was normal, with no complications, no evidence of fetal distress, and no difficulties in the delivery of blood to the infant through the umbilical cord. Her conviction was overturned by the Florida Supreme Court in 1992, holding that the statute relating to the delivery of controlled substances was not meant to apply to drug delivery via the umbilical cord (*Johnson v. State*, 1992).

The case of *Whitner v. State* (1997) provides an example of how the prosecution of a pregnant woman for substance use during pregnancy may proceed under child abuse statutes. This case involved an African-American woman. While only 14 years old, she witnessed the death of her mother. Traumatized and without any other support system, she turned to marijuana, alcohol, and other drugs. She first became pregnant at the age of 15; her youngest child was born with cocaine in his system. Whitner was arrested, charged, and prosecuted for child abuse because she had used cocaine while pregnant, despite the fact that the baby was born healthy and with no detectable injury. The Supreme Court of South Carolina, finding that the word "child" as used in the state's child abuse and endangerment statute encompassed "viable fetuses," convicted Whitner and sentenced her to 8 years in prison. Although other states have brought charges against women for child endangerment due to substance use during pregnancy, many courts have held that the statutes on which the prosecutions rest do not encompass harm to a fetus (e.g., *Reinesto v. State*, 1995; *Reyes v. Superior Court*, 1977).

South Carolina has successfully brought prosecutions for homicide by child abuse. In 2003, the Supreme Court of South Carolina affirmed the conviction of Regina McKnight for homicide by child abuse based on the determination by a pathologist that McKnight had exposed the stillborn fetus to cocaine and the pathologist's ruling that the death was a homicide (*State v. McKnight*, 2003). This decision was only recently overturned (Associated Press, 2008). In doing so, Chief Justice Toal noted that the death of the fetus could have resulted from factors other than cocaine exposure (*McKnight v. State*, 2008).

In some cases, courts have ordered the incarceration of women because of their substance use while pregnant but for crimes unrelated to their substance use. As an example, in 1988, a judge in Washington, DC sentenced Brenda Vaughn "to jail for the duration of her pregnancy" after she pled guilty to a charge of forging checks. However, the imprisonment, according to the judge, was ordered to protect the fetus from the woman's substance abuse (Roberts, 1991; *United States v. Vaughn*, 1988). Similarly, in sentencing an addicted woman to prison for the duration of her pregnancy, a judge in a New Jersey court stated that it was not "because we want to punish her, but because we want to save the baby" (*New Jersey v. Ikerd*, 2004, p. 219).

Prosecutions have been brought not only for the use of illegal substances during pregnancy but for legal ones as well. South Carolina, for example, arrested one woman for the use of alcohol during pregnancy (Paltrow, 1999).

This course of action raises significant issues for clinicians who provide care to pregnant women and to the pregnant women themselves (Jos, Perlmutter, & Marshall, 2003). For example, a physician may prescribe a controlled legal drug for its therapeutic effect, but a prosecutor may later decide to prosecute the woman for the use of that drug, even though its use was legal.

Responses in the Civil Context

States have more frequently utilized civil mechanisms to address the issue of maternal ingestion of substances during pregnancy. This may occur for several reasons. First, to criminally prosecute an individual successfully, the state must prove its case beyond a reasonable doubt, which is a relatively high standard to have to meet. In contrast, the state must establish its case in a civil matter, in most instances, by a preponderance of the evidence, a substantially lower threshold. As in the case of criminal prosecutions, civil cases are often initiated against the mother on the basis of toxicology screens that are performed on the infant at birth.

As of 2004, approximately 10 states included maternal substance abuse or infant substance exposure within their statutory definitions of abuse, and 15 states mandated the reporting of maternal substance use during pregnancy as child abuse or neglect (Lester, et al., 2004). The definition of maternal substance use as a form of child abuse or neglect provides the basis for severe criminal and/or civil penalties. Although the processing of civil abuse and neglect cases differs across states, there is a similar pattern:

> All states have laws requiring the reporting of suspected cases of abuse and neglect. Child welfare agencies and sometimes law enforcement agencies receive and investigate these reports. If coercive state intervention is deemed warranted, an abuse or neglect proceeding can be instituted in a juvenile or family court. When a court adjudicates a child to be abused or neglected, it has several dispositional alternatives. These alternatives range from allowing the child to remain in his or her home with in-home monitoring and services, to placement of the child in foster care or other out-of-home placement. In some cases a court may terminate parental rights without parental consent, which frees a child for adoption. Child welfare agencies are responsible for the provision of services to children who are abused and neglected, or who are at risk of abuse and neglect, the provision of services to families, and the arrangement of foster care placements, other out of home placements, and adoptions. (Gittler, 2003, pp. 239–240)

Termination of Parental Rights/Removal of Child

As of 2004, 16 states had implemented legislation permitting the removal of a child from its home based on a positive toxicology screen at birth or a confirmed report of substance use in the home (Lester, et al., 2004). The Illinois statute, for example, characterizes a mother as unfit if the "child's blood, urine, or meconium contained any amount of a controlled substance . . . or a metabolite of such substances . . . and the mother of this child is the biological mother of at least one other child who was adjudicated as a neglected minor" (Illinois Compiled Statutes Annotated, §, 2008). Ohio law includes in its definition of an abused child "any child who . . . because of the acts of his [or her] parents . . . suffers physical or mental injury that harms or threatens to harm the child's health or welfare" (Ohio Revised Code, 2008). An Ohio court held that a child will be considered to be "per se abused" if a toxicology test detects the presence of illegal drugs (*In re Baby Boy Blackshear*, 2000).

Involuntary Civil Commitment

More than 30 states now permit the civil commitment of a pregnant woman based on her use of alcohol and drugs during pregnancy (Fentiman, 2006), and some state statutes explicitly provide for the involuntary civil commitment of pregnant women who are dependent on illegal drugs and/or alcohol (Minnesota Statutes Annotated, 2007; South Dakota Codified Laws, 2007; Wisconsin Statutes Annotated, 2007). The case of *Wisconsin ex rel. Angela v. Kruzicki* (1995) exemplifies the use of involuntary civil commitment.

In this case, Angela M. W.'s physician found that she had tested positive for cocaine during her pregnancy and reported these findings to the County Department of Health and Human Services after his patient refused to seek treatment for substance abuse and failed to present at subsequent appointments with him. The Department petitioned the juvenile court, requesting that the court place the unborn child in custody for its own protection. Angela's physician provided an affidavit in support of the petition, stating that:

> (10) As a licensed obstetrician, it is my opinion that [Angela's] active cocaine usage presents a real and immediate danger to the health[,] safety and continued viability of her unborn child.

> (11) It is my opinion that without intervention forcing [Angela] to cease her drug use that she will continue using cocaine and other drugs with the following likely effects on her unborn child: low weight gain, abruption placentae, increased infectious disease, hypertension and tachycardia, preterm labor and delivery, possible precipitous delivery, and increased risks for pregnancy loss, including spontaneous abortion and still birth, SIDS, congenital malformations, intraventricular hemorrhage and precipitous labor. (*Wisconsin ex rel. Angela v. Kruzicki*, 1995, p. 486)

The court ordered that the woman be detained by the sheriff's department and transported to the hospital for treatment and protection. The decision was later overturned by the Wisconsin Supreme Court, finding that the legislature had not intended that the then-existing statute encompass an unborn fetus in its definition of "child" (*Wisconsin ex rel. Angela v. Kruzicki*, 1997).

The Wisconsin legislature subsequently amended the statute to provide specifically for the inclusion of fetuses in its provisions. Wisconsin's current statute allows police officers to "hold an expectant mother in physical custody" if:

there is probable cause to believe that the adult expectant mother is within the jurisdiction of the court, to believe that if the expectant mother is not held, there is a substantial risk that the physical health of the unborn child, and of the child when born, will be seriously affected or endangered by the adult expectant mother[’]s habitual lack of self-control in the use of alcohol beverages, controlled substances or controlled substance analogs, exhibited to a severe degree, and to believe that the expectant adult mother is refusing or has refused to accept any alcohol or other drug abuse services offered to her or is not making or has not made a good faith effort to participate in any alcohol or other drug abuse services offered to her (Wisconsin Statutes Annotated § 48.205(d), 2007)

THE EPIDEMIOLOGIST AND LAW ENFORCEMENT

The Potential Roles of an Epidemiologist

An epidemiologist may be asked to play any one of several roles in the context of a civil action related to child welfare or a criminal prosecution of the mother. This request could be initiated at either the request of the governmental entity, such as the child welfare agency or the prosecuting authority, or at the request of the pregnant woman against whom the legal action is directed.

A consulting expert–epidemiologist might be retained for ongoing advice during the course of the criminal trial. For example, the defense attorney might retain an epidemiologist to assist with the evaluation of any scientific information that might be presented. As one example, the epidemiologist could explain the concepts of sensitivity and specificity and negative and positive predictive value as they relate to specific tests that may have been utilized. The epidemiologist could also be helpful in drafting motions or jury instructions. Those experts retained as consultants may or may not be those who are retained to testify during the course of the trial.

Methodological Issues for the Testifying or Consulting Expert

The epidemiology or other public health expert who testifies or provides consultation in a civil or criminal action that has been brought against a woman for substance use during pregnancy must be cognizant of the various methodological issues that exist in cases involving maternal substance use during pregnancy, regardless of whether they have been retained by the governmental entity or the woman. Depending upon the type of action that is being pursued, these methodological issues may include:

- Gestational age at the time of substance use
- Quantity and frequency of maternal substance ingestion
- Type of substance
- Assessing/measuring fetal exposure to ingested substance
  - Bodily specimen used for testing
  - Source of specimen (mother or infant)
  - Type of assay
  - Use of confirmatory testing
- Nature of harm to fetus or infant
  - Individual fetal susceptibility to harm
  - Type of harm (e.g., death, delayed development, physical abnormalities)
  - Sensitivity and specificity of outcome measures
- Potential confounding factors
  - Poverty
  - Maternal malnutrition
  - Maternal weight gain and caloric intake
  - Maternal state of health
  - Genetic factors
- Alternative causes

Several of these issues are discussed in greater detail in the following paragraphs.

Drug Testing

One of the primary issues that may be raised is the accuracy of the drug testing. The government entity is likely to produce the results of testing that has been conducted in its effort to support its requested action, while the woman who is the object of these efforts may dispute the accuracy of the test findings that provide a basis for the government action. There will be no basis for pursuing a civil or a criminal case against the mother if it were to be found that she had actually not ingested the substance of concern during her pregnancy.

Numerous subissues relate to the larger issue of drug testing. These include the bodily substance utilized for the test, for example, blood or urine; whether the substance was drawn from the mother or the infant; the assay utilized to detect substances; and sensitivity, specificity, and positive and negative predictive values of the assay that was used.

The importance of this issue cannot be stressed enough; one study found, for example, a 43% false positive rate for cocaine when a screening test was used without the use of a confirmatory procedure (Moore, Lewis, & Leikin, 1995). Although gas chromatography/mass spectrometry is the forensic standard for confirmation of presumptive positive screens, one research group found that 25% of a sample of 8500 persons was incorrectly identified (Lester, elSohly, Wright, & Smeriglio, 2001).

It is likely that either side of the legal case would rely on toxicologic evidence and/or testimony to support or refute the findings. Other healthcare professionals may also be called upon, as well. For example, the case of *Johnson v. State* (1992) involved testimony by a toxicologist, a pathologist, and a neonatologist. An epidemiologist might be called upon to explain the concepts of specificity, sensitivity, and positive and negative predictive values and how they relate to a determination that the mother did or did not ingest a particular substance.

Establishing Causation

Although exposure to a specific drug in utero may have been found to be associated with a specific adverse outcome, exposure by itself is insufficient to establish that the exposure was responsible for a specific outcome to a specific child. Consequently, regardless of the nature of the proceeding, causation is likely to be a critical and contentious issue.

First, even where there exists an association between the maternal substance use during pregnancy and a specific outcome, that association may not be indicative of causation. Various aspects of that association require evaluation before a determination of causation can be made. These include the strength and consistency of the association as demonstrated by research findings, the temporal ordering between the exposure to the substance and the outcome, the dose-response relationship, and the biological plausibility of the observed association (Button, et al., 2007).

Second, in utero substance exposure varies in its timing, duration, and intensity. For example, whether maternal ingestion of cocaine results in a detectable injury to the newborn and the nature of that injury may depend on whether it was used, for example, during the development of the fetal brain or during the last days of pregnancy and whether it was used on only one occasion or whether it was used more frequently, such as every weekend. The effects of a drug may be transient or longer lasting.

Third, variables other than in utero exposure to a specific substance may also have the potential to result in the same outcome as that associated with the maternal substance use. As an example, smoking has been found to be responsible for 20% to 30% of all low birth weight infants. Infants born to mothers who smoke weigh, on average, 150 to 250 grams less than infants born to mothers who did not smoke during pregnancy (Andres & Day, 2000). This suggests that other factors may be responsible for the majority of the low birth weight babies. Smokers may be different from nonsmokers with respect to various sociodemographic and other health characteristics, suggesting that problems found in the offspring of smoking mothers, such as low birth weight, may be a reflection of these maternal characteristics apart from the exposure to smoking (Carter, Paterson, Gao, & Lusitini, 2007). These maternal characteristics may be unknown, may not have been measured, or may not have been adequately controlled for in the analysis (cf. Maughan, Taylor, Caspi, & Moffitt, 2004). Consequently, in any given case, it may be difficult, if not impossible, to determine whether the low birth weight of the infant resulted from maternal smoking during pregnancy or from any of the other potentially causative factors that may have existed contemporaneously, such as poverty or maternal malnutrition.

Similarly, although fetal alcohol syndrome has been attributed specifically to alcohol ingestion during pregnancy, research suggests that characteristics of children that have been linked to fetal alcohol syndrome may not be specific to that syndrome. The facial appearance of children who were born to mothers with phenylketonuria (Lipson, Yu, O'Halloran, & Williams, 1981) and those who were born to epileptic women who used Dilantin during pregnancy (Hill, 1976) resembles that of children who are believed to have fetal alcohol syndrome. Other factors may produce features that are compatible with fetal alcohol syndrome, including marijuana use during pregnancy, weight gain of less than 5 pounds, and exposure to X-rays (Hingson, et al., 1982).

Fourth, numerous other postnatal factors share responsibility for the infant's development. The postnatal caregiving environment is critical to a child's development regardless of whether the mother ingested substances during pregnancy. An environment that is characterized by disorganization and abuse will be detrimental to a child, while one that reflects stability, emotional connectedness, and consistent parental supervision will be more likely to be beneficial (National Research Council, 1993). As an example, the later behavioral problems of children who were exposed in utero to methamphetamine may also be attributable to environmental factors (Billing, Eriksson, Jonsson, & Steneroth, 1994).

This constellation of methodological difficulties is evident in attempts to interpret findings relating to the association between maternal prenatal smoking and the later development in the offspring of conduct disorders. Despite growing evidence of an association between the exposure and the outcome, researchers have advised caution in interpreting these findings because of the likelihood of substantial confounding. Consider, as an example, the multitude of factors involved in assessing the effects of prenatal smoking. First, the same factors associated with prenatal smoking—lower levels of education, younger age, adverse social circumstances, and depression—are also associated with the development of behavioral problems in children (Breslau, Kilbey, & Andreski, 1993; Hill, 2002; Matthews, 2001; Ventura, Matthews, Curtin, Matthews, & Park, 2000). Second, smoking is more common among women who exhibit antisocial behavior (Bardone, et al., 1998), a known risk factor for the development of antisocial behavior in their offspring as a result of both genetic and environmental influences (Maughan, et al., 2004). Finally, smoking may be a proxy variable for genetic risk for antisocial behavior so that, regardless of whether or not the fetus was exposed to smoking in utero, the child's later development of a conduct disorder would have been the result of the genetic influence, rather than the in utero exposure to smoking (Maughan, et al., 2004).

Case Study 2: The Medical Examination of Aliens and the Exclusion Provisions

MENTAL ILLNESS IN THE CONTEXT OF IMMIGRATION LAW

Individuals who are seeking entry into the United States, who are not already US citizens or permanent resident aliens ("green card" or "mica" holders), are potentially inadmissible to the United States if the person is determined:

> (I) to have a physical or mental disorder and behavior associated with the disorder that may pose, or has posed, a threat to the property, safety, or welfare of the alien or others, or

> (II) to have had a physical or mental disorder and a history of behavior associated with the disorder, which behavior has posed a threat to the property, safety, or welfare of the alien or others and which behavior is likely to recur or lead to other harmful behavior; or

> (III) who is determined . . . to be a drug abuser or addict (Immigration and Nationality Act, 2008a)

If the individual is trying to become a permanent resident of the United States, he or she will be required to undergo a medical examination conducted by a physician authorized by the US government to serve as a civil surgeon, if the individual is in the United States, or a physician authorized by the US government to serve as a panel physician, if the individual is applying for an immigrant visa from outside of the United States. If the authorized physician finds that the person has a mental illness that falls within these statutory parameters, the physician will issue what is called a Class A certificate, which renders the alien inadmissible to the United States, meaning that he or she will be permanently barred, in most cases, from ever entering the country legally. In some cases, the physician may issue a Class B medical certificate, which signifies that an illness or disorder is present but that the individual is not inadmissible.

The *Technical Instructions for Medical Examinations of Aliens* guides the examinations of the panel physicians, while the *Technical Instructions for Medical Examinations of Aliens in the United States* guides the examinations performed by the civil surgeons. Both of these publications utilize the same definitions as the basis for this assessment:

> mental disorder—a currently accepted psychiatric disorder, as evidenced by inclusion in the current Diagnostic and Statistical Manual of Mental Disorders (DSM-III-R or subsequent revision), published by the American Psychiatric Association

> harmful behavior—for purposes of this examination, a dangerous action or series of actions by the alien that has resulted in injury (psychological or physical) to the alien or another person, or that has threatened the health or safety of the alien or another person, or that has resulted in property damage (Public Health Service, n.d.a, b)

The physician will premise his or her evaluation of the individual on a physical examination, the individual's medical history, and an interview with the individual.

The physician must find either of the following to issue a Class A medical certificate:

- That the client has a "mental disorder" as identified in the current version of the DSM as well as associated harmful behavior or a history of harmful behavior
- A history of a "mental disorder" and a history of associated harmful behavior and that harmful behavior is likely to recur

The *Diagnostic and Statistical Manual of Mental Disorders* (DSM) was developed by the American Psychiatric Association for the diagnosis of mental illnesses. Both sets of instructions distinguish between "Major Diagnostic Categories," which "may be associated" with harmful behavior according to the third revision of the DSM (DSM-III-R) and other diagnostic categories that invariably include harmful behavior as part of the diagnostic criteria. The instructions indicate that the following diagnoses "may be associated" with harmful behavior:

- Mental retardation
- Personality disorders
- Autistic disorders
- Adult antisocial behavior
- Organic mental disorders (dementias)
- Conduct disorders
- Schizophrenic, paranoid, and other psychotic disorders

- Adjustment disorders
- Delusional disorders
- Sexual disorders
- Mood disorders
- Impulse control disorders
- Dissociative disorders
- Psychoactive substance use disorders
- Anxiety-related disorders
- Somatoform disorders

The instructions refer to the DSM-III-R. However, the DSM is currently in its fourth revised edition, and some of the diagnostic categories and the criteria for such diagnoses have changed since the publication of the DSM-III-R.

Individuals who are issued a Class A medical certificate because of mental illness may apply for a waiver of inadmissibility which, if granted, would allow them to obtain their permanent resident status (Immigration and Nationality Act, 2008b). The application for this waiver is filed with the application for permanent residence either at the consulate, if the individual is outside of the United States (immigrant visa processing), or in the United States, if the individual is in the country (adjustment of status). The waiver application will be forwarded to the Division of Global Migration and Quarantine (DGMQ) within the Centers for Disease Control and Prevention (CDC).

In general, individuals who apply for such waivers often enlist the assistance of an attorney because of the complexity of the process, although they are not required to have an attorney. Because the waiver application must be supplemented with other evidence as required by the instructions, the attorney will often obtain consultation from a psychiatrist and other healthcare professionals. Depending upon the situation, an epidemiologist may also be consulted.

The Role of the Epidemiologist
In such cases, it is highly likely that an attorney who represents the prospective immigrant would wish to retain an epidemiologist both to assist with the preparation of the arguments to be made and to provide an affidavit in support of those arguments. Issues that the epidemiologist may be asked to address include:

- The risk of violence to self and others in the context of the client's specific diagnosis, age, and other factors.
- The ability of individuals with this diagnosis to engage in employment
- The prevalence of adherence or risk of nonadherence to medication required for this illness

For the epidemiologist to prepare an affidavit that addresses these or other issues, he or she would necessarily review the relevant literature relating to these issues. One of the inherent difficulties, however, is that the epidemiologist can speak only to what the risks and rates are in a population context; he or she cannot make predictions relating to the behavior of any specific individual on the basis of such data. To address this gap, it is likely that the attorney for the prospective immigrant would also seek the expertise of a psychologist or psychiatrist who could provide insight with respect to the particular proclivities of the individual client. While not determinative of the outcome of the case, it is highly likely that the data provided by the epidemiologist and the evaluation provided by the psychologist or psychiatrist would be critical to the ultimate decision in the case.

Exercise

A significant body of research has consistently observed the relative lack of availability of treatment programs for pregnant women who abuse substances and the questionable quality of care that pregnant women receive while incarcerated in jails and prisons. Assume that your state legislature is considering the adoption of a statute that would permit the criminal prosecution of a pregnant woman for child abuse based upon her use of alcohol during her pregnancy. You have been asked to testify before the state legislature with respect to the potential advantages and deficiencies or drawbacks of such a law.

Prepare your draft testimony for the legislature. Consider, at a minimum, the following issues: (1) the legality of alcohol use; (2) the availability of alcohol treatment for the alcohol-abusing pregnant woman both outside of the prison system and within the prison system; (3) measurement of risk to the fetus; (4) the availability and quality of prenatal care and labor and delivery services to the woman within the prison system; and (5) the larger public health consequences if such a law were to be implemented.

References

1. Acuff-Smith, K. D., George, M., Lorens, S. A., & Vorhees, C. V. (1992). Preliminary evidence for methamphetamine-induced behavioral and ocular effects in rat offspring following exposure during early organogenesis. *Psychopharmacology, 109,* 255–263.

2. Andres, R. L., & Day, M. C. (2000). Perinatal complications associated with maternal tobacco use. *Seminars in Neonatology, 5,* 231–241.

3. Arria, A. M., Derauf, C., LaGasse, L. L., Gant, P., Shah, R., Smith, L., et al. (2006). Methamphetamine and other substance use during pregnancy: Preliminary estimates from the Infant Development, Environment, and Lifestyle (IDEAL) study. *Maternal and Child Health Journal*, 10, 293–302.

4. Associated Press. (2008, May 13). South Carolina: Verdict overturned in baby's death. *The New York Times*. Retrieved August 10, 2008, from http://www.nytimes.com/2008/05/13/us/13brfs-VERDICTOVERT_BRF.html.

5. Bardone, A. M., Moffitt, T. E., Caspi, A., Dickson, N., Stanton, W. R., & Silva, P. A. (1998). Adult physical health outcomes of adolescent girls with conduct disorder, depression, and anxiety. *Journal of the American Academy of Child and Adolescent Psychiatry*, 37, 594–601.

6. Bauer, C. R., Shankaran, S., Bada, H., & Lester, B. M. (2002). The maternal lifestyle study: Drug exposure during pregnancy and short-term maternal outcomes. *American Journal of Obstetrics and Gynecology*, 186, 487–495.

7. Billing, L., Eriksson, M., Jonsson, B., & Steneroth, G. (1994). The influence of environmental factors on behavioral problems in 8-year-old children exposed to amphetamine during fetal life. *Child Abuse & Neglect*, 18, 3–9.

8. Billing, L., Eriksson, M., Steneroth, G., & Zetterstrom, R. (1985). Preschool children of amphetamine-addicted mothers. I. Somatic and psychomotor development. *Acta Paediatrica Scandinavia*, 74, 179–184.

9. Billing, L., Eriksson, M., Steneroth, G., & Zetterstrom, R. (1988). Predictive indicators for adjustment in 4-year-old children whose mothers used amphetamine during pregnancy. *Child Abuse & Neglect*, 12, 503–507.

10. Breslau, N., Kilbey, M., & Andreski, P. (1993). Nicotine dependence and major depression: New evidence from a prospective investigation. *Archives of General Psychiatry*, 50, 31–35.

11. Büttner, A., Mall, G., Penning, R., & Weis, S. (2000). The neuropathology of heroin use. *Forensic Science International*, 113, 435–442.

12. Button, T. M. M., Maughan, B., & McGuffin, P. (2007). The relationship of maternal smoking to psychological problems in the offspring. *Early Human Development*, 83, 727–732.

13. Carter, S., Paterson, J., Gao, W., & Lusitini, L. (2007). Maternal smoking during pregnancy and behaviour problems in a birth cohort of 2-year-old Pacific children in New Zealand. *Early Human Development*, 84, 59–66.

14. Cho, D. H., Lyu, H. M., Lee, H. B., Kim, P. Y., & Chin, K. (1991). Behavioral teratogenicity of methamphetamine. *Journal of Toxicology Science Supplement*, 1, 37–49.

15. Delaney-Black, V., Covington, C., Templin, T., & Ager, J. (1998). Prenatal cocaine exposure and child behaviors. *Pediatrics*, 102, 945–950.

16. Faden, V. B., & Graubard, B. I. (2000). Maternal substance use during pregnancy and developmental outcome at age three. *Journal of Substance Abuse*, 12, 329–340.

17. Fentiman, L. C. (2006). The new "fetal protection": The wrong answer to the crisis of inadequate health care for women and children. *Denver University Law Review*, 84, 537–599.

18. Fergusson, D. M., Horwood, L. J., Northstone, K., & ALSPAC Study Team. (2002). Maternal use of cannabis and pregnancy outcome. *BJOG: An International Journal of Obstetrics and Gynaecology*, 109, 21–27.

19. Finn, S. P., Leen, E., English, L., & O'Briain, D. S. (2003). Autopsy findings in an outbreak of severe systemic illness in heroin users following injection site

inflammation: An effect of *Clostridium novyi* exotoxin? *Archives of Pathology Laboratory Medicine, 127,* 1465–1470.

20. Floyd, R. L., Zahniser, C., Gunter, E. P., & Kendrick, J. S. (1991). Smoking during pregnancy: Prevalence, effects, and intervention strategies. *Birth, 18,* 48–53.

21. Fried, P. A., & O'Connell, C. M. (1987). A comparison of the effects of prenatal exposure to tobacco, alcohol, cannabis, and caffeine on birth size and subsequent growth. *Neurotoxicology & Teratology, 9,* 79–85.

22. Ganapathy, V., Prasad, P. D., Ganapathy, M. E., & Leibach, L. H. (1999). Drugs of abuse and placental transport. *Advances in Drug Delivery Review, 38,* 99–110.

23. Gilchrist, L. D., Hussey, J. M., Gillmore, M. R., Lohr, M. J., & Morrison, D. M. (1996). Drug use among adolescent mothers: Pregnancy to 18 months postpartum. *Journal of Adolescent Health, 19,* 337–344.

24. Gittler, J. (2003). The American drug war, maternal substance abuse and child protection: A commentary. *Journal of Gender, Race, & Justice, 7,* 237–265.

25. Harris, L. H., & Paltrow, L. (2003). The status of pregnant women and fetuses in U.S. criminal law. *Journal of the American Medical Association, 289,* 1697–1698.

26. Hill, J. (2002). Biological, psychological, and social processes in the conduct disorders. *Journal of Child Psychology & Psychiatry, 43,* 133–164.

27. Hill, R. M. (1976). Fetal malformations and antiepileptic drugs. *American Journal of Disabilities in Children, 130,* 923–925.

28. Hingson, R., Alpert, J., Day, N., Dooling, E., Kayne, H., Morelock, S., et al. (1982). Effects of maternal drinking and marijuana use on fetal growth and development. *Pediatrics, 70,* 539–546.

29. Illinois Compiled Statutes Annotated 50/1-1(D)(k)(2008).

30. Immigration and Nationality Act § § 212(a)(1)(iii), (iv) 8 U.S.C. § § 1182 (a)(1)(iii), (iv) (2008a).

31. Immigration and Nationality Act § § 212(g)(1)(3) 8 U.S.C. § § 1182(g)(1)(3) (2008b).

32. In re Baby Boy Blackshear, 736 N.E.2d 462 (Ohio 2000).

33. Johnson v. State, 602 So. 2d 1288 (Fla. S.Ct. 1992).

34. Jos, P. H., Perlmutter, M., & Marshall, M. F. (2003). Substance abuse during pregnancy: Clinical and public health approaches. *Journal of Law, Medicine, & Ethics, 31,* 340–347.

35. Kaiser, M. M., & Hays, B. J. (2005). Health-risk behaviors in a sample of first-time pregnant adolescents. *Public Health Nursing, 22,* 483–493.

36. Kilby, J. W. (1997). A smoking cessation plan for pregnant women. *Journal of Obstetrical, Gynecological, and Neonatal Nursing, 26,* 397–402.

37. Krulewitch, C. J. (2001). Science update: Alcohol use and pregnancy. *Journal of Midwifery & Women's Health, 46,* 394.

38. Leech, S. L., Richardson, G. A., Goldschmidt, L., & Day, D. L. (1999). Prenatal substance exposure: Effects on attention and impulsivity of 6-year-olds. *Neurotoxicology and Teratology, 21,* 109–118.

39. Lester, B. M., Andreozzi, L., & Appiah, L. (2004). Substance use during pregnancy: Time for policy to catch up with research. *Harm Reduction Journal, 1.* Retrieved January 17, 2008, from http://www.harmreductionjournal.com/content/1/1/5.

40. Lester, B. M., elSohly, M. A., Wright, L. L., & Smeriglio, V. L. (2001). The maternal lifestyle study: Drug use by meconium toxicology and maternal self-report. *Pediatrics, 107,* 309–317.

41. Lester, B. M., LaGasse, L., Freier, C., & Brunner, S. (1996). Human studies of cocaine exposed infants. In C. L. Wethering, V. Smeriglio, & L. Finnegan (Eds.). *NIDA monograph series: Behavioral studies of drug-exposed offspring: Methodological issues in human and animal research* (Vol. 164, pp. 175–210). Rockville, MD: National Institute on Drug Abuse.

42. Lester, B. M., LaGasse, L., & Seifer, R. (1998). Cocaine exposure and children: The meaning of subtle effects. *Science, 282,* 633–634.

43. Lester, B. M., & Tronick, E. Z. (1994). The effects of prenatal cocaine exposure and child outcome: Lessons from the past. *Infant Mental Health Journal, 15,* 107–120.

44. Lester, B. M., Tronick, E. Z., LaGasse, L., Seifer, R., Bauer, C. R., Shankaran, S., et al. (2002). The Maternal Lifestyle Study: Effects of substance exposure during pregnancy on neurodevelopmental outcome in 1-month-old infants. *Pediatrics, 110,* 1182–1192.

45. Levin, E. D., & Slotkin, T. A. (1998). Developmental neurotoxicity of nicotine. In W. Slikker, Jr. & L.W. Chang (Eds.), *Handbook of developmental neurotoxicity* (pp. 587–615). San Diego, CA: Academic Press.

46. Lewis, K. W., & Bosque, E. M. (1995). Deficient hypoxia awakening response in infants of smoking mothers: Possible relationship to sudden infant death syndrome. *Journal of Pediatrics, 127,* 691–699.

47. Linden, P. (1995). Drug addiction during pregnancy: A call for increased social responsibility. *American University Journal of Gender & the Law, 4,* 105–139.

48. Lipson, A. H., Yu, J. S., O'Halloran, M. T., & Williams, R. (1981). Alcohol and phenylketonuria. *Lancet, 1,* 717–718.

49. Matthews, T. J. (2001). *Smoking during pregnancy in the 1990s.* Hyattsville, MD: National Center for Health Statistics.

50. Mattson, S. N., Riley, E. P., Sowell, E. R., & Jernigan, T. L. (1996). A decrease in size of the basal ganglia in children with fetal alcohol syndrome. *Alcoholism: Clinical and Experimental Research, 20,* 1088–1093.

51. Maughan, B., Taylor, A., Caspi, A., & Moffitt, T. E. (2004). Prenatal smoking and early childhood conduct problems: Testing genetic and environmental explanations of the association. *Archives of General Psychiatry, 61,* 836–843.

52. McKnight v. State (2008). Opinion No. 26484, State of South Carolina Supreme Court. Retrieved August 10, 2008, from http://www.judicial.state.sc.us/opinions/displayOpnion.cfm?caseNo=26484.

53. Minnesota Statutes Annotated § 253B.02 (2007).

54. Mitchell, E. A., Ford, R. P., Stewart, A. W., & Taylor, B. J. (1993). Smoking and the sudden infant death syndrome. *Pediatrics, 91,* 893–896.

55. Moore, C., Lewis, D., & Leikin, J. (1995). False-positive and false-negative rates in meconium drug testing. *Clinical Chemistry, 41,* 1614–1616.

56. National Research Council. (1993). *Understanding child abuse and neglect.* Washington, DC: National Academy Press.

57. New Jersey v. Ikerd, 850 A.2d 516 (N.J. Super. Ct. App. Div. 2004).

58. Office of Applied Statistics, Substance Abuse and Mental Health Services Administration. (2005). Substance use during pregnancy: 2002 and 2003 update. *The National Survey on Drug Use and Health (NSDUH) report.* Retrieved January 2008, from http://www.oas.samhsa.gov.

59. Ohio Revised Code § 2151.031(D)(2008).

60. Olson, H. C., O'Connor, M. J., & Fitzgerald, H. E. (2001). Lessons learned from study of the developmental impact of parental alcohol abuse. *Infant Mental Health Journal, 22*, 271–290.

61. Paltrow, L. (1999). Pregnant drug users, fetal persons, and the threat to Roe v. Wade. *Albany Law Review, 62*, 1029–1055.

62. Plessinger, M. A. (1998). Prenatal exposure to amphetamines. Risks and adverse outcomes in pregnancy. *Obstetrics and Gynecology Clinics of North America, 25*, 119–138.

63. Public Health Service. (n.d.a). *Technical instructions for medical examination of aliens.* Atlanta, GA: Centers for Disease Control and Prevention. Retrieved January 21, 2008, from http://www.cdc.gov/ncidod/dq/technica.htm.

64. Public Health Service. (n.d.b). *Technical instructions for medical examination of aliens in the United States.* Atlanta, GA: Centers for Disease Control and Prevention. Retrieved January 21, 2008, from http://www.cdc.gov/ncidod/dq/technica.htm.

65. Rayburn, W. F. (2007). Maternal and fetal effects from substance use. *Clinical Perinatology, 34*, 559–571.

66. Reinesto v. State, 894 P.2d 733 (Ariz. Ct. App. 1995).

67. Reyes v. Superior Court, 75 Cal. App. 3d 214 (1977).

68. Richardson, K. K. (1999). Adolescent pregnancy and substance use. *Journal of Obstetrical, Gynecological, and Neonatal Nursing, 28*, 623–627.

69. Riley, E. P., Mattson, S. N., Sowell, E. R., & Jernigan, T. L. (1995). Abnormalities of the corpus callosum in children perinatally exposed to alcohol. *Alcoholism: Clinical and Experimental Research, 19*, 1198–1202.

70. Roberts, D. E. (1991). Punishing drug addicts who have babies: Women of color, equality, and the right of privacy. *Harvard Law Review, 104*, 1419–1482.

71. Schoendorf, K. C., & Kiely, J. L. (1992). Relationship of sudden infant death syndrome to maternal smoking during and after pregnancy. *Pediatrics, 90*, 905–908.

72. Schueller, J. (1999). The use of cocaine by pregnant women: Child abuse or choice? *Journal of Legislation, 25*, 163–165.

73. Senate Bill 1337, Statement of Purpose, 58th leg., 2d Reg. Sess. (Idaho, 2006). Retrieved June 2007, from http://www3.state.id.us/oasis/2006/S1337.html.

74. Sherwood, R. A., Keating, J., Kavvadia, V., Greenough, A., & Peters, T. J. (1999). Substance misuse in early pregnancy and relationship to fetal outcome. *European Journal of Pediatrics, 158*, 488–491.

75. Slotkin, T. A. (1998). Fetal nicotine or cocaine exposure: Which one is worse? *Journal of Pharmacology and Experimental Therapeutics, 285*, 932–945.

76. South Dakota Codified Laws § 34-20A-63(3)(2007).

77. State v. McKnight, 576 S.E.2d 168 (S.C. 2003).

78. Suzuki, K., Minei, L. J., & Johnson, E. E. (1980). Effect of nicotine upon uterine blood flow in the pregnant rhesus monkey. *American Journal of Obstetrics and Gynecology, 136*, 1009–1013.

79. Swayze, V. W., II, Johnson, V. P., Hanson, J. W., & Piven, J. (1997). Magnetic resonance imaging of brain anomalies in fetal alcohol syndrome. *Pediatrics, 99*, 232–240.

80. United States v. Vaughn, Crim. No. 2172-88 B (D.C. Super. Ct. Aug. 23, 1988).

81. Ventura, S., Matthews J., Curtin, S., Matthews, T., & Park, M. (2000). *Births: Final data for 1998.* Hyattsville, MD: National Center for Health Statistics.

82. Weissman, A. D., & Caldecott-Hazard, S. (1995). Developmental neurotoxicity to methamphetamines. *Clinical and Experimental Pharmacology & Physiology, 22*, 372–374.

83.   Whitner v. State, 492 S.E.2d 777 (S.C. 1997).

84.   Wisconsin ex rel. Angela v. Kruzicki, 541 N.W.2d 482 (Wis. Ct. App. 1995), *overruled by Wisconsin ex rel. Angela v. Kruzicki*, 561 N.W.2d 729 (Wis. 1997).

85.   Wisconsin Statutes Annotated § § 48.193(1)(d)(2), 48.205 (2007).

86.   Wood, E., Kerr, T., Montaner, J. S., Strathdee, S. A., Wodak, A., Hankins, C. A., et al. (2004). Rationale for evaluating North America's first medically supervised safer-injecting facility. *Lancet, 4*, 301–306.

87.   Zuckerman, B., Frank, D. A., Hingson, R., Amaro, H., Levenson, S. M., Kayne, H., et al. (1989). Effects of maternal marijuana and cocaine on fetal growth. *New England Journal of Medicine, 320*, 762–768.

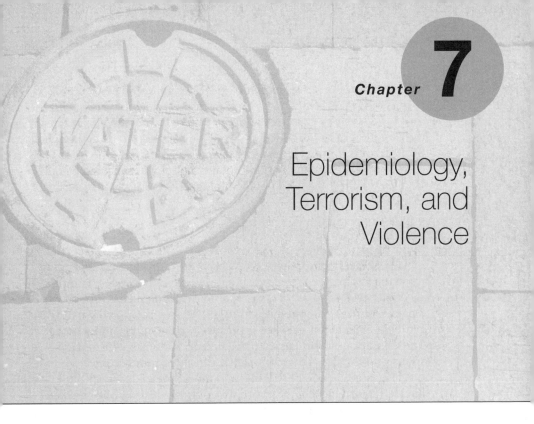

Chapter 7

Epidemiology, Terrorism, and Violence

Although one does not immediately conceive of epidemiology as a tool for solving crimes, Chapter 3, Epidemiology and Criminal Law, underscores the importance of epidemiologic methods in some criminal investigations. The potential usefulness of epidemiologic methods and the skills of the epidemiologist are further examined in these two case studies that involve violence and bioterrorism.

Case Study 1: Partner Violence, Epidemiology, and the Law

Both prosecutors who seek the conviction of individuals who are accused of battering and defense attorneys who seek the acquittal of battering victims who have killed their batterers have attempted to utilize expert testimony relating to the battered woman syndrome (BWS). Most frequently, that testimony has been sought from a psychologist, a psychiatrist, or a sociologist who is familiar with BWS. However, the testimony of an epidemiologist may be valuable in some circumstances. This case study first provides an overview of intimate partner violence, the frequency of its occurrence, and its consequences. This is followed by a discussion of the battered woman syndrome and the evolution of its introduction through expert testimony in the context of criminal prosecutions. The chapter then explains the bases for the admissibility of expert testimony and the approach that can be utilized for the introduction of epidemiologic data relating to battering.

DEFINING INTIMATE PARTNER VIOLENCE

"Intimate partner violence," also referred to as domestic violence, family violence, and wife battering, has been variously defined depending upon the discipline of reference and the elements believed to comprise the violence. Denzin (1984, pp. 483–484) has defined domestic violence as "situated, emotional, and cognitive activity involving negative symbolic interaction between intimates, usually in the family home." The definition encompasses marital rape; sadomasochistic rituals; spouse abuse; inflicted emotionality; threats of murder; physical torture; harassment; acts of striking; and mock, pretended, or playful violence (Denzin, 1984). Kornblit, in contrast, distinguishes between abuse, violence and maltreatment:

> The former [abuse] refers to actions which are harmful for the victim, both physically as well as mentally, omitted or resulting from omission, carried out intentionally or not.

> Violence in a limited sense is used to refer to physical aggression.

> Maltreatment includes abuse (physical, sexual, and/or emotional) and neglect (physical, educational, and/or affective). (Kornblit, 1994, p. 1181)

Brown (1992, p. 1) uses the term "wife-beating" and defines it as "A man intentionally inflicting pain on a woman, within a non-transient, male-female relationship, whether or not the partners are officially married. The subject is further restricted to physical aggression." Brown distinguishes between a "beating," which is conceived of as a physical reprimand that is generally culturally expected and tolerated by the beating victim, and a "battering," which is said to refer to extraordinary behavior that is neither usual nor acceptable within the specified society and may result in severe injury, disability, or death.

Variation similarly exists across state laws that define domestic violence and serve as the basis for prosecutions for this crime. Ohio's statute relating to domestic violence encompasses physical harm, serious physical harm, and using threat of force to cause the individual to believe that he or she will suffer imminent physical harm (Ohio Revised Code, 2008).

THE INCIDENCE, PREVALENCE AND CONSEQUENCES OF INTIMATE PARTNER VIOLENCE

The Incidence and Prevalence of Partner Violence in the United States
A woman in the United States is beaten every 15 seconds (Steele & Sigman, 1991); every 9 seconds, a husband abuses his wife (*Weiand v. State*, 1999). Women are abused in approximately 12% of all marriages in the United States (Koons, 2006), while approximately 1 out of every 32 households is affected by intimate partner violence (Klaus, 2007). The American Psychological Association has indicated that almost one-third of all women in the United States will be assaulted by a partner during their adulthood (Federal Bureau of Investigation, 2003). All told, it has been estimated that nearly 5.3 million separate episodes of intimate partner victimization occur each year in the United States, resulting in nearly 2 million injuries and 1300 deaths (National Center for Injury Prevention and Control, 2003).

The majority of these incidents involve victimizations of females. For example, between 2001 and 2005, nonfatal intimate partner victimizations represented 22% of nonfatal violent victimizations against females aged 12 years and older, but 4% of those directed against males of the same age range (Catalano, 2007). Females between the ages of 20 and 24 years, those who are separated or divorced from their intimate partners, and those who reside in rental housing compared to owned housing, appear to be at greater risk of nonfatal partner violence (Catalano, 2007). Partner violence is more likely to occur between the hours of 6 p.m. and 6 a.m. (Catalano, 2007), in neighborhoods characterized by relatively high levels of disorder (Cunradi, 2007), and in urban areas (Catalano, 2007). Compared to male victims of intimate partner violence, female victims are seven times more likely to be confronted by their partner with a firearm during the course of the incident and almost twice as likely to report that their partner explicitly threatened to kill them (Catalano, 2007).

Consequences of Partner Violence
The consequences of even nonfatal intimate partner violence are both varied and severe. Over 50% of female victims of nonfatal intimate partner violence have been found to have suffered some physical injury; this includes 5% who suffered serious injury, such as broken bones, severe internal injury, and/or unconsciousness; 44% who experienced more minor injuries; and 3% who suffered rape or sexual assault (Catalano, 2007). Outcomes that appear to be less severe in comparison include partial loss of vision or hearing, burns, bites, hematomas, fractures, cuts or abrasions, inflammation, penetrating puncture wounds, dislocation, and sprains (Balakrishnan, Imell, Bandy, & Prasad, 1995; Bates, Redman, Brown, & Hancock, 1995; Beck,

Frietag, & Singer, 1996; Browne & Williams, 1993; Hartzell, Botek, & Goldberg, 1996). However, it has been suggested that less than one-fifth of the female victims who report an injury have sought medical treatment following the injury (Catalano, 2007).

The occurrence of partner violence is associated with adverse health conditions in addition to the immediate injury that is the direct effect of the violence. In comparison with those who have not experienced partner violence, females who report partner violence have been found to be more likely to smoke (Hathaway, et al., 2000; McNutt, Carlson, Persaud, & Postmus, 2002); consume greater amounts of alcohol (Lemon, Verhoek-Ofredahl, & Donnelly, 2002); and to experience sexually transmitted infections (Letourneau, Holmes, & Chasedunn-Roark, 1999), pelvic inflammatory disease, invasive cervical cancer, and preinvasive cervical neoplasia (Coker, Sanderson, Fadden, & Pirisi, 2000). Women in abusive relationships have been found to be less likely to use condoms and more likely to experience threats of violence when they discussed condoms, resulting in an increased risk of HIV infection (Wingood & DiClemente, 1997). Partner violence has also been found to be associated with increased rates of depression, anxiety, posttraumatic stress disorder, and the occurrence of suicide (Herman, 1997; Olson, et al., 1999; Rodriguez, et al., 2008; Sanford, et al., 2006; Walker, 1979).

Death is the most severe consequence of intimate partner violence. Research indicates that of all adult women who are murdered, one-third to more than one-half are killed by an intimate or former intimate; of these, the majority were battered before their deaths (Paulozzi, Saltzman, Thompson, & Holmgreen, 2001; Sanford, et al., 2006). Female murder victims are significantly more likely to have been killed by an intimate or former intimate partner, as compared with male murder victims (Fox & Zawitz, 2005); of those women who were killed by their intimate partner, almost one-half (44%) had visited an emergency department within 2 years of the homicide; of these, 93% had at least one injury visit (Crandall, Nathens, Kernic, Hold, & Rivara, 2004). A study of female intimate partner homicide conducted in North Carolina over a 3-year period found that almost one-half (46.1%) of the 293 murdered women had been killed by their marital partners, 80% had been killed in their own homes, and 66% had been killed with guns (Moracco, Runyan, & Butts, 2003). Homicide committed by an intimate partner or former intimate partner is the leading cause of death of pregnant women in the United States (Chang, Berg, Saltzman, & Herndon, 2005). Studies conducted in New York and Chicago indicate that the leading cause of maternal mortality is trauma; the highest proportion of these traumatic deaths are attributable to homicide (Fildes, Reed, Jones, Martin, & Barrett, 1992).

Third parties may also experience serious consequences. Several studies have suggested that low infant birth weight may be associated with physical abuse during pregnancy, although the causal pathway remains unclear (Bullock & McFarlane, 1989; Campbell, et al., 1999; Parker, McFarlane, & Soeken, 1994). Children who witness the violence may themselves experience anxiety, depression, preoccupation with aggression, suicidal ideation, sleep disorders, headaches, bedwetting, and digestive difficulties, sometimes resulting in social withdrawal and truancy (Attala, Bauza, Pratt, & Viera, 1995; Holden & Ritchie, 1991; Hughes, 1986, 1988; Humphreys, 1993).

The consequences of intimate partner violence inure to society at large, in addition to the victim of the attack and other family members. Victims of intimate partner violence lose almost 8 million days of paid work annually; this represents the equivalent of more than 32,000 full-time job positions and 5.6 million days of household productivity (National Center for Injury Prevention and Control, 2003). In 2003, the costs of intimate partner violence exceed $8.3 billion annually, reflecting $460 million for rape, $6.2 billion for physical assaults other than rape, $461 million for stalking, and $1.2 billion for the value of lives lost (Max, Rice, Finkelstein, Bardwell, & Leadbetter, 2004).

THE BATTERED WOMAN SYNDROME

The battered woman syndrome (BWS), a psychological theory developed during the 1970s and 1980s, represents an attempt to explain why battered women remain with their abusive partners. The theory is premised on the work of Lenore Walker who, based on her interviews with battered women, postulated that the battering relationship often reflects a three-stage cycle of violence (Walker, 1979). The first stage, labeled the "tension building phase," is characterized by a minimal amount of verbal and physical attacks by the intimate partner. The woman often minimizes the significance of these incidents and attempts to placate her partner. During the second phase, termed the "battering phase," however, the battering escalates and the woman may undergo an acute battering incident. This second stage is followed by the "honeymoon phase," during which the batterer seeks the forgiveness of the battered partner. Walker (1979) maintained that repeated cycles of violence could potentially result in the development of learned helplessness, akin to that observed in laboratory dogs who learned that they were helpless after being repeatedly subjected to shocks that they were powerless to control (Seligman, Maier, & Geer, 1968). BWS refers to the effects of this cycle of violence: learned helplessness, reexperiencing of the trauma, intrusive recollections, generalized anxiety, low self-esteem, and social withdrawal (Giles-Sims, 1998).

Walker's research has been heavily criticized as being methodologically and analytically unsound due to interviewer bias, the lack of specificity with respect to the temporal sequencing of the phases, the lack of a comparison group, and the lack of support in her data for her conclusions relating to the existence of the abusive cycle (Faigman, 1986). Additional criticisms have been leveled against the use of BWS in the context of trials of women who are accused of killing their batterers. It has been argued that the use of the theory to explain a woman's circumstances relies on and perpetuates stereotypes of femininity that ultimately harm women who do not conform to racial and gender stereotypes held by judges and jurors (Ferraro, 2003; Schneider, 2000).

BWS has also been critiqued for its oversimplification of the range of potential responses to stress and violence and the nuances that are inherent in relationships. While the theory explains the violent act, it fails to acknowledge and integrate alternative strategies that the battered individual may have employed in an attempt to alleviate the frequency or intensity of the violence or to protect children in the home (Baker, 2005). One scholar observed that BWS:

> paints a simplistic emotional picture, one of a woman who is helpless, not one who is struggling. Expert testimony [on BWS] generally focuses on women's "learned helplessness" and passivity. It tells a story of a woman who is so broken that she no longer cares that she is mistreated. This defense often fails because when real women get into court, the jury hears a story of a woman who struggles, emotionally if not physically. Such struggles show signs of initiative and agency that are inconsistent with [BWS]. When the woman fails to choose the emotionally simplistic background option—leave—or conform to the emotionally simplistic alternative—give up completely—the law has no place for her and thus assumes that she must be culpable when she finally fights back. (Baker, 2005, pp. 459–460)

Because the theory depicts the women who killed as mental or emotional wrecks, suffering from a "syndrome," it may also be used by the prosecution to challenge the woman's credibility and the validity of her perceptions, decisions, and responses (*People v. Dillard*, 1996).

THE EPIDEMIOLOGIST AND PARTNER VIOLENCE

In general, there are four situations in which expert testimony regarding BWS may be sought: (1) by the prosecution when seeking the conviction of an individual for acts alleged to constitute battering; (2) by the defense when seeking the acquittal of a woman for the killing of her intimate partner during a violent confrontation; (3) by the defense when seeking the acquittal of a woman for the killing of her intimate partner during a period of nonconfrontation, such as when the battering partner is sleeping; and (4) at the time of the defendant's sentencing.

Research relating to battering and its effects are relevant to these legal issues as they relate to (1) the battered woman's perception of danger within the battering relationship, which bears on the issue of self-defense; (2) a woman's state of mind as a consequence of the battering as it existed at the time of the alleged killing; and (3) patterns of violent and coercive behavior in battering relationships and patterns of coping behavior (United States Department of Justice, National Institute of Justice, United States Department of Health and Human Services, & National Institute of Mental Health, 1996). Although expert testimony is usually solicited from a psychologist or psychiatrist who can testify regarding the syndrome and how it may shape behavior, and such testimony would be critical with respect to the first two issues listed, testimony from an epidemiologist may be helpful in promoting an understanding of patterns of behavior in similarly situated samples of persons. The epidemiologist can provide testimony that is based on scientific knowledge. Many courts, for example, permit "generic" expert testimony to explain battering and its effects generally (United States Department of Justice, et al., 1996). The potential role of the epidemiologist in each such situation is examined in the following paragraphs.

The Use of Expert Testimony
The admissibility of expert testimony in a case depends, in general, upon whether the testimony will meet the requirements of the Federal Rules of Evidence or similar evidentiary rules that apply in a particular jurisdiction. Three rules, in particular, are relevant to this discussion. Federal Rule 401 requires that the proffered evidence be relevant; relevancy is found if the testimony has "any tendency to make the existence of any fact that is of consequence to the determination of the action more or less probable than it would be without the evidence."

Expert testimony must also conform to the standard enunciated by Federal Rule 702, which provides:

> If scientific, technical, or other specialized knowledge will assist the trier of fact to understand the evidence or to determine a fact in issue, a witness qualified as an expert by knowledge, skill, experience, training, or education, may testify thereto in the form of an opinion or otherwise, if (1) the testimony is based upon sufficient facts or data, (2) the testimony is the product of reliable principles and methods, and (3) the witness has applied the principles and methods reliably to the facts of the case.

There must be appropriate validation of the scientific testimony if it is to be considered reliable (*Daubert v. Merrell-Dow Pharmaceuticals, Inc.*, 1993). To assess the legal validity of the potential testimony, in contrast to the scientific validity of the theory or the studies that provide the basis for the testimony, the court must (1) determine whether the theory or technique at issue could have been tested; (2) determine whether the methodology has been subjected to peer review; (3) consider the potential rate of error associated with a particular method or technique; and (4) assess the extent to which the proffered methodology has been accepted within the identified relevant scientific community.

Even if the proposed testimony meets the requirements of Federal Rules 401 and 702, it may be excluded under Federal Rule 403 "if its probative value is substantially outweighed by the danger of unfair prejudice, confusion of the issues, or misleading the jury, or by considerations of undue delay, waste of time, or needless presentation of cumulative evidence."

BWS Evidence and Defending the Battered Spouse

Despite media-sounded alarms of killing sprees by battered women of their abusive partners (Yepsen, 2004), relatively few abused women kill their batterers. When they do, it is most often as a last resort (Jones, 1996; Maguigan, 1991; Walker, 1989). In 1992, for example, it was estimated that between 800 and 1000 of the women who were battered each year were charged with the murder of their abusive partners (Andersen & Read-Andersen, 1992). Between 1993 and 2001, 4% of all male murder victims, compared to approximately one-third of all female murder victims, were killed by their intimate partners (Rennison, 2003). Battered women are more likely to kill or attempt to kill their abusive intimates in situations that involve greater frequency of abuse, forced or threatened sexual acts, or threats of death by the batterer; more severe injuries resulting from the abuse; the batterer's drug use or frequent intoxication; an immediate threat to the lives or safety of any children; the batterer's injury or killing of pets; or the women's threat of suicide (Browne, 1987; Ferraro, 2006; Gagne, 1998).

In general, a successful claim of "perfect" self-defense requires (1) a reasonable belief on the part of the apparently assaultive individual that she was in imminent danger of great bodily harm or death at the time the defensive act was committed; (2) that she used only a reasonable amount of force to counter the aggression; (3) that she was not the aggressor; and (4) in some circumstances, that the only means of escape was through the use of deadly force (Faigman, 1986). As an example, a woman who kills a man may claim that the act was one of self-defense, and because it is found to be in self-defense, the killing is found to be justified (Krause, 2007). In such a situation, the acceptance of self-defense as a justification means that, despite the legal prohibition against homicide, the killing will be viewed as "at least not wrong" (Dressler, 2006, § 16.03, pp. 218–219).

Most states follow what has been called the objective test, meaning that the defendant believed that self-defense was necessary and that this belief would have been reasonable from the perspective of the ordinary person (LaFave & Scott, 1986). Claims of self-defense that are "imperfect" because they do not meet all of the requirements of a perfect claim may serve to mitigate the killing but will not justify it. This will not result in an acquittal, but it may bring about a reduction in the charges (Joice, 2006).

Despite the concerns raised with respect to the introduction of BWS-related testimony, most jurisdictions now permit its introduction to at least some extent, due to past court decisions or the codification of its use by state statute (Fernandez, 2007). BWS testimony may be used to support the defendant's credibility by helping the jury to analyze the claim of self-defense objectively rather than through the lens of stereotypes pertaining to abused women; to prove that the defendant honestly believed that she needed to defend herself against imminent death or great bodily injury; and to demonstrate the reasonableness of the defendant's behavior (*People v. Jaspar*, 2002). Justice Alice Resnick of the Ohio Supreme Court explained the need for expert testimony relating to BWS as follows:

> Expert testimony on the battered woman syndrome would help dispel the ordinary lay person's perception that a woman in a battering relationship is free to leave at any time. The expert evidence would counter any "common sense" conclusions by the jury that if the beatings were really that bad the woman would have left her husband much earlier. Popular misconceptions about battered women would be put to rest, including the beliefs that women are masochistic and enjoy the beating and that they intentionally put their husbands into fits of rage. (*State v. Koss*, 1990, p. 973)

Expert testimony, she stated,

> is aimed at an area where the purported common knowledge of the jury may be very much mistaken, an area where jurors' logic, drawn from their own experience, may lead to a wholly incorrect conclusion, an area where expert knowledge would enable the jurors to disregard their prior conclusions as being common myths rather than common knowledge. (*State v. Koss*, 1990, p. 974)

Ohio's statute that permits the introduction of expert testimony regarding BWS specifically recognizes:

> (1) That the syndrome [BWS] currently is a matter of commonly scientific knowledge;
> (2) That the subject matter and details of the syndrome are not within the general understanding or experience of a person who is a member of the general populace and are not within the field of common knowledge. (Ohio Revised Code § 2901.06(A), 2008)

The statute further provides that:

> If a person is charged with an offense involving the use of force against another and the person, as a defense to the offense charged, raises the affirmative defense of self-defense, the person may introduce expert testimony of the "battered woman syndrome" and expert testimony that the person suffered from that syndrome as evidence to establish the requisite belief of an imminent threat of death or great bodily harm that is necessary, as an element of the affirmative defense, to justify the person's use of the force in question. (Ohio Revised Code § 2901.06(B), 2008)

Although the authors of a report released by the United States Department of Justice et al. (1996) rejected the use of BWS testimony, they affirmed the need for expert testimony to assist judges and juries (Dutton, 1996).

BWS Evidence and Prosecuting the Batterer

Although the introduction of BWS testimony has been used primarily in situations that involve claims of self-defense by women alleged to have killed their batterers, there has been an increasing reliance on the theory by prosecutors who seek conviction of the batterer. As an example, in one Washington case, the prosecution sought the conviction of a man who had been charged with four counts of rape during a 23-month long relationship with a woman (*State v. Ciskie*, 1988). The defense claimed that the sex had been consensual, pointing to the alleged victim's failure to report the incidents immediately after their occurrence or to terminate the relationship. The prosecution countered this argument with expert testimony indicating that "the failure of the woman in the hypothetical to report the sexual assaults until two days after the last incident and nine months after the first was characteristic of a person suffering from battered woman syndrome" (*State v. Ciskie*, 1988, p. 1173).

Case Study 2: Biological Terrorism, Law Enforcement, and the Epidemiologist

DEFINING BIOTERRORISM

Acts of terrorism are designed to induce fear and panic in civilian populations through the use of means that will bring about illness and/or death. Terrorism may be effectuated using any of a multitude of mechanisms, such as the use of conventional weaponry, chemical weapons, nuclear or radiological weapons, and/or the manipulation and exploitation of computer systems and through a variety of potential avenues, such as the contamination of food and/or water supplies and/or aerosolization (Shermer, 2005). US law defines bioterrorism as an act of terror that utilizes biological agents, which may be bacterial, viral, and/or fungal in nature, to cause illness and/or death in a civilian population for the express or implied purpose of causing fear or panic in the country's citizens (28 U.S.C. § 1605(a)(7), 2001).

Biological weapons, which consist of living organisms that can potentially infect victims and bring about their illness, incapacitation, and death (Guesnier, 2001), are considered to be potentially one of the most dangerous weapons in the world (Remarks, 2002). The threat of bioterrorism has been called a "plague more monstrous than anything we have experienced" (Bacevich, 2000, p. 221, quoting Secretary of Defense William S. Cohen) that, because of its insidious nature and potentially widespread and devastating consequences, can induce "nightmares of primal fear" (Kellman, 2001, p. 419).

One of the easiest ways to distribute pathogens is through their introduction into food and water supplies. The World Health Organization (2002) refers to the use of food to effectuate terrorism as "food terrorism" and defines it as "an act or threat of deliberate contamination of food for human consumption with chemical, biological or radionuclear agents for the purpose of causing injury or death to civilian populations and/or disrupting social, economic or political stability." Other scholars have referred to this form of terrorism as "agroterrorism" (Stirrup, 2007), meaning "the deliberate introduction of a disease agent, either against livestock or into the food chain, for purposes of undermining stability and/or generating fear" (Chalk, 2001). Consider the following situations throughout history in which food and/or water were deliberately contaminated to effectuate the goals of warfare and/or terrorism:

- During the sixth century BC, the Assyrians used rye ergot to poison the wells of their enemies (Kornfield, 2003).

▓ In 1346, the Tartar army threw plague-ridden dead bodies over the walls of Kaffa, leading to the contamination of bogs and waters supplies, which ultimately forced the defenders of the city to surrender (Kornfield, 2003).

▓ During the 1960s, during the course of the Vietnam War, the Vietcong used fecally contaminated water to sicken American servicemen (Kornfield, 2003).

▓ In 1972 in Chicago, members of the group known as The Order of the Rising Sun planned to poison the water supply in Chicago, St. Louis, and other Midwestern cities by introducing typhoid cultures into the cities' water supplies, but they were arrested prior to carrying out their plans (Arizona Department of Health Services, 2005).

▓ In 1978, the Arab Army Palestinian Commandos used mercury to contaminate citrus products from Israel that were destined for European markets, resulting in the discovery of poisoned oranges in Belgium, Germany, Sweden, the Netherlands, and the United Kingdom, and cases of illness in at least three countries (Ban, 2000; Purver, 1995).

▓ In 1984, outside of Antelope, Oregon members of the Rajneesh cult introduced *Salmonella* into open salad bars at numerous restaurants, resulting in the poisoning of 750 people (Garrett, 1998).

▓ In January 2003, more than 90 people in Michigan became ill following their purchase and ingestion of ground beef that had intentionally been contaminated with nicotine by a disgruntled employee of the supermarket (Boulton, et al., 2003; Dyckman, 2003).

The large number of disease outbreaks that are caused by the unintentional contamination of food sources underscore the vulnerability of our food sources and supply chain to their intentional contamination for the purpose of causing widespread illness or death (Bledsoe & Rasco, 2002; Center for Science in the Public Interest, 2004). A total of 3500 outbreaks of foodborne illness, involving 115,700 cases, were reported from 1990 to 2003 (Center for Science in the Public Interest, 2004). This likely represents an undercount of the actual number of outbreaks and cases due to underreporting and misdiagnosis. Several of these outbreaks are of particular note due to their severe and far-reaching health and economic consequences.

▓ The consumption of spinach contaminated by E. coli that originated from a California-based company resulted in the illness of at least 199 people across 26 states and one person in Canada, as well as the deaths of two elderly women in Wisconsin and Nebraska and the death of a young child in Idaho (United

States Food and Drug Administration, 2006; Preston & Davey, 2006; Sander, 2006). The spinach industry suffered an estimated loss of $50 million in less than 1 month as a result of the outbreak (Philips, 2006).

- In 1994, more than 200,000 people in 41 states became ill after they ate Schwann's ice cream that had been contaminated with *Salmonella* (Hennesy, et al., 1996).

- In 2002, 46 people in eight states became ill, seven people died, and three women suffered stillbirths or miscarriages as the result of the contamination of ready-to-eat chicken and turkey products manufactured in Pennsylvania that were found to be contaminated by *Listeria monocytogenes* (Dyckman, 2003).

- In 2003, 605 people became ill and 3 died in Pittsburgh in the largest outbreak of hepatitis A in the United States. The outbreak was ultimately traced to the contamination of scallions that had been imported from Mexico (Boodman, 2003).

- In 2008, the contamination of jalapeño peppers imported from Mexico resulted in illness in 1294 people in 43 states, the District of Columbia, and Canada (United States Food and Drug Administration, 2008). Individuals were found to be infected with the same genetic strain of *Salmonella saintpaul*. The initial erroneous attribution of the epidemic to tomatoes resulted in a loss to tomato growers of more than $100 million (Jones, 2008).

Accordingly, this case study focuses on the introduction of biological contaminants into food and/or water supplies for the purpose of terrorism and the possible roles that the epidemiologist may play in such investigations.

EPIDEMIOLOGY AND BIOTERRORISM

The Bioterrorist

The terrorists themselves must have a more sophisticated understanding of the epidemiology of disease, as compared to the general public, to effectuate their goal. In deciding which biological agent to use and how to disseminate that agent to cause harm, the terrorist must consider the agent's pathogenicity, the degree to which the agent is infectious or contagious, the process through which the contagion will be most effective and protective measures least effective, the level of the agent's lethality, and the potential risk to the terrorist him- or herself as a result of handling the biological agent (Kellman, 2001). For example, the agent of choice will differ in the degree of its pathogenicity and lethality depending on whether the intent of the terrorist is to sicken as many people as possible or to kill as many people as possible.

The introduction of an agent into the air to effectuate the terrorist's goals is, to some degree, dependent on the weather; the potential for weather conditions that are adverse to the dispersion of the introduced substance may provide an incentive to utilize an alternate route by which to effectuate the intended contamination.

The motivation for the bioterrorist acts varies greatly. Some groups may hold an apocalyptic ideology, believing that the world will soon end (Tucker, 2000). Others, such as members of the Rajneesh cult, may use bioterrorism in an attempt to achieve their political goals. Still others may view their activities as defensive in nature, although objectively the actions may appear to be paranoid in nature (Tucker, 2000).

The Foodborne Investigation

The United States Food and Drug Administration bears significant responsibility, together with other federal and state agencies, for the investigation of foodborne disease outbreaks. These agencies are to work collaboratively in "traceback investigations" to identify the source of the outbreak-causing product, its distribution, and the source of contamination (Guzewich & Salsbury, 2001). These investigations consist of epidemiological, laboratory, and environmental components.

The principles of epidemiology and the skills of the epidemiologist are critical in the conduct of such investigations, as well as to law enforcement personnel in assisting them in the detection of an outbreak, the source of the outbreak, and potentially the characterization of that outbreak as accidental or intentional.

Detecting an Outbreak

Recall from Chapter 3, Epidemiology and Criminal Law, how the methods employed in disease surveillance and outbreak investigation could be utilized in investigations of "epidemics" of death. We noted that epidemiologic investigation of an apparent outbreak requires a determination as to whether the number of persons who died during a defined period of time is in excess of what would be expected. Existing mechanisms for disease surveillance and reporting may prove to be critical in facilitating a determination as to whether cases of illness resulting from specified biological agents are in excess of what would be expected. This is because the systematic reporting of disease incidence helps to establish a baseline or background rate of disease against which "spikes" can be detected.

The Centers for Disease Control and Prevention (2001) has compiled a list of 24 biological agents that are deemed to be critical because of the harm to the public health that could result from their use in terrorist acts. Factors that were considered in the development of this list include the morbidity and mortality that could result from the particular agent; the potential for population-wide distribution of the agent based in view of its stability, the ease with which it could be mass produced and distributed, and the ease with which it could be transmitted from person to person; the potential for instilling fear in the public and causing civil disruption; and the existence of any special public health preparedness needs, in view of diagnostic needs, surveillance requirements, and other factors.

Each of the 24 agents and/or their resulting diseases were categorized as Category A, B, or C diseases based upon their potential to create harm, with Category A including the seven most harmful classes of agents: anthrax, arenaviruses such as Lassa fever and Argentine hemorrhagic fever, botulism, *Filoviruses* such as Ebola and Marburg hemorrhagic fevers, plague, smallpox, and tularemia. Category B includes many of the agents that have been used in the past in deliberate terrorist acts, or that have been implicated in unintentional epidemics, such as *Salmonella* and *Shigella*.

Disease reporting requirements related to these biological agents fall within the purview of the state, rather than the federal, governments. Consequently, the reporting requirements for each of these 24 agents differ across states. Consider, for example, the variation that exists with respect to *Salmonella*, which has been widely implicated as the contaminant in numerous intentionally caused and unintentionally occurring epidemics. The Centers for Disease Control and Prevention (2001) found that only 15 states (28%) require the reporting of *Salmonella* infection within 24 hours. An additional 39 jurisdictions, or 72% of states, require reporting of the infection within a time frame ranging from 48 hours to 7 days or within an unspecified time frame (Centers for Disease Control and Prevention, 2001). The wide variation between states' reporting requirements increases the difficulty of quickly detecting illness resulting from the intentional introduction of a biological agent into the food chain. Reporting may be further hampered as the result of the administrative burden associated with reporting and the existence of minimal or no penalties for noncompliance with the reporting requirements (Horton, Misrahi, Matthews, & Kocher, 2002).

Discovering the Source of the Outbreak

The outbreak investigation will also focus on the characterization of the cases, for example, by demographic features and exposures; the development of various hypotheses that might explain the apparent outbreak; and the testing of these hypotheses to determine which should be accepted or rejected in the face of newly available data from the progressing investigation (Roht, Selwyn, Holguin, & Christensen, 1982).

The development of an epidemic curve would help in such instances to identify periods of time, whether days or blocks of hours in days, during which the cases of illness were likely to occur and to focus attention on the circumstances that prevailed during such time periods. (For a review of how to construct an epidemic curve, readers are referred to Roht, et al., 1982.) The first person who becomes ill during the defined time period would constitute the primary case, while the first case of illness brought to the attention of the epidemiologist would be the index case. The primary and index cases of illness may or may not be one and the same. Individuals who became ill during the defined period of time and whose illnesses were suspected to be associated with the potential pathogen would be considered suspect cases.

The epidemiological investigation will verify the diagnosis through interviews and appropriate laboratory tests, provide a case definition, and, through the use of epidemiological study methods, determine whether an association exists between the illness and one or more ingested foods. The findings from the investigation essentially serve as a road map for further inquiry by law enforcement personnel, should that be deemed necessary.

Characterizing the Outbreak

In some situations, it may be difficult to ascertain whether a sudden and/or prolonged increase in the numbers of cases of a particular disease or the presence of a particular disease agent results from natural causes or a deliberate act. Consider, for example, a scenario in which the water source for a large metropolitan area has been contaminated with *Campylobacter*. The contamination has resulted in widespread illness, characterized by bloody stools and vomiting and numerous deaths. However, *Campylobacter* occurs naturally within the environment, and many cases are reported annually. Epidemiological methods may be critical to determine whether there actually exists an increase in the concentration of the bacteria, an increase in the numbers of persons becoming ill, and an increase in the number of deaths. If it is determined that there is, in fact, an increase in the concentration of bacteria, epidemiologists and other scientists may be able to determine whether it is the same strain that would naturally occur in the region that is the original source of the outbreak; these findings, in turn, would suggest whether the increase may have naturally occurred or whether the supply was deliberately contaminated (Williamson, 2002).

DESIGNING THE SURVEILLANCE SYSTEM FOR THE DETECTION OF FOOD TERRORISM-RELATED DISEASE

The development of an effective surveillance system for the early detection of food terrorism will require input from epidemiologists to both governmental and nongovernmental organizations. The need for such expertise has been widely recognized. For example, researchers who conducted a systematic review of surveillance systems for the early detection of bioterrorism-related diseases found that relatively few such systems provide for the collection of foodborne disease data (Bravata, et al., 2004). In discussing the need for timeliness, specificity, and sensitivity of a surveillance system, the authors noted:

> Most surveillance systems routinely analyze the data by calculating rates of cases over time. Few included reports described the methods for calculating the expected rate of disease or for setting thresholds to determine when the observed rate differs significantly from expected. Several authors described methods for stochastically modeling the spread of communicable disease . . . The use of these methods may allow for more accurate determination of the expected rates of disease and deviations from expected. (Bravata, et al., 2004, p. 917)

Safe Food International, an international coalition of consumer organizations formed by the Center for Science in the Public Interest, the World Health Organization, and the United Nations' Food and Agriculture Organization, developed in June 2005 *The Guidelines for Consumer Organizations to Promote National Food Safety Systems* (DeWaal, 2007). The guidelines included as critical elements in the development of an effective food safety program both the establishment of foodborne disease surveillance systems and the provision of appropriate information, education, communication, and training. (Training to assist professionals to recognize the need for cross-disciplinary consultation is discussed in Chapter 9, Looking Toward the Future.)

FOOD TERRORISM AND QUARANTINE

Depending upon the degree of infectiousness and lethality of the illness caused by an act of food terrorism and, accordingly, its potential impact on the public health, it is conceivable that the relevant public health authority would pursue quarantine and/or isolation measures to protect the public health from further risk. In fact, the Model State Emergency Health Powers Act, drafted by the Centers for Disease Control and Prevention in collaboration with the Center for Law and the Public's Health of Georgetown and Johns Hopkins Universities, specifically authorizes the quarantine or isolation of affected individuals in addition to the collection and reporting of private health information, the care of those who are ill, and the appropriation of necessary supplies (O'Leary, 2006). Despite widespread criticism that the powers granted to the government by the act are overly broad (Annas, 2003; Chen, 2005; O'Leary, 2006) in the attempt to provide "state and local officials with the ability to prevent, detect, manage and contain emergency health threats without unduly interfering with civil rights and liberties" (Model State Emergency Health Powers Act, 2001,

p. 6), as of 2003, 37 states had enacted bills or resolutions adopting the act or similar provisions (Gostin, 2003).

It is likely that epidemiologists may play an important role in working with government officials to assess the extent of the threat to the public health and the need for a quarantine or isolation order in response to the threat (cf. Barbera, et al., 2001). The epidemiologist's role in the context of quarantine and isolation orders is discussed more fully in Chapter 5, Law, Epidemiology, and Communicable Disease. An examination of the balance between individual rights and liberties and the need to protect the public health in such circumstances is examined in Chapter 9, Looking Toward the Future.

Exercise

As an expert in epidemiology, you have been asked to comment on the adequacy of your state's provisions relating to quarantine and isolation measures in the event of a bioterrorist threat resulting from the intentional dissemination of anthrax into the population. Prepare a commentary, making sure to address the extent to which the existing provisions:

- Provide guidance to law enforcement and public health authorities in determining whether a large-scale quarantine is necessary and feasible
- Provide guidance in determining who should be quarantined and the duration of the quarantine
- The availability of resources to enforce the quarantine
- The availability of resources to provide necessary food, medical care, and other necessary support to those individuals who have been quarantined
- The potential benefits to be derived from the imposition of a quarantine in such circumstances
- The potential adverse consequences that could result from such a quarantine

In view of your responses to the foregoing, should a large-scale quarantine be considered if a bioterrorist threat from anthrax were present? What, if any, alternatives should be considered and why?

References

1. Andersen, E. P., & Read-Andersen, A. (1992). Constitutional dimensions of the battered woman syndrome. *Ohio State Law Journal, 53,* 363–411.
2. Annas, G. J. (2003). Blinded by bioterrorism: Public health and liberty in the 21st century. *Health Matrix, 13,* 33–70.

3. Arizona Department of Health Services. (2005). History of biowarfare and bioterrorism. Retrieved November 12, 2008 from http://www.azdhs.gov/phs/edc/edrp/es/bthistor2.htm.

4. Attala, J. M., Bauza, K., Pratt, H., & Viera, D. (1995). Integrative review of effects on children of witnessing domestic violence. *Issues in Comprehensive Pediatric Nursing, 18*, 163–175.

5. Bacevich, A. J. (2000). Bad medicine for biological terror. *Orbis, 44*, 221–236.

6. Baker, K. K. (2005). Gender and emotion in criminal law. *Harvard Journal of Law & Gender, 28*, 447–466.

7. Balakrishnan, C., Imell, L. L., Bandy, A. T., & Prasad, J. K. (1995). Perineal burns in males secondary to spouse abuse. *Burns, 21*, 34–35.

8. Ban, J. (2000). Agricultural biological warfare: An overview. *The Chemical & Biological Arms Control Institute, 9*, 1–8.

9. Barbera, J., Macintyre, A., Gostin, L., Inglesby, T., O'Toole, T., DeAtley, C., et al. (2001). Large-scale quarantine following biological terrorism in the United States: Scientific examination, logistic and legal limits, and possible consequences. *Journal of the American Medical Association, 286*, 2711–2717.

10. Bates, L., Redman, S., Brown, W., & Hancock, L. (1995). Domestic violence experienced by women attending an accident and emergency department. *Australian Journal of Public Health, 19*, 292–299.

11. Beck, S. R., Freitag, S. K., & Singer, N. (1996). Ocular injuries in battered women. *Ophthalmology, 103*, 148–151.

12. Blesdoe, G. E., & Rasco, B. A. (2002). Addressing the risk of bioterrorism in food production. *Food Technology, 56*(2), 43–47.

13. Boodman, S. (2003, November 25). Raw menace: Major hepatitis A outbreak tied to green onions. *The Washington Post*, p. F01.

14. Boulton, M., Stanbury, M., Wade, D., Tilden, J., Bryan, D., Payne, J., et al. (2003, May 9). Nicotine poisoning after ingestion of contaminated ground beef—Michigan, 2003. *Morbidity & Mortality Weekly Report, 52*(18), 413–416.

15. Bravata, D. M., McDonals, K. M., Smith, W. M., Rydzak, C., Szeto, H., Buckeridge, D. L., et al. (2004). Systematic review: Surveillance systems for early detection of bioterrorism-related diseases. *Annals of Internal Medicine, 140*, 910–922.

16. Brown, J. K. (1992). Introduction: Definitions, assumptions, themes, and issues. In D. A. Counts, J. K. Brown, & J. C. Campbell (Eds.), *Sanctions and sanctuary: Cultural perspectives on the beating of wives* (pp. 1–18). Boulder, CO: Westview Press.

17. Browne, A. (1987). *When battered women kill*. New York: Free Press.

18. Browne, A., & Williams, K. R. (1993). Gender, intimacy, and lethal violence: Trends from 1976 through 1987. *Gender & Society, 7*, 78–98.

19. Bullock, L. F., & McFarlane, J. (1989). The birthweight/battering connection. *American Journal of Nursing, 89*, 1153–1155.

20. Campbell, J. C., Torres, S., Ryan, J., King, C., Campbell, D. W., Stallings, R. Y., et al. (1999). Physical and nonphysical partner abuse and other risk factors for low birthweight among full term and preterm babies: A multiethnic case-control study. *American Journal of Epidemiology, 150*, 714–726.

21. Catalano, S. (2007). *Intimate partner violence in the United States*. Washington, DC: Bureau of Justice Statistics, Office of Justice Programs, United States Department of Justice.

22. Center for Science in the Public Interest. (2004). *Outbreak alert! Closing the gaps in our federal food-safety net*. Washington, DC: Author. Retrieved July 29, 2008, from http://cspinet.org/new/pdf/outbreakalert2004.pdf.

23. Centers for Disease Control and Prevention. (2001). *The public health response to biological and chemical terrorism: Interim planning guidance for state public health officials.* Retrieved July 19, 2008, from http://www.bt.cdc.gov/Documents/Planning/PlanningGuidance.pdf.

24. Chalk, P. (2001). Testimony. *Terrorism, infrastructure protection, and the U.S. food and agriculture sector: Hearing before the Senate Subcommittee on Oversight of Government Management, Restructuring, and the District of Columbia,* 107th Cong., 1st Sess.

25. Chang, J., Berg, C., Saltzman, L., & Herndon, J. (2005). Homicide: A leading cause of injury deaths among pregnant and postpartum women in the United States, 1991–1999. *American Journal of Public Health, 96*(3), 471–477.

26. Chen, K. C. (2005). Pennsylvania's bioterrorism act: Better prevention from better preparation. *Temple Political & Civil Rights Law Review, 15,* 165–198.

27. Coker, A. L., Sanderson, M., Fadden, M. K., & Pirisi, L. (2000). Intimate partner violence and cervical neoplasia. *Journal of Women's Health & Gender-Based Medicine, 9*(9), 1015–1023.

28. Crandall, M., Nathens, A. B., Kernic, M. A., Hold, V. L., & Rivara, F. P. (2004). Predicting future injury among women in abusive relationships. *Journal of Trauma-Injury Infection and Critical Care, 56*(4), 902–912.

29. Cunradi, C. B. (2007). Drinking level, neighborhood social disorder, and mutual intimate partner violence. *Alcoholism: Clinical and Experimental Research, 31*(6), 1012–1019.

30. Daubert v. Merrell-Dow Pharmaceuticals, Inc., 509 U.S. 579 (1993).

31. Denzin, N. K. (1984). Toward a phenomenology of domestic, family violence. *American Journal of Sociology, 90,* 483–513.

32. DeWaal, C. S. (2007). Food protection & defense: Preparing for a crisis. *Minnesota Journal of Law, Science, & Technology, 8,* 187–198.

33. Dressler, J. (2006). *Understanding criminal law* (4th ed.). Albany, NY: Matthew Bender.

34. Dutton, M. A. (1996). Impact of evidence concerning battering and its effects in criminal trials involving battered women. In *The validity and use of evidence concerning battering and its effects in criminal trials (section 1).* Washington, DC: United States Department of Justice, National Institute of Justice, United States Department of Health and Human Services, & National Institute of Mental Health. Retrieved March 28, 2008, from http://www.ncjrs.org/pdffiles/batter.pdf.

35. Dyckman, L. J. (2003). *Bioterrorism: A threat to agriculture and the food supply: Testimony before the Committee on Governmental Affairs, U.S. Senate.* Washington, DC: General Accounting Office. Retrieved July 31, 2008, from http://www.gao.gov/new.items/do4259t.pdf.

36. Faigman, D. L. (1986). The battered woman syndrome and self-defense: A legal and empirical dissent. *Virginia Law Review, 72*(3), 619–647.

37. Federal Bureau of Investigation, United States Department of Justice. (2003). *Crime in the United States: Violence among family members and intimate partners.* Retrieved March 24, 2008, from http://www.fbi.gov/ucr/cius_03/pdf/03sec5.pdf.

38. Federal Rules of Evidence 401, 403, 702 (2006).

39. Fernandez, L. K. (2007). Eighth annual review of gender and sexuality law: Battered woman syndrome. *Georgetown Journal of Gender & Law, 8,* 235–249.

40. Ferraro, K. J. (2003). The words change but the melody lingers: The persistence of the battered woman syndrome in criminal cases involving battered women. *Violence Against Women, 9*(1), 110–129.

41. Ferraro, K. J. (2006). *Neither angels nor demons.* Lebanon, NH: University Press of New England.

42. Fildes, J., Reed, L., Jones, N., Martin, M., & Barrett, J. (1992). Trauma: The leading cause of maternal death. *Journal of Trauma, 32,* 643–645.

43. Fox, J. A., & Zawitz, M. W. (2005). *Homicide trends in the United States.* Washington, DC: United States Department of Justice.

44. Gagne, P. (1998). *Battered women's justice: The movement for clemency and the politics of self-defense.* New York: Twayne.

45. Garrett, L. (1998, April 6). Weapons in the hands of a cult/group plotted attack to influence election. *Newsday,* p. A24.

46. Giles-Sims, J. (1998). The aftermath of partner violence. In J. L. Jasinski & L. M. Williams (Eds.), *Partner violence: A comprehensive review of 20 years of research* (pp. 44–72). Thousand Oaks, CA: Sage Publications.

47. Gostin, L. O. (2003). The Model State Emergency Health Powers Act: Public health and civil liberties in a time of terrorism. *Health Matrix, 13,* 3–32.

48. Guesnier, F. M. (2001). World Trade Center attacks: Fears of biological warfare stand in the wake. *Colorado Journal of International Environmental Law & Policy, 2001,* 181–190.

49. Guzewich, J. J., & Salsbury, P. A. (2001). FDA's role in traceback investigations for produce. *Food Safety Magazine.* Retrieved July 31, 2008, from http://www.cfsan.fda.gov/~acrobat/prodtra2.pdf.

50. Hartzell, K. N., Botek, A. A., & Goldberg, S. H. (1996). Orbital fractures in women due to sexual assault and domestic violence. *Ophthalmology, 103,* 953–957.

51. Hathaway, J. E., Mucci, L. A., Silverman, J. G., Brooks, D. R., Mathews, R., & Pavlos, C. A. (2000). Health status and health care use of Massachusetts women reporting partner abuse. *American Journal of Preventive Medicine, 19*(4), 302–307.

52. Hennesy, T. W., Hedberg, C. W., Slutsker, L., White K. E., Besser-Wiek, J. M., Moen, M. E., et al. (1996). A national outbreak of *Salmonella enteritidis* infections from ice cream. *New England Journal of Medicine, 334,* 1281–1286.

53. Herman, J. L. (1997). *Trauma and recovery: The aftermath of violence: From domestic abuse to political terror.* New York: Basic Books.

54. Holden, G. W., & Ritchie, K. L. (1991). Linking extreme marital discord, child rearing, and child behavior problems: Evidence from battered women. *Child Development, 62,* 311–327.

55. Horton, H. H., Misrahi, J. J., Matthews, G. W., & Kocher, P. L. (2002). Critical biological agents: Disease reporting as a tool for determining bioterrorism preparedness. *Journal of Law, Medicine, & Ethics, 30,* 262–266.

56. Hughes, H. M. (1986). Research with children in shelters: Implications for clinical services. *Children Today, 15,* 21–25.

57. Hughes, H. M. (1988). Psychological and behavioral correlates of family violence in child witnesses and victims. *American Journal of Orthopsychiatry, 58,* 77–90.

58. Humphreys, J. (1993). Children of battered women. In J. C. Campbell & J. Humphreys (Eds.), *Nursing care of survivors of family violence.* St. Louis, MO: Mosby.

59. Joice, V. J. (2006). A restraining order and a handgun: North Carolina's attempt to "empower" victims of domestic violence. *Howard Law Journal, 50,* 289–317.

60. Jones, A. (1996). *Women who kill: A social history of women murderers in the U.S.A. from colonial times to the present.* Boston: Beacon Press.

61. Jones, C. (2008, July 19). FDA OK's eating tomatoes; jalapenos suspected. *The Kaleidoscope.* Retrieved July 29, 2008, from http://www.uabkaleidoscope.com/kaleidoscope-article-698.html.

62. Kellman, B. (2001). Biological terrorism: Legal measures for preventing catastrophe. *Harvard Journal of Law and Public Policy, 24,* 417–488.

63. Klaus, P. (2007). *National Crime Victimization Survey: Crime and the nation's households,* 2005. Washington, DC: Bureau of Justice Statistics, United States Department of Justice.

64. Koons, J. E. (2006). Gunsmoke and legal mirrors: Women surviving intimate battery and deadly legal doctrines. *Journal of Law and Policy,* 14, 617–693.

65. Kornblit, A. L. (1994). Domestic violence—An emerging health issue. *Social Science and Medicine,* 39, 1181–1188.

66. Kornfield, I. E. (2003). Combating terrorism in the environmental trenches: Responding to terrorism: Terror in the water: Threats to drinking water and infrastructure. *Widener Law Symposium Journal,* 9, 439–483.

67. Krause, J. H. (2007). Distorted reflections of battered women who kill: A response to Professor Dressler. *Ohio State Journal of Criminal Law,* 4, 555–572.

68. LaFave, W., & Scott, A. (1986). *Handbook on criminal law* (2nd ed.). Rochester, NY: West.

69. Lemon, S. C., Verhoek-Ofredahl, W., & Donnelly, E. F. (2002). Preventive healthcare use, smoking, and alcohol use among Rhode Island women experiencing intimate partner violence. *Journal of Women's Health & Gender-Based Medicine,* 11(6), 555–562.

70. Letourneau, E. J., Holmes, M., & Chasedunn-Roark, J. (1999). Gynecologic health consequences to victims of interpersonal violence. *Women's Health Issues,* 9(2), 115–120.

71. Maguigan, H. (1991). Battered women and self-defense: Myths and misconceptions in current reform proposals. *University of Pennsylvania Law Review,* 140, 379–486.

72. Max, W., Rice, D. P., Finkelstein, E., Bardwell, R. A., & Leadbetter, S. (2004). The economic toll of intimate partner violence against women in the United States. *Violence and Victims,* 19(3), 259–272.

73. McNutt, L. A., Carlson, B. E., Persaud, M., & Postmus, J. (2002). Cumulative abuse experiences, physical health, and health behaviors. *Annals of Epidemiology,* 12(2), 123–130.

74. Model State Emergency Health Powers Act. (2001). Retrieved July 31, 2008, from http://www.publichealthlaw.net/MSEHPA/MSEHPA2.pdf.

75. Moracco, K. E., Runyan, C. W., & Butts, J. D. (2003). Female intimate partner homicide: A population-based study. *Journal of the American Medical Women's Association,* 58, 20–25.

76. National Center for Injury Prevention and Control. (2003). *Costs of intimate partner violence against women in the United States.* Atlanta, GA: Centers for Disease Control and Prevention.

77. Ohio Revised Code §§ 2901.06, 2929.25 (2008).

78. O'Leary, N. P. M. (2006). Bioterrorism or avian influenza: California, the Model State Emergency Health Powers Act, and protecting civil liberties during a public health emergency. *California Western Law Review,* 42, 249–286.

79. Olson, L., Huylar, F., Lynch, A. W., Fullerton, L., Werenko, D., Sklar, D. et al. (1999). Guns, alcohol, and intimate partner violence: The epidemiology of female suicide in New Mexico. *Crisis,* 20, 121–126.

80. Parker, B., McFarlane, J., & Soeken, K. (1994). Abuse during pregnancy: Effects of maternal complications and birthweight in adult and teenage women. *Obstetrics & Gynecology,* 84, 323–328.

81. Paulozzi, L. J., Saltzman, L. E., Thompson, M. P., & Holmgreen, P. (2001). Surveillance for homicide among intimate partners—United States, 1981–1998. *Morbidity & Mortality Weekly Report,* 50, 1–16.

82. People v. Dillard, 53 Cal. Rptr. 2d 456 (Cal. Ct. App. 1996).

83. People v. Jaspar, 119 Cal. Rptr. 2d 470 (2002).

84. Philips, M. (2006, October 2). They're seeing red over greens. *Newsweek*, p. 43.

85. Preston, J., & Davey, M. (2006, September 16). Possible source of bad spinach is named as outbreak widens. *The New York Times*, p. A1.

86. Purver, R. (1995). *Chemical and biological terrorism: The threat according to the open literature.* Retrieved July 31, 2008, from http://www.csis-scrs.gc.ca/pblctns/thr/cbtrrrsm01-eng.asp.

87. Remarks at the signing of the Public Health Security and Bioterrorism Preparedness and Response Act of 2002. (2002, June 17). Weekly Comp. Pres. Doc. 38, 998.

88. Rennison, C. M. (2003). *Intimate partner violence, 1993–2001.* Washington, DC: United States Department of Justice. Retrieved November 12, 2008 from http://www.ojp.usdoj.gov/bjs/pub/pdf/ipv01.pdf.

89. Rodriguez, M. A., Heilmann, M. S. V., Fielder, E., Ang, A., Nevarez, F., & Mangione, C. M. (2008). Intimate partner violence, depression, and PTSD among pregnant Latina women. *Annals of Family Medicine, 6*(1), 44–52.

90. Roht, L. H., Selwyn, B. J., Holguin, A. H., & Christensen, B. L. (1982). *Principles of epidemiology: A self-teaching guide.* New York: Academic Press.

91. Sander, L. (2006, September 28). Company acts to stem E. coli risk. *The New York Times*, p. A21.

92. Sanford, C., Marshall, S. W., Martin, S. L., Coyne-Beasley, T., Waller, A. E., Cook, P. J., et al. (2006). Deaths from violence in North Carolina, 2004: How deaths differ in females and males. *Injury Prevention, 12,* ii10–ii16.

93. Schneider, E. M. (2000). *Battered women and feminist lawmaking.* New Haven, CT: Yale University Press.

94. Seligman, M., Maier, S. F., & Geer, J. (1968). Alleviation of learned helplessness in the dog. *Journal of Abnormal Psychology, 73,* 256–262.

95. Shermer, S. D. (2005). The Drinking Water Security and Safety Amendments of 2002: Is America's drinking water infrastructure safer four years later? *UCLA Journal of Environmental Law & Policy, 24,* 355–457.

96. *State v. Ciskie,* 751 P.2d 1165 (Wash. 1988).

97. *State v. Koss,* 551 N.E.2d 970 (Ohio 1990).

98. Steele, W. W., Jr., & Sigman, C. W. (1991). Reexamining the doctrine of self-defense to accommodate battered women. *American Journal of Criminal Law, 18,* 169–185.

99. Stirrup, A. (2007). Comment, hidden cargo: A cautionary tale about agroterrorism and the safety of imported produce. *San Joaquin Agricultural Law Review, 16,* 171–189.

100. Tucker, J. B. (2000). Historical trends related to bioterrorism: An empirical analysis. *Emerging Infectious Diseases, 5*(4), 1–7. Retrieved July 29, 2008, from http://origin.cdc.gov/ncidod/EID/vol5no4/tucker.htm.

101. United States Department of Justice, National Institute of Justice, United States Department of Health and Human Services, & National Institute of Mental Health. (1996). *The validity and use of evidence concerning battering and its effects in criminal trials: Report responding to section 40507 of the Violence Against Women Act.* Washington, DC: Authors.

102. United States Food and Drug Administration. (2006). *FDA news: FDA statement on foodborne E. coli O157:H7 outbreak in spinach.* Retrieved July 31, 2008, from http://www.fda.gov/bbs/topics/NEWS/2006/NEW01486.html.

103. United States Food and Drug Administration. (2008). *Salmonella saintpaul outbreak.* Retrieved July 29, 2008, from http://www.fda.gov/oc/opacom/hottopics/tomatoes.html.

104. Walker, L. E. (1979). *The battered woman.* New York: Harper and Row.

105. Walker, L. E. (1989). *Terrifying love: Why battered women kill and how society responds.* New York: Harper & Row.

106. Weiand v. State, 732 So. 2d 1044 (Fla. 1999).

107. Williamson, K. M. (2002). Comment, Proving causation in acts of bioterrorism. *Cumberland Law Review, 33,* 709–726.

108. Wingood, G. M., & DiClemente, R. J. (1997).The effects of an abusive primary sexual partner on the condom use and sexual negotiation practices of African-American women. *American Journal of Public Health, 87,* 1016–1018.

109. World Health Organization. (2002). *Food safety issues: Terrorist threats to food guidance for establishing and strengthening prevention and response systems.* Retrieved November 12, 2008 from http://www/who.int/foodsafety/publications/general/en/terrorist.pdf.

110. Yepsen, D. (2004, May 16). Op-Ed, Let Shanahan case run course. *Des Moines Register,* p. 3 OP.

111. 28 U.S.C. § 1605(a)(7)(2001).

Chapter 8

Environmental Concerns

Epidemiology has become increasingly important in informing legislative and regulatory efforts to control environmental exposures that are believed to be injurious to public health. Epidemiologists may be called upon to provide relevant testimony to legislative and/or administrative bodies that are responsible for determining the parameters of permissible exposure and the penalties to be imposed for violation of the limitations imposed.

Case Study 1: Regulating Environmental Tobacco Smoke

THE EFFECTS OF SECONDHAND SMOKE

Cigarette smoking has been referred to as "the single leading preventable cause of death in the United States" (United States Department of Health and Human Services, 2000), resulting on an annual basis in more deaths than the combined total of deaths due to AIDS, alcohol, cocaine, heroin, homicide, suicide, motor vehicle accidents, and fires (Institute of Medicine, 2001). Tobacco has been linked to deaths due to cardiovascular disease, cancer, and respiratory disease (Centers for Disease Control and Prevention, 1993) and has been found to be responsible for a reduction in life expectancy among smokers in comparison with nonsmokers (Lew & Garfinkel, 1987).

Secondary smoke, also known by the term "passive smoking," has been found to result in significant adverse health effects to the tobacco nonuser. These include the development of lung cancer, chronic obstructive pulmonary disease, adverse birth outcomes, and childhood difficulties, as well as the exacerbation of existing conditions, such as asthma symptoms.

Researchers who conducted a review of nine studies related to lung cancer mortality concluded that on an annual basis, secondhand smoke results in anywhere from 2600 to 7400 deaths due to lung cancer within the United States (Repace & Lowrey, 1990). Nonsmoking women who live with smoker–husbands have been found to have an increased risk of developing lung cancer, as compared with women whose husbands did not smoke (Fontham, et al., 1991; Lee & Forey, 1998). An elevated risk of lung cancer among nonsmokers has also been found to be associated with high levels of exposure to tobacco smoke during childhood (Stockwell, et al., 1992).

The association between environmental tobacco smoke (ETS) and the occurrence of chronic obstructive pulmonary disease appears to be less well established. A population-based survey of adults conducted by Whittemore and colleagues (1995) concluded that somewhere between 4% and 6% of nonsmokers may be affected by ETS, based on self-reporting of symptoms. Reduced pulmonary function among nonsmokers who are married to smokers and exposed to smoke in the workplace has been reported (Berglund, Abbey, Lebowitz, Knutsen, & McDonnell, 1999; Hole, Gillis, Chopra, & Hawthorne, 1989). However, other studies that relied on a cross-sectional design (Schottenfeld, 1984) or cohort design (Jones, Higgins, Higgins, & Keller, 1983) failed to find such an association.

Research findings indicate that children are affected by exposure to parental smoking. As early as 1986, the National Academy of Sciences concluded from its review of scientific evidence that children of smokers were twice as likely as children of nonsmokers to suffer from respiratory infections, bronchitis, and pneumonia (United States Department of Health and Human Services, 1986).

In utero exposure to tobacco smoke has been found to be associated with various adverse prenatal outcomes, including spontaneous abortion, placenta previa, and placental abruption (Castles, Adams, Melvon, Lelsch, & Boulton, 1999). It is believed that these pregnancy complications may account for as much as one-fifth of all prenatal deaths (Ananth, Savitz, & Luter, 1996). Other adverse outcomes have been noted in connection with in utero exposure to tobacco smoke: preterm delivery (Shah & Bracken, 2000), the delivery of a low birth weight or premature infant, sudden infant death syndrome (American College of Obstetricians and Gynecologists, 1997; Dwyer, Posonby, & Couper, 1999; Lewis & Bosque, 1995; Mitchell, Ford, Stewart, & Taylor, 1993; Schoendorf & Kiely, 1992), later learning and behavior problems (Button, Maughan, & McGuffin, 2007), and respiratory difficulties, including asthma (Floyd, Zahniser, Gunter, & Kendrick, 1991; Kilby, 1997; Richardson, 1999) and decreased lung function in school-age children (Gilliland, et al., 2000).

Exposure to secondary smoke has also been found to be associated with the worsening of already-existing conditions in addition to constituting a risk factor for the development of specified conditions, previously noted. Several studies have noted a dose–effect relationship between cotinine levels and asthma severity in children who are exposed to parental smoke (Chilmonczyk, et al., 1993; Ehrlich, et al., 1996; Rylander, Pershagen, Eriksson, & Bermann, 1995). Conversely, lung function of asthmatic children who are exposed to parental smoking was found to have improved following maternal cessation of smoking (Murray & Morrison, 1989).

It has been argued that it was the recognition of the harm from smoking to third parties, "innocent bystanders," rather than the harm to smokers themselves, that brought about the transformation of cultural perceptions and regulation of smoking in the United States (Anonymous, 1978; Brandt, 2007). This perspective is reflected in the comment by an editor of a prestigious scientific journal:

> The principal effects of smoking are borne by the smokers themselves. They pay for their habit with chronic disease and shortened life. Involved are the individual's decisions and his life. However, when the individual smokes in a poorly ventilated space in the presence of others, he infringes on the rights of others and becomes a serious contributor to air pollution. (Abelson, 1967, p. 1527)

APPROACHES TO HARM REDUCTION FROM ETS AND THE EPIDEMIOLOGIST

A variety of harm reduction measures have been utilized in an attempt to reduce the potential risks to smokers themselves. The concept of harm reduction rests on the idea that any behavior change that reduces the aggregate harmful effects of a particular behavior to the individual and society is beneficial (Institute of Medicine, 2001). Harms encompassed in this calculation are many and varied and include morbidity and mortality of the individual him- or herself, the economic and human costs of enforcement and regulation, crime resulting from the use of the particular substance, and lost wages. The total harm has been expressed by MacCoun and Reuter (2001) as follows:

$$\text{Total harm} = \text{Harmfulness (per use)} \times \text{Intensity (per user)} \times \text{Prevalence (of use)}$$

Harm can be reduced through reliance on any of four approaches: (1) lowering the inherent harmfulness of a particular class of products; (2) changing the mode of ingestion as a means of reducing harm; (3) modifying behavior; or (4) adding a less harmful component to the constellation of available products, which, although less harmful, also creates dependency. The concept of harm reduction has been applied to interventions to reduce alcohol use, such as with controlled drinking; illicit drug use, such as the use of methadone to treat heroin addiction or needle exchange to reduce the potential harm from the sharing of injection equipment; and automobile safety regulation to reduce the harm from motor vehicle accidents. The assessment of the extent to which any harm reduction intervention is effective must consider the mechanism by which the intervention is believed to operate; whether the intervention appears to convey approval of the behavior that it is designed to reduce, resulting in conflicting messages; and the effect of the intervention on the prevalence of the targeted behavior, the intensity of use, and on third parties.

Harm reduction approaches that have been utilized in the context of tobacco use to reduce the potential harm to the smoker have included the production of filtered and light cigarettes, modified tobacco, and nicotine replacement therapy. Some tobacco companies appeared to exploit in their advertising the notion that such product modifications would result in lower risks to the smoker and to others. As an example, a 1999 advertisement for Merit Ultra Lights urged the smoker to "Discover the rewards of thinking light," while Accord advertisements highlighted "a smooth satisfying taste with less smoke around you, virtually no lingering odor, and no ashes" (Institute of Medicine, 2001, p. 65). However, the use of both light and filtered cigarettes and modified tobacco has actually led to an increase in cigarette consumption, an increase in harm to third persons, and in apparently conflicting messages: it is not okay to smoke, but it is okay to smoke light/filtered cigarettes or modified tobacco. Nicotine replacement therapy has been found to bring about a reduction in smoking and a reduction in harm to others (Institute of Medicine, 2001).

These harm reduction measures, when effective, may reduce not only the harm to smokers themselves but also to third parties, such as family members, coworkers, and others who share space with the smoker. One harm reduction measure that more directly impacts the nonsmoker is the establishment and enforcement of smoking regulations aimed at reducing environmental tobacco smoke. Control of smoking in the workplace was suggested as an initial measure to protect nonsmokers by then-Surgeon General Koop:

> The right of the smoker to smoke stops at the point where his or her smoking increases the disease risk in those occupying the same environment. . . . [T]he simplest, least expensive and most effective way to accomplish this protection is to establish a smoke-free work-site. (Milotsky, 1986, quoting then-Surgeon General Koop)

SMOKING REGULATIONS, LAW ENFORCEMENT, AND THE EPIDEMIOLOGIST

Almost every state has implemented legislation prohibiting or limiting smoking to varying degrees in public venues, such as restaurants, stadiums, nightclubs, airports, and places of employment (American Lung Association, 1998). Advocates for ETS regulation have advanced a three-pronged argument to support their position: the threat to the public health and safety, such as the effects on nonsmokers and other third parties; the risk assumed by adolescents who may initiate smoking or progress from experimentation to regular tobacco usage; and the risk assumed by consenting adults (Jacobson & Zapawa, 2001). Opponents of such regulation have argued that it serves to limit individual choice and freedom, is a manifestation of governmental paternalism, and that a policy relating to smoking or nonsmoking in a particular venue should be left to the determination of market forces (Sullum, 1998). (See Chapter 9, Looking Toward the Future, for a discussion of the balance between individual rights, government authority, and protection of the public health.)

Findings from epidemiological studies lend critical support to the need for such regulation and its consistent enforcement. A longitudinal study involving 3834 Massachusetts youths between the ages of 12 and 17 years at baseline found that those who lived in towns characterized by strong smoking regulation, that is, a complete smoking ban for restaurants, were significantly less likely to progress from experimenting with cigarette smoking to established smoking behavior (Siegel, Albers, Cheng, Hamilton, & Biener, 2008). This has implications not only for the health of the youths themselves but for their family members, their future family members, and employees of the restaurants that they patronize.

As an example of such legislation, Ohio's law provides: "No proprietor . . . shall permit smoking in the public place or place of employment or in the areas directly or indirectly under the control of the proprietor immediately adjacent to locations of ingress or egress to the public place or place of employment" (Ohio Administrative Code § 3701-52-02, 2008).

A "proprietor" is defined as "an employer, owner, manager, operator, liquor permit holder, or person in charge or control of a public place or place of employment" (Ohio Administrative Code § 3701-52-01(P), 2008). The statute provides for several exemptions, including private clubs, private residences, and family-owned and operated businesses. Violation of the statutory provision will result in the issuance of a warning letter for the first violation and, for subsequent violations, the imposition of a civil fine, which increases in amount with an increasing number of violations by the same establishment (Ohio Administrative Code § 3701-52-09, 2008).

The proprietor of an establishment may, however, request administrative review of the proposed finding and civil fine to be imposed. At the time of this hearing, which must be held before a board of health, its designee, or an impartial decision maker licensed to practice law in Ohio, the proprietor may present its case and cross-examine any adverse witnesses. Conceivably, the proprietor might argue that the state's imposition of a no-smoking ban on his or her restaurant essentially constitutes an infringement on his privacy interests and those of the patrons and, because of a reduction in business due to the smoking ban, an unconstitutional taking of property. Although this argument would not be relevant to whether a violation occurred, it would be relevant to the ultimate constitutionality, and therefore legality, of the law itself. Epidemiological evidence relating to the association between environmental tobacco smoke and the dangers to the public health could be introduced to support legal counterarguments related to the state's authority and responsibility to protect the public health. Although the administrative body does not have jurisdiction to review or decide constitutional arguments, these must be raised to preserve them for future review in a court that does have such authority.

Case Study 2: Television, Violence, and Aggression

VIOLENCE AND PUBLIC HEALTH

There has been increasing concern voiced in recent years about violence committed by young persons. Evidence suggests that the rate at which young persons are perpetrating violent crimes has increased dramatically (Fox, 1993). As an example, in the United States, the rate of arrests of individuals 18 years of age and older for murder and non-negligent manslaughter increased by 10.5% between 1981 and 1991. Juvenile arrests during the same period of time for these same crimes increased by 92.7%, while arrests for all offenses committed by juveniles increased by 5.6%. Alarmingly, involvement in violent crime appears to be increasing among younger-aged juveniles. Between 1985 and 1991, the arrest rates for criminal homicide increased among 13- and 14-year-old males by 140%; among 15-year-old males by 217%; among 16-year-old males by 158%; and among 17-year-old males by 121% (Ruttenberg, 1994).

The World Health Organization has advocated the adoption of a public health approach to the prevention of violence and the reduction of morbidity and mortality (Krug, Dahlberg, Mercy, Zwi, & Lozano, 2002) in lieu of the more traditional criminal justice approach to dealing with violence (Ruttenberg, 1994). Epidemiology is thought to be a critical component of such an approach (Mercy, Rosenberg, Powell, Broome, & Roper, 1993). One scholar has asserted that "violence, like smallpox and many other infectious diseases, is a problem that can be addressed and perhaps prevented through the application of epidemiological methods" (Rosenberg, 1989, p. 148).

Browne and Hamilton-Giachritsis (2005, pp. 702–703) explained what a public health approach to addressing violence in the media might look like:

> A public-health perspective on media violence might be defined as considering the effects of violent imagery on the child within the broader context of child welfare, families, and communities. Hence, in addition to the habits and behaviour of the child or adolescent viewer, the behaviour of parents in monitoring the use of televisions and computers and knowingly or unknowingly allowing access to violent imagery should be considered. Furthermore, the role of communities and societies in providing standards, guidelines, and education to families also needs assessment. Attention can then be directed to public-health interventions to reduce the extent and effect of violence in the media for the whole population (universal interventions) and high-risk individuals (targeted interventions), respectively.

Others have visualized a public health approach to violence that more specifically relies on epidemiologic methodology, requiring:

> (i) development of surveillance systems for morbidity and mortality associated with interpersonal violence, (ii) identification of those who are at risk for non-fatal events, (iii) the application of case control methods to the exploration of modifiable risk factors for victims and perpetrators, and (iv) rigorous evaluation of trial programs. (Prothrow-Stith & Weissman, 1991, p. 138)

Various strategies have been proposed as potential interventions to reduce the incidence of violent crime and the resulting individual, social, and economic costs of such violence. Foremost among these is the implementation of one or more types of media restrictions. This case study examines the effects, if any, of television depictions of violence on viewers, proposed interventions to reduce exposure and/or the impact of such exposure, and the role of the epidemiologist in the context of related administrative and/or criminal enforcement functions.

TELEVISION VIEWING AND VIOLENCE: IS THERE A LINK?

The Effects of Exposure to Television Violence

Television ownership and, consequently, television viewing, was once a relatively rare occurrence. In 1950, almost 1 decade after the licensing and approval of commercially available television stations by the Federal Communications Commission, only 9% of households in the United States could boast television ownership (Nielsen Media Research, 1998). By 1985, however, approximately 98% of US households had at least one television set.

Not surprisingly, in view of this increase in access to television, children in the United States now spend a large portion of their lives watching television. It has been estimated that the average American child between the ages of 2 and 15 years views more than 27 hours of television each week (Centerwall, 1992). The US National Television Study found that 61% of television programs contained violence, but only 4% of shows had an antiviolence theme (Federman, 1998). Additional research suggests that by the time a child has reached the seventh grade, he or she will have witnessed 8000 murders and more than 10,000 acts of other violence (Huston, et al., 1992). On any given day, a child may witness 138 murders, 333 gunfights, and almost 175 stabbings, not including acts of violence that are televised in news programs or feature films (Schorr, 1993).

Although much of the violence that is witnessed may be set in realistic settings, there are no negative long-term consequences depicted in the vast majority of the programs, the perpetrator is frequently unpunished, there is no criticism of the violence in a large majority of the violent scenes, and much of the violence is associated with humor (Federman, 1998). More than one-half of violent programs have been found to contain lethal violence, often committed by attractive people (Federman, 1998).

There are numerous anecdotal reports of violence perpetrated by youths who attempt to imitate scenes from television programming.

As an example, a 17-year-old boy in France died following his attempt to manufacture a homemade bomb using a technique that had been demonstrated on the television show *MacGyver* (Simons, 1993). In 1993, a 5-year-old boy in Ohio set a fire in imitation of a scene that he had viewed on the MTV cartoon show *Beavis and Butt-Head*; his sister died as a result (Anonymous, 1993). A joint statement of the American Psychological Association, the American Academy of Pediatrics, the American Academy of Child and Adolescent Psychiatry, the American Medical Association, the American Academy of Family Physicians, and the American Psychiatric Association (2000) contended that "the data point overwhelmingly to a causal connection between media violence and aggressive behavior in some children."

Research findings suggest that an association does exist between the viewing of violence on television and later aggressive and/or violent behavior; such findings have been consistent across experimental and observational studies and short-term and long-term studies. These studies have been conducted both in the United States and in other countries (Bachrach, 1986; Centerwall, 1989; Fraczek, 1986; Sheehan, 1986). It is beyond the scope of this chapter to review all such studies, but a brief summary of those undertaken in the United States is presented.

Drabman and Thomas (1974) reported from an early experimental study that was conducted with male and female third and fourth grade students. The child participants were told that they were responsible for watching younger children. The children participating in the study who had viewed an aggressive film delayed seeking adult assistance with their disruptive charges longer than those children who had not witnessed an aggressive film, and they were more likely to tolerate increased levels of aggression prior to seeking help.

Joy and colleagues (1986) compared the aggression levels of children in an isolated Canadian town following the introduction of television in the mid-1970s with two comparable Canadian towns that were already accustomed to television. The children were observed during first and second grade and then again 2 years later. The investigators found that the level of verbal and physical aggression had increased in all three of the towns, but the greatest increase was observed in the children residing in the town in which television had been more recently introduced.

Researchers who conducted a 17-year study of 707 individuals in a community sample reported finding a significant association between the amount of time individuals spent watching television during adolescence and early adulthood and the occurrence of later behaviors such as threats of aggression, robbery, and physical fights resulting in injury (Johnson, Cohen, Smailes, Kasen, & Brook, 2002). The investigators had controlled for a number of other factors that have been found to be associated with the commission of violent acts, including previous aggression, childhood neglect, parental education, family income level, neighborhood violence, and psychiatric illness. A later cohort study conducted by Huesmann and colleagues (2003) with 557 children aged 6 to 9 years that focused specifically on exposure to media violence, in contrast to exposure to television, reported similar findings after controlling for various factors including socioeconomic status, intelligence level, parental viewing behaviors, and parental aggression. Meta-analyses have also found a statistically significant association between exposure to television violence and aggression (Paik & Comstock, 1994; Wood, Wong, & Chachere, 1991).

Despite the large body of research that suggests a link, and possibly a causal link at that, between television exposure to violence and the later commission of violent acts, television executives consistently decry the findings. One common argument suggests that the level of violence depicted in television programming merely reflects the level of violence that exists in our society today. However, it appears that the rate at which violent crime occurs in television dramas far exceeds that in real life. A study that compared the frequency of violent and nonviolent crimes in six reality-based law enforcement television programs with the crime rates reported by the United States Federal Bureau of Investigation (FBI) found large discrepancies between what occurs in real life and what was portrayed on television (Oliver, 1994). Data from the FBI indicated that approximately 0.2% of crimes reported by the FBI were murders, and 87% of the crimes were nonviolent. However, 50% of the crimes depicted in these television shows were murders, and only 13% were nonviolent crimes (Oliver, 1994). One film critic has countered the television industry's claim with the observation that:

> If this were true, then why do so few people witness murders in real life but everyone sees them on TV and in the movies? . . . About 350 characters appear each night on prime-time TV, but studies show an average of seven of these people are murdered every night. If this rate applied in reality, then in just 50 days everyone in the United States would be killed and the last left could turn off the TV. (Medved, 1995, pp. 156–157, quoted in Bushman & Anderson, 2001, p. 479)

Other media executives have argued that the witnessing of violence on television serves as a cathartic release, analogous to the emotional release that was achieved by audiences that viewed the tragic downfall of protagonists in Greek dramas (Bushman & Anderson, 2001).

Bushman and Anderson (2001) have drawn parallels between exposure to television violence and later violent behavior, on the one hand, and exposure to cigarette smoking and cancer, on the other. These similarities include the following:

- Just as not all smokers develop lung cancer, so, too, not all viewers of television violence become violent themselves.
- Just as smoking is neither a sufficient nor a necessary cause of lung cancer, exposure to television violence is neither a necessary nor sufficient cause for the later commission of violent acts.
- Just as repeated exposure to cigarettes may reduce or eliminate initial feelings of nausea and continued exposure may increase craving for cigarettes, so, too, might repeated exposure to violence result in increased desire for violence.
- Just as the short term effects of smoking are relatively innocuous, so, too, are the short term effects of exposure to television violence generally benign.
- Just as the long term effects of smoking can be devastatingly harmful, so, too, can the longer term effects of exposure to television violence prove to be injurious.
- Just as economic motives drove tobacco company executives to repeatedly deny a causal link between cigarette smoking and lung cancer, so, too, are there economic incentives to refute or deny the possibility of an association between television violence and the later commission of violent acts by viewers. (Bushman & Anderson, 2001)

Although a large number of studies have reported finding a causal association between exposure to television violence and later acts of violence by at least some viewers, there have been significant questions raised with respect to these findings, even apart from the objections raised by media representatives. One such concern centers on the varying definitions and outcomes measures that have been utilized across studies. As an example, Browne and Hamilton-Giachritsis (2005), in their review of the relevant literature that addresses exposure to violent media, focused on violence as the outcome of interest, defining it as "the exercise of physical force so as to injure or damage persons or property in such a way that causes bodily injury and/or forcibly interferes with personal freedom" (Browne & Hamilton-Giachritsis, 2005, p. 703). In contrast, Bushman and Anderson examined aggression as the outcome of interest, conceiving of it as "any behavior intended to harm another individual who is motivated to avoid that harm" (Bushman & Anderson, 2001, p. 483).

This discrepancy goes far beyond a matter of semantics because, unlike the usual conceptualization of violence, aggression may assume only a nonverbal form and may, in some instances, constitute an appropriate response to environmental provocation/stimuli. One scholar explained:

> In spite of ethical and legal restrictions on aggression that are so often at the forefront of our thinking, aggression is sometimes normal and sometimes abnormal or pathological. This is determined by the context of the aggression in relation to expected behavior within the species, and so requires judgments by others of the species . . . The significance of context implies that the same behavior can be aggressive in one context but not in another. (Young, Brasic, Sheitman, & Studnick, 1994 p. 17)

The confusion between violence and aggression, however, is understandable because:

> aggression is a form of social behavior studied by ethologists, biologists, and psychologists, whereas violence is more about the interpretation that is given to a form of social behavior, an interpretation that is essentially determined by the social context in which we live. At times both the terms are interchangeable but at other times they are not: an interaction deemed abusive or violent in one culture may be considered "normal" in another. (de Zulueta, 1993, p. ix)

Confusion may also result from a failure to distinguish clearly between the various outcome variables: behavior, thoughts, and emotions (Anderson, Berkowitz, Donnerstein, Huesmann, Johnson, Linz, et al., 2003).

THEORETICAL UNDERPINNINGS

Various theories have been advanced in an attempt to explain the mechanism underlying the apparent association between exposure to television violence and later aggression or violence. Foremost among these are cognitive priming, arousal processes, social-cognitive observational-learning theory, desensitization theory, aggression seeking, and the surrogate variable theory.

Adherents to the idea of cognitive priming maintain that exposure to aggressive ideas and acts on television can activate other aggressive thoughts in the viewers through their association in memory pathways (Berkowitz, 1993). Accordingly, the viewing of aggressive acts will activate memory traces that relate to aggressive schemas and beliefs so that it becomes more likely that the viewer will utilize them (Berkowitz, 1993). Therefore, a television viewer would be primed to react more aggressively after having viewed violence because the violence observed on television would have retrieved a network of memories that involves aggression or violence (Bushman & Green, 1990; Felson, 1996).

Experts believe that this effect is relatively short lived (Huesmann, et al., 2003).

It is also possible that some viewers are aroused by observing violence. Because of the level of arousal, they are unable to restrain aggression (Berkowitz, 1993).

Social-cognitive observational-learning theory posits that children who view aggressive behaviors are more likely to replicate that behavior (Bandura, 1977). Accordingly, even though children appear to engage in aggressive behaviors spontaneously between the ages of 2 and 4 years old (Tremblay, 2000), it is more likely that they will develop more entrenched, automatic, complex, and abstracted scripts of violence in response to their environments if they witness violent behavior during that stage of their development (Huesmann, 1988). Additionally, as the children grow older, their observation of violence in their environments will foster a belief that the actions of others arise from hostility, resulting in an increased likelihood that they will respond to the encounter in an aggressive manner (Comstock & Paik, 1991). Gradually, the children may become unable to distinguish between those behaviors that are socially acceptable and those that are inappropriate.

Desensitization theory essentially holds that individuals who frequently view television violence become less sensitive to violence and its effects and, consequently, are more likely to engage in aggressive behavior or violence (Zillman, 1983). Desensitization can occur emotionally and/or cognitively. Emotional desensitization occurs when an individual's emotional reaction is numb or blunted in response to an occurrence that would typically evoke a strong response (Funk, Baldacci, Pasold, & Baumgardner, 2004). Cognitive desensitization reflects the belief that violence is both mundane and inevitable.

Yet another theory suggests that children who are more aggressive are more likely to seek out aggressive programming than their less aggressive peers (Atkin, Greenberg, Korzenny, & McDermott, 1979). Viewing such violence provides these children with needed justification for their violence because it convinces them that they are not the only ones who have such feelings (Huesmann, 1998). Research also suggests, however, that a bidirectional relationship may be involved, whereby more aggressive children are more likely to seek out depictions of violence that then, in turn, results in an increase in the children's level of aggression from what it was at baseline (Black & Bevan, 1992).

As indicated previously, numerous factors other than exposure to television violence have been found to be associated with later violence and/or aggression. Researchers have suggested that exposure to television violence is actually a stand-in or surrogate variable for another, yet unidentified factor that is associated with both aggressive/violent behavior and exposure to television violence (Huesmann, et al., 2003).

REGULATING TELEVISION VIOLENCE

> Beaten up and strapped to a chair, once again it looks like the end
> for Jack Bauer, the hero of Fox Network's hot show "24." Using
> his wits (and his teeth), Bauer goes for the jugular—literally.
>
> In the scene, Bauer, played by Kiefer Sutherland, chomps on
> the neck of the terrorist holding him captive; he spits the blood
> out and makes his escape. (Associated Press, 2007)

It is unlikely that such violence would have appeared in the first
days of television's existence. At that time, the National Association of
Broadcasters, formerly known as the National Association of Radio
and Television Broadcasters (NARTB), had adopted a code of standards
to govern its practices. Effective March 1, 1952, the NARTB Television
Code included the following provisions specific to the depiction of
violence and aggression:

> (o) The presentation of cruelty, greed and selfishness as worthy
> motivations is to be avoided. . . .

> (q) Criminality shall be presented as undesirable and unsympathetic.
> The condoning of crime and the treatment of the commission of
> crime in a frivolous, cynical, or callous manner is unacceptable.

> (r) The presentation of techniques of crime in such detail as to
> invite invitation shall be avoided.

> (s) The use of horror for its own sake shall be eliminated; the use
> of visual or aural effects which would shock or alarm the viewer,
> and the detailed presentation of brutality or physical agency by
> sight or by sound are not permissible. . . .

> (u) The presentation of murder or revenge as a motive for mur-
> der shall not be justifiable. (National Association of Radio and
> Television Broadcasters, 1952)

Further provisions, partially noted as follows, emphasized the role
of television in the lives of children and the need to guard against
undue influence:

> 1. The education of children involves giving them a sense of
>   the world at large. Crime, violence and sex are a part of the
>   world they will be called upon to meet, and a certain
>   amount of proper presentation of such is helpful in ori-
>   enting the child to his surroundings. However, violence
>   and explicit sex shall not be presented in an attractive man-
>   ner, nor to such an extent such as will lead a child to believe
>   that they play a greater part in life than they do. They should
>   not be presented, without indications of the resultant retri-
>   bution and punishment.

2. It is not enough that only those programs which are intended for viewing by children shall be suitable to the young and immature. Television is responsible for insuring the programs of all sorts which occur during the times of the day when children may normally be expected to have the opportunity of viewing television shall exercise care in the following regards: . . .

(d) In eliminating reference to kidnapping of children or threats of kidnapping

(e) In avoiding material which is excessively violent or would create morbid suspense, or other undesirable reactions in children (National Association of Radio and Television Broadcasters, 1952)

Current regulations prohibit the broadcasting of obscene material and, between the hours of 6:00 a.m. and 10:00 p.m., when children are most likely to watch television, material that is deemed to be indecent (47 Code of Federal Regulations, 2008). Material will be considered to be obscene if it meets three criteria enunciated by the United States Supreme Court:

- An average person, applying contemporary community standards, finds that the material, taken as a whole, appeals to the prurient interest;
- The material describes or depicts in a patently offensive way sexual conduct specifically defined by the relevant law; and
- The material when considered as a whole lacks serious literary, artistic, political, or scientific value (Federal Communications Commission, 2008a, 2008b)

In contrast, materials or language will be found to be indecent when:

In context, [it] depicts or describes, in terms patently offensive as measured by contemporary community standards for the broadcast medium, sexual or excretory organs or activities. Indecent programming contains patently offensive sexual or excretory material that does not rise to the level of obscenity. (Federal Communications Commission, 2008a, 2008b)

The broadcasting of indecent material can be restricted, but it cannot be prohibited entirely in view of the protections guaranteed by the First Amendment of the United States Constitution. (See Chapter 1, Epidemiology and Law, for a review of the amendments to the Constitution.) Language will be found to rise to the level of profanity if it is "so grossly offensive to members of the public who actually hear it as to amount to a nuisance" (Federal Communications Commission, 2008a, 2008b).

These legally-imposed restrictions clearly do not encompass the depiction of violence or aggression. Although several jurisdictions have attempted to regulate the portrayal of violence in a variety of media, these efforts have been found by the reviewing courts to be unconstitutional, again based on First Amendment protections of freedom of speech (Chaffee, 2005). Currently, regulation of television violence is effectuated through a voluntary rating system of programming by television networks, using 1997 standards that outline appropriate audiences. This schema utilizes the following categories:

TV-Y   appropriate for all children

TV-Y7   appropriate for children aged 7 years and older

TV-G   general audience; suitable for all ages

TV-PG   parental guidance suggested; material may be unsuitable for younger children and may contain moderate violence (V), some sexual situations (S), infrequent coarse language (L), and/or suggestive dialogue (D)

TV-14   contains materials that may be unsuitable for children under the age of 14 years; may contain intense violence (V), intense sexual situations (S), strong coarse language (L), and/or intensely suggestive dialogue (D)

TV-MA   mature audience only; contains graphic violence (V), explicit sexual activity (S), and/or crude indecent language (L)

Additionally, as of January 1, 2000, the Federal Communications Commission required that all new television sets 13 inches or larger contain V-chip technology, which permits parents to block undesirable television programming (Telecommunications Act of 1996).

Recent evaluations have found these regulations to be largely ineffective due to a lack of understanding and knowledge on the part of many parents of the existence and the operation of the standards and the V-chip (Buhayar, 2007; Labaton, 2007) and the ineffectiveness of the rating system itself (Associated Press, 2007; Bushman & Cantor, 2003; Bushman & Stack, 1996; Cantor, 1998). Advocates for increased regulation of violence on television have called for both the availability of à la carte purchasing of access to television broadcasting, which would allow parents to select for purchase only that programming that they deem suitable, and the imposition of increased restrictions on depictions of violence (Buhayar, 2007; Labaton, 2007). Broadcasters have argued that it is impossible to define "violence" adequately for the purpose of such regulation and that such limitations would infringe on their First Amendment protections. Supporters of such legislation counter by noting that the industry must have already developed working definitions of violence to rate the suitability of programming for various audiences (Labaton, 2007).

Research findings relating to children's understanding of advertising and the effects of television commercials on children have played a critical role in the past in the formulation and implementation of standards for advertising during children's programming (Kunkel, 1990). It is likely that epidemiologists who have been involved in the design and conduct of studies relating to the effects of television violence on children's aggression and violence levels will have the opportunity to provide input into these standards.

Exercise

Assume that Congress has passed legislation authorizing the FCC to develop regulations relating to the depiction of violence on television and children's access to such programming. As an expert in epidemiology and the association between viewing violence on television and children's own behavior, you have been asked by the FCC to provide input into the drafting of appropriate regulations. Prepare a set of draft regulations. You must consider in formulating these standards: (1) definitions of violence and aggression and a clear distinction between the two; (2) the audience that is to be targeted for protection by these regulations; (3) the audience to be subject to these regulations, for example, cable, regular television, etc.; and (4) the availability of programming with violent or aggressive content to individuals who are not targeted for protection.

References

1. Abelson, P. H. (1967). A damaging source of air pollution. *Science*, 158(808), 1527.
2. American College of Obstetricians and Gynecologists. (1997). Educational bulletin: Smoking and women's health. *International Journal of Gynecology & Obstetrics*, 60, 71–82.
3. American Lung Association. (1998). *State legislated actions on tobacco issues.* Washington, DC: Author.
4. American Psychological Association, American Academy of Pediatrics, American Academy of Child and Adolescent Psychiatry, American Medical Association, American Academy of Family Physicians, & American Psychiatric Association. (2000). Joint statement on the impact of entertainment violence on children: Congressional public health summit. Retrieved July 7, 2008, from http://www.aap.org/advocacy/releases/jstmtevc.htm.
5. Ananth, C. V., Savitz, D. A., & Luter, E. R. (1996). Maternal cigarette smoking as a risk factor for placental abruption, placenta previa, and uterine bleeding in pregnancy. *American Journal of Epidemiology*, 144(9), 881–889.

6. Anderson, C.A., Berkowitz, L., Donnerstein, E., Huesmann, L.R., Johnson, J., Linz, D. et al. (2003). The influence of media violence on youth. *Psychological Science in the Public Interest*, 4(3), 81–110.

7. Anonymous. (1978, May 5). The right not to smoke [Editorial]. *The New York Times*.

8. Anonymous. (1993, October 10). Cartoon on MTV blamed for fire. *The New York Times*, p. 30.

9. Associated Press. (2007, February 15). FCC report suggests possible regulation of TV violence, allowing 'à la carte' cable choice. FoxNews. Retrieved July 22, 2008, from http://www.foxnews.com/printer_friendly_story/0,3566,252259,00.html.

10. Atkin, C., Greenberg, B., Korzenny, F., & McDermott, S. (1979). Selective exposure to televised violence. *Journal of Broadcasting*, 23, 5–13.

11. Bachrach, R. S. (1986). The differential effect of observation of violence on kibbutz and city children in Israel. In L. R. Huesmann & L. D. Eron (Eds.), *Television and the aggressive child: A cross-national comparison* (pp. 201–238). Hillsdale, NJ: Erlbaum.

12. Bandura, A. (1977). *Social learning theory*. Englewood Cliffs, NJ: Prentice Hall.

13. Berglund, D. J., Abbey, D. E., Lebowitz, M. D., Knutsen, S. F., & McDonnell, W. F. (1999). Respiratory symptoms and pulmonary function in an elderly non-smoking population. *Chest*, 115(1), 49–59.

14. Berkowitz, L. (1993). *Aggression: Its causes, consequences, and control*. New York: McGraw-Hill.

15. Black, S. L., & Bevan, S. (1992). At the movies with Buss and Durkee: A natural experiment on film violence. *Aggressive Behavior*, 18, 37–45.

16. Brandt, A. M. (2007). *The cigarette century: The rise, fall, and deadly persistence of the product that defined America*. New York: Basic Books.

17. Browne, K. D., & Hamilton-Giachritsis, C. (2005). The influence of violent media on children and adolescents: A public-health approach. *Lancet*, 365, 702–710.

18. Buhayar, N. (2007, May 2). Federal government calls for regulation of TV violence. *NewsHour Extra*. Retrieved July 22, 2008, from http://www.pbs.org/newshour/extra.

19. Bushman, B. J., & Anderson, C.A. (2001). Media violence and the American public: Scientific facts versus media misinformation. *American Psychologist*, 56, 477–489.

20. Bushman, B. J., & Cantor, J. (2003). Media ratings for violence and sex: Implications for policymakers and parents. *American Psychologist*, 58(2), 130–141.

21. Bushman, B. J., & Green, R. G. (1990). Role of cognitive-emotional mediators and individual differences in the effects of media violence on aggression. *Journal of Personality and Social Psychology*, 58, 156–163.

22. Bushman, B. J., & Stack, A. D. (1996). Forbidden fruit versus tainted fruit: Effects of warning labels on attraction to television violence. *Journal of Experimental Psychology: Applied*, 2(3), 207–226.

23. Button, T. M. M., Maughan, B., & McGuffin, P. (2007). The relationship of maternal smoking to psychological problems in the offspring. *Early Human Development*, 83, 727–732.

24. Cantor, J. (1998). Ratings for program content: The role of research findings. *Annals of the American Academy of Political and Social Science*, 557, 54–69.

25. Castles, A., Adams, E. K., Melvon, C. L., Lelsch, C., & Boulton, M. L. (1999). Effects of smoking during pregnancy. Five meta-analyses. *American Journal of Preventive Medicine*, 16(3), 208–215.

26. Centers for Disease Control and Prevention. (1993). Cigarette-smoking attributable mortality and years of potential life lost—United States, 1990. *Morbidity and Mortality Weekly Report*, 42, 645–649.

27. Centerwall, B. S. (1989). Exposure to television as a cause of violence. In G. Comstock (Ed.), *Public communication and behavior* (Vol. 2, pp. 1–58). Orlando, FL: Academic Press.

28. Centerwall, B. S. (1992). Television and violence: The scale of the problem and where to go from here. *Journal of the American Medical Association*, 267, 3059–3063.

29. Chaffee, E. C. (2005). Sailing toward safe harbor hours: The constitutionality of regulating television violence. *University of Michigan Journal of Legal Reform*, 39, 1–35.

30. Chilmonczyk, B. A., Salmun, L., Megathlin, K. N., Neveux, L. M., Palomaki, G. E., Knight, G. J., et al. (1993). Association between exposure to environmental tobacco smoke and exacerbations of asthma in children. *New England Journal of Medicine*, 328, 1665–1669.

31. Comstock, G. A., & Paik, H. (1991). *Television and the American child*. San Diego, CA: Academic Press.

32. de Zulueta, F. (1993). *The traumatic roots of destructiveness from pain to violence*. London: Whurr Publishers.

33. Drabman, R. S., & Thomas, M. H. (1974). Does media violence increase children's tolerance of real-life aggression? *Developmental Psychology*, 10(3), 418–421.

34. Dwyer, T., Posonby, A. L., & Couper, D. (1999). Tobacco smoke exposure at one month of age and subsequent risk of SIDS—A prospective study. *American Journal of Epidemiology*, 149(7), 593–602.

35. Ehrlich, R. J., Du Toit, D., Jordaan, E., Zwarenstein, M., Potter, P., Volmink, J. A., et al. (1996). Risk factors for childhood asthma and wheezing. Importance of maternal and household smoking. *American Journal of Respiratory Critical Care Medicine*, 154(3 Pt. 1), 681–688.

36. Federal Communications Commission. (2008a). *Obscene, indecent, and profane broadcasts*. Retrieved July 22, 2008, from http://www.fcc.gov/cgb/consumerfacts/obscene.html.

37. Federal Communications Commission. (2008b). *Regulation of obscenity, indecency, and profanity*. Retrieved July 22, 2008, from http://www.fcc.gov/eb/oip.

38. Federman, J. (Ed.). (1998). *National Television Violence Study: Executive summary*. Santa Barbara, CA: The Center for Communication and Social Policy, University of California.

39. Felson, R. B. (1996). Mass media effects on violent behavior. *Annual Review of Sociology*, 22, 103–128.

40. Floyd, R. L., Zahniser, C., Gunter, E. P., & Kendrick, J. S. (1991). Smoking during pregnancy: Prevalence, effects, and intervention strategies. *Birth*, 18, 48–53.

41. Fontham, E. T., Correa, P., WuWilliams, A., Reynolds, P., Greenberg, R. S., Buffler, P. A., et al. (1991). Lung cancer in nonsmoking women: A multicenter case-control study. *Cancer Epidemiology Biomarkers and Prevention*, 1(1), 35–43.

42. Fox, J. A. (1993, January 31). Murder most common. *Boston Globe*, pp. 65, 68.

43. Fraczek, A. (1986). Socio-cultural environment, television viewing, and the development of aggression among children in Poland. In L. R. Huesmann & L. D. Eron (Eds.), *Television and the aggressive child: A cross-national comparison* (pp. 119–160). Hillsdale, NJ: Erlbaum.

44. Funk, J. B., Baldacci, H. B., Pasold, T., & Baumgardner, J. (2004). Violence exposure in real-life, video games, television, movies, and the Internet: Is there desensitization? *Journal of Adolescence*, 27, 23–39.

45. Gilliland, F. D., Berhane, K., McConnell, R., Gauderman, W. J., Vora, H., Rapaport, E. B., et al. (2000). Maternal smoking during pregnancy, environmental tobacco smoke exposure and childhood lung function. *Thorax, 55*(4), 271–276.

46. Hole, D. J., Gillis, C. R., Chopra, C., & Hawthorne, V. M. (1989). Passive smoking and cardiorespiratory health in a general population in the west of Scotland. *British Medical Journal, 299*, 423–427.

47. Huesmann, L. R. (1988). An information processing model for the development of aggression. *Aggressive Behavior, 14*, 13–24.

48. Huesmann, L. R. (1998). The role of social information processing and cognitive schemas in the acquisition and maintenance of habitual aggressive behavior. In R. G. Geen & E. Donnerstein (Eds.), *Human aggression: Theories, research, and implications for policy* (pp. 73–109). New York: Academic Press.

49. Huesmann, L. R., Moise-Titus, J., Podolski, C. L., & Eron, L. D. (2003). Longitudinal relations between children's exposure to TV violence and their aggressive and violent behavior in young adulthood: 1977–1992. *Developmental Psychology, 39*, 201–221.

50. Huston, A. C., Donnerstein, E., Fairchild, H., Feshbach, N. D., Katz, P. A., Murray, J. P., et al. (1992). *Big world, small screen: The role of television in American society.* Lincoln, NE: University of Nebraska Press.

51. Institute of Medicine. (2001). *Clearing the smoke: Assessing the science base for tobacco harm reduction.* Washington, DC: National Academy Press.

52. Jacobson, P. D., & Zapawa, L. M. (2001). Clean indoor air restrictions: Progress and promise. In R. L. Rabin & S. D. Sugarman (Eds.), *Regulating tobacco* (pp. 207–244). New York: Oxford University Press.

53. Johnson, J. G., Cohen, P., Smailes, E. M., Kasen, S., & Brook, J. S. (2002). Television viewing and aggressive behavior during adolescence and adulthood. *Science, 295*, 2468–2471.

54. Jones, J. R., Higgins, I. T., Higgins, M. W., & Keller, J. B. (1983). Effects of cooking fuels on lung function in nonsmoking women. *Archives of Environmental Health, 38*(4), 219–222.

55. Joy, L. A., Kimball, M. M., & Zaback, M. L. (1986). Television and children's aggressive behavior. In T. M. Williams (Ed.), *The impact of television: A natural experiment in three communities* (pp. 303–360). New York: Academic Press.

56. Kilby, J. W. (1997). A smoking cessation plan for pregnant women. *Journal of Obstetrical, Gynecological, and Neonatal Nursing, 26*, 397–402.

57. Krug, E. G., Dahlberg, L. L., Mercy, J. A., Zwi, A. B., & Lozano, R. (Eds.), (2002). *World report on violence and health.* Geneva, Switzerland: World Health Organization.

58. Kunkel, D. (1990). The role of research in the regulation of U.S. children's television advertising. *Science Communication, 12*(1), 101–119.

59. Labaton, S. (2007, April 26). F.C.C. moves to restrict TV violence. *The New York Times.* Retrieved July 22, 2008, from http://www.nytimes.com/2007/04/26/business/media/26fcc.html?pagewanted=print.

60. Lee, P. N., & Forey, B. A. (1998). Trends in cigarette consumption cannot fully explain trends in British lung cancer rates. *Journal of Epidemiology & Community Health, 52*, 82–92.

61. Lew, E. A., & Garfinkel, L. (1987). Differences in mortality and longevity by sex, smoking habits, and health status. *Journal of the Society of Actuaries, 39*, 107–130.

62. Lewis, K. W., & Bosque, E. M. (1995). Deficient hypoxia awakening response in infants of smoking mothers: Possible relationship to sudden infant death syndrome. *Journal of Pediatrics, 127*, 691–699.

63. MacCoun, R. J., & Reuter, P. (2001). *Drug war heresies: Learning from other vices, times and places.* Cambridge, England: Cambridge University Press.

64. Medved, M. (1995). Hollywood's 3 big lies. *Reader's Digest, 147*(882), 155–159. Quoted in B. J. Bushman & C. A. Anderson. (2001). Media violence and the American public: Scientific facts versus media misinformation. *American Psychologist, 56,* 477–489.

65. Mercy, J.A., Rosenberg, M.L., Powell, K.E., Broome, C.V., & Roper, W.L. (1993). Public health policy for preventing violence, *Health Affairs, 12*(4), 7–29.

66. Milotsky, I. (1986, December 17). Surgeon general, citing risks, urges smoke-free workplace. *The New York Times.*

67. Mitchell, E. A., Ford, R. P., Stewart, A. W., & Taylor, B. J. (1993). Smoking and the sudden infant death syndrome. *Pediatrics, 91,* 893–896.

68. Murray, A. B., & Morrison, B. J. (1989). Passive smoking by asthmatics: Its greater effect on boys than on girls and on older than on younger children. *Pediatrics, 84*(3), 451–459.

69. National Association of Radio and Television Broadcasters. (1952). *Television code.* Washington, DC: Author. Retrieved July 22, 2008, from http://chnm.gmu .edu/exploring/20thcentury/regulatingtelevision/Pop_report.html.

70. Nielsen Media Research. (1998). *Galaxy explorer.* New York: Author.

71. Ohio Administrative Code § § 3701-52-01, -02, -09 (2008).

72. Oliver, M. B. (1994). Portrayals of crime, race, and aggression in "reality-based" police shows: A content analysis. *Journal of Broadcasting and Electronic Media, 38,* 179–192.

73. Paik, H., & Comstock, G. (1994). The effects of television violence on antisocial behavior—A metaanalysis. *Communication Research, 21,* 516–546.

74. Prothrow-Stith, D., & Weissman, M. (1991). *Deadly consequences.* New York: HarperCollins.

75. Repace, J. L., & Lowrey, A. H. (1990). Risk assessment methodologies for passive smoking-induced lung cancer. *Risk Analysis, 10*(1), 27–37.

76. Richardson, K. K. (1999). Adolescent pregnancy and substance use. *Journal of Obstetrical, Gynecological, and Neonatal Nursing, 28,* 623–627.

77. Rosenberg, M.L. (1989). Violence is a public health problem. In R.C. Maulitz (Ed.). *Unnatural causes: The three leading killer diseases in America* (pp. 147–168). New Brunswick, NJ.

78. Ruttenberg, H. (1994). The limited promise of public health methodologies to prevent youth violence. *Yale Law Journal, 103,* 1885–1912.

79. Rylander, E., Pershagen, G., Eriksson, M., & Bermann, G. (1995). Parental smoking, urinary cotinine, and wheezing bronchitis in children. *Epidemiology, 6*(3), 289–293.

80. Schoendorf, K. C., & Kiely, J. L. (1992). Relationship of sudden infant death syndrome to maternal smoking during and after pregnancy. *Pediatrics, 90,* 905–908.

81. Schorr, D. (1993, September 7). TV violence—What we know but ignore. *Christian Science Monitor,* p. 19.

82. Schottenfeld, D. (1984). Epidemiology of cancer of the esophagus. *Seminars in Oncology, 11*(2), 92–100.

83. Shah, N. R., & Bracken, M. B. (2000). A systematic review and meta-analysis of prospective studies on the association between maternal cigarette smoking and preterm delivery. *American Journal of Obstetrics & Gynecology, 182*(2), 465–472.

84. Sheehan, P. W. (1986). Television viewing and its relation to aggression among children in Australia. In L. R. Huesmann & L. D. Eron (Eds.), *Television and the aggressive child: A cross-national comparison* (pp. 161–200). Hillsdale, NJ: Erlbaum.

85. Siegel, M., Albers, A. B., Cheng, D. M., Hamilton, W. L., & Biener, L. (2008). Local restaurant smoking regulations and the adolescent smoking initiation process: Results of a multilevel contextual analysis among Massachusetts youth. *Archives of Pediatric & Adolescent Medicine, 162*(5), 477–483.

86. Simons, M. (1993, August 30). Blaming TV for son's death. *The New York Times,* p. 30.

87. Stockwell, H. G., Goldman, A. L., Lyman, G. H., Noss, C. I., Armstrong, A. W., Pinkham, P. A., et al. (1992). Environmental tobacco smoke and lung cancer risk in nonsmoking women. *Journal of the National Cancer Institute, 84*(18), 1417–1422.

88. Sullum, J. (1998). *For your own good: The anti-smoking crusade and the tyranny of public health.* New York: Free Press.

89. Telecommunications Act of 1996, Pub. L. No. 104-104, codified at 47 U.S.C. § 303 et seq.

90. Tremblay, R. E. (2000). The development of aggressive behavior during childhood: What have we learned in the past century? *International Journal of Behavioral Development, 24,* 129–141.

91. United States Department of Health and Human Services. (1986). *The health consequences of involuntary smoking: A report of the surgeon general.* Washington, DC: Government Printing Office.

92. United States Department of Health and Human Services. (2000). *Healthy people 2010.* Retrieved November 12, 2008 from http://www.health/gov/healthypeople/Document/tableofcontents.htm.

93. Whittemore, A. S., Perlin, S. A., & DiCiccio, Y. (1995). Chronic obstructive pulmonary disease in lifelong nonsmokers: Results from NHANES. *American Journal of Public Health, 85*(5), 702–706.

94. Wood, W., Wong, F. Y., & Chachere, J. G. (1991). Effects of media violence on viewers' aggression in unconstrained social-interaction. *Psychological Bulletin, 109,* 371–383.

95. Young, J. G., Brasic, J. R., Sheitman, B., & Studnick, M. (1994). Brain mechanisms mediating aggression and violence. In C. Chiland & J. G. Young (Eds.), *Children and violence* (pp. 29–72). Northvale, NJ: Jason Aronson.

96. Zillman, D. (1983). Arousal and aggression. In R. G. Geen & E. I. Donnerstein (Eds.), *Aggression: Theoretical and empirical reviews, vol. 1: Theoretical and methodological issues* (pp. 75–101). New York: Academic Press.

97. 47 Code of Federal Regulations § 73.3999 (2008).

Chapter 9

Looking Toward the Future

The previous chapters have raised significant issues that must be addressed from a broader perspective. Foremost among these are how to achieve a balance between individual rights, public health concerns, and the interests of the government and how to train professionals in diverse fields of endeavor to recognize and address those situations that demand professional expertise in unrelated disciplines to augment investigational efforts, whether in the epidemiologic or law enforcement context. This final chapter provides an overview of various perspectives and offers additional possibilities for consideration.

Finding Balance

The tension that exists between individual interests and those of the government and/or public health are reflected throughout the diverse topics in this text. It may be helpful to recount the contexts in which the use of epidemiologic data in conjunction with law enforcement efforts gives rise to this conflict:

- In administrative actions to seize goods or products, creating a conflict between the individual's constitutional right to be free from unwarranted searches and seizures and the need to protect the public health
- In criminal prosecutions for HIV transmission, in which the right of the HIV-infected individual to privacy and confidentiality is challenged by the need to protect the public health
- In efforts to involuntarily quarantine individuals who may transmit tuberculosis to others, resulting in conflict between the individual's right to privacy, freedom of movement, and right of association, and the need to protect the public health
- Disease surveillance and reporting, functions that potentially create conflict between individuals' interest in privacy and the public health
- In civil and criminal actions that are commenced against pregnant women for the ingestion of legal and/or illicit substances during their pregnancies, bringing into conflict the mothers' interest in privacy and the state's interest in the child's welfare
- In administrative proceedings to determine the admissibility of intending immigrants with a diagnosis of mental illness, bringing into conflict the individual's right to privacy and the interests of the government in maintaining the safety of its citizens
- In the context of incidents involving biological terrorism, during which the government may impose measures such as mandated vaccination and/or involuntary quarantine and/or isolation and/or seize and destroy goods in an attempt to reduce the likelihood of disease transmission, creating conflict with individuals' privacy and property interests, freedom of religion, freedom of movement, and freedom of association
- In the regulation of environmental tobacco smoke, underscoring the conflict between both the government's police power and its obligation to protect its citizens from harm and smokers' freedom of speech and association
- In the attempted regulation of television programming to reduce or eliminate child exposure to violence and aggression, implicating freedom of speech, on the one hand, and the need to protect children from harm, on the other

The right of the government to act in each of these situations, whether it is the local, state, or federal government, derives from the police power of the state. This concept has been subject to several definitions:

the inherent authority of the state (and through delegation, local government to enact laws and promulgate regulations to protect, preserve, and promote the health, safety, morals, and general welfare of the people. To achieve these communal benefits, the state retains the power to restrict, within federal and state constitutional limits, private interests—personal interests in autonomy, privacy, association, and liberty as well as economic interests in freedom to contract and uses of property (Gostin, 2000).

coercive action under states authority to encourage educational efforts . . . seize property, close businesses, destroy animals, or involuntarily treat or even lock away individuals (Richards & Rathbun, 1977, p. 42)

the inherent authority of all sovereign governments to enact laws and promote regulations that safeguard the health, welfare, and morals of its citizens (Misrahi, Matthews, & Hoffman, 2003, p. 196)

The government's right to act also derives from the concept of *parens patriae*, which originates from English common law. This principle holds that the State may exercise its sovereign power to act as the guardian of persons and their property if they are unable to do so themselves (Schwartz & Costanzo, 1987). These two principles—the protection of citizenry through the reliance on the police power of the State and the protection of individuals on the basis of *parens patriae*—may converge in fulfillment of a particular function or activity, such as quarantine and isolation and restrictions on the distribution and use of tobacco products.

As was evident from the case studies, overzealous protection of society from harm may lead to not only a violation of individual liberties but also a loss of rights altogether. Conversely, overemphasis on individual liberties could potentially result in significant irreversible harm to the public. The balance that has been struck between these interests has varied in relation to the level of perceived threat. One scholar observed, "The safer the nation feels, the more weight judges will be willing to give to the liberty interest. The greater the threat that an activity poses to the nation's safety, the stronger will be the grounds for seeking to repress that activity even at some cost to liberty" (Posner, 2003, p. 26).

Kass (2001) formulated six issues to be addressed in evaluating the ethical implications of any public health action: the goals of the proposed program; the effectiveness of the proposed program in achieving its goals; the known or potential burdens of the proposed program; the possibility of minimizing the burdens to be imposed by the proposed program and the availability of any suitable alternatives; the fairness of implementation; and the fairness with which the benefits and burdens of the program are to be distributed. These factors are equally relevant in considering the application of epidemiology in the law enforcement context. It is important, as well, to consider the egregiousness or severity of the harm that is to be avoided. Each of these elements is discussed in greater detail in the following paragraphs.

ASSESSING THE SEVERITY OF HARM

The potential severity of the harm that is to be avoided through the law enforcement action may be difficult to determine. It is clear that many decisions that necessitate a balancing of individual and governmental or public health interests must be made on the basis of what is acknowledged to be incomplete knowledge, or significant disagreement may exist with respect to the potential for harm. Consider the following situations.

As noted in Chapter 5, Law, Epidemiology, and Communicable Disease, many states have instituted laws rendering varying types of sexual activity of an HIV-infected person a crime in the absence of disclosure of HIV status and/or use of protective measures designed to reduce the likelihood of transmission. The promulgation of these laws, and the conviction of HIV-positive individuals for even spitting at another individual, creates the impression that such contact creates an inordinately high level of transmission risk. However, epidemiological data suggest that the risk is actually quite low, certainly much lower than the risk associated with the transmission of hepatitis or syphilis.

There is considerable disagreement among scholars as to the harm that would result to the populace as a result of bioterrorism, intended to terrorize the civilian population, as distinguished from biological warfare, intended to conquer a country. Gostin, for example, has asserted that "a single gram of crystalline botulinum toxin, evenly dispersed and inhaled, could kill more than one million people" (Gostin, 2003, p. 1119). Annas (2003b) implicitly challenges this evaluation of the threatened danger in noting that the effort by the Japanese terrorist cult of Aum Shinrikyo to kill individuals at Japanese military installations using botulinum toxin was a futile one for the cult.

In other situations, the potential severity of the harm may be more easily assessed. As an example, the inability to detain individuals with infectious tuberculosis or to mandate appropriate treatment could result in the transmission of multidrug-resistant tuberculosis to numerous other individuals. Such was the case involving a gentleman in England who had infectious tuberculosis; the relevant laws did not permit either extended detention or mandated treatment, and his free movement in the absence of precautions to others resulted in the infection of an additional 12 people (Meikle, 2005). It was estimated that the cost of treatment for each of the individuals who developed drug-resistant tuberculosis could range between £6000 and £60,000 (Meikle, 2005), or approximately $12,000 to $120,000.

THE GOALS OF THE PROPOSED ACTIVITY

In many cases, the goals of the proposed activity, whether in the administrative or criminal law context, will be to reduce morbidity and mortality. These goals are reflected, for example, in efforts to seize adulterated food and drug products; in the promulgation of statutes and regulations that are designed to reduce exposure to secondary tobacco smoke; and in attempts to reduce media portrayal of violence as a means of reducing the incidence of violent crime. In other circumstances, however, the motivation underlying both the substance and procedure of the law enforcement effort may be less clear. Such is the case, for example, of the regulations relating to the examination and inadmissibility of intending immigrants who have been deemed to have mental illnesses. These regulations ostensibly are designed to protect the public from physical harm and the government from potential financial harm as a result of the individual's potential inability to obtain gainful employment. One must question if such regulations also rest on a fear of the foreign and the foreigner and the irrational belief that the exclusion of foreigners will insulate Americans from disease themselves.

It has been asserted that "if public health action is to be based on science and epidemiology, draconian public health measures should not be used until there is some evidence they will be effective" (Annas, 2003b p. 1180). In many instances, reliance on epidemiological data and epidemiologists as experts has been critical to the effectiveness of the law enforcement efforts. The isolation in appropriate facilities of individuals with multidrug-resistant tuberculosis who are unwilling or unable to adhere to their prescribed medication regimens serves to decrease the risk of disease transmission to other, unknowing persons. As seen in the discussion in Chapter 3, Epidemiology and Criminal Law, the calculation of disease incidence and identification of excess cases of death enabled prosecutors to identify the likely perpetrators of patient murders and the risk factors for such occurrences and also facilitated the establishment of safety measures to reduce the likelihood that future murders of patients would occur.

In other situations, however, it appears that reliable epidemiological data have been ignored in the pursuit of law enforcement goals. Consider, as an example, the use of quarantine and isolation measures in the context of bioterrorism. Although some scholars have called for consideration of quarantine or isolation as a means of combating bioterrorism (Gostin, 2003), it is clear that such a course of action may not be effective. Because anthrax, for example, is not transmitted from person to person, quarantine or isolation will do little to stem the threat of larger-scale injury. In other cases, the illness symptoms caused by the biological agent used by the terrorists may so closely resemble the symptoms of other illnesses that healthcare workers will be unable to distinguish between those who should be subject to a quarantine advisory or order and those who should not (O'Leary, 2006).

Consider, as well, that a number of states continue to maintain laws criminalizing, to varying degrees, sexual activity by HIV-infected persons despite the relatively low risk of HIV transmission associated with various sexual activities (Campo, et al., 2006; Downs & De Vincenzi, 1996; Royce, Seña, Cates, & Cohen, 1997; Vittinghoff, et al., 1999) and research findings indicating that such laws fail to bring about the desired behavior change (Burris, Beletsky, Burleson, Case, & Lazzarini, 2007; Lazzarini, Bray, & Burris, 2002). In this instance, it appears that the balance between the individual and public health has been shifted to the latter, despite the lack of effectiveness of the law enforcement efforts. This necessarily raises issues as to the existence of other underlying motivations for the promulgation and perpetuation of such provisions that have not been verbalized.

THE POTENTIAL IMPACT OR BURDEN

We can begin to consider the potential impact or burden that can result from the integration of epidemiology and law enforcement efforts by examining the burdens imposed by a widespread and generally accepted activity within the domain of epidemiology, that of disease surveillance and reporting. In many instances, such activities entail a loss of privacy for the individuals involved and the loss of confidentiality with respect to the information about themselves. Although it was conducted within the context of health care, rather than epidemiology, a joint health-law enforcement effort that was undertaken in South Carolina is illustrative of such dangers. This joint effort was developed and implemented ostensibly for the purpose of protecting unborn children from harm. In that situation, a hospital in Charleston, South Carolina tested pregnant women for drugs; those women who tested positive were presented with the choice of entering a recovery program or being reported to the police for prosecution (Anonymous, 2001; Denniston, 2001; Greenberg, 2001; Lane, 2001). Law enforcement was actively involved at every stage, from the time of the mothers' initial presentation for prenatal care through labor and delivery of the newborns (Denniston, 2001). The joint effort by healthcare personnel, who were legitimately concerned about the high prevalence of substance use found among their patients, and law enforcement personnel not only resulted in the loss of privacy for the women involved, but it may have discouraged others from seeking care (Lane, 2001).

This loss of privacy and confidentiality was also evident in the case of Nushawn Williams, detailed in Chapter 5, Law, Epidemiology, and Communicable Disease, when his identity and HIV serostatus were released to the public in an attempt to interrupt HIV transmission. Later, even his mental illness diagnosis was made available to the public, although the possible threat to the public health from his sexual activities had abated. The media coverage that was provided at the urging of public health authorities may have resulted in a loss of privacy, as well, for the young women who were known to others to have had sexual relations with Williams; their HIV status may have become known or presumed as a result of the media reports that were disseminated.

The potential—and likely unintended—burden may be even more draconian in some instances. Suppose, hypothetically, that an individual presented for HIV testing prior to the promulgation of the state law that criminalized sexual activity by HIV-infected persons. He or she was found to be HIV positive and was counseled on how to prevent transmission of the infection to others. In accordance with disease surveillance and reporting mechanisms, his name was provided to the state and was also retained by the local public health authority. Several years later, following the passage of such a criminal law provision and during the course of conducting contact tracing, a public health official discovered that this same individual had unprotected intercourse with an individual who tested positive for syphilis, clearly indicating that barrier protection was not used. A lapse in the confidentiality protections could now leave this individual vulnerable to an intrusive investigation into the most intimate details of his relations and possible criminal prosecution. And, depending upon the particular circumstances and one's moral stance, the initiation of law enforcement activity on the basis of epidemiologic findings may or may not be warranted, not only because of the burden on these particular individuals but also because of the potential deterrent effect that such policy and practice could have on people's willingness to present for HIV testing.

Consider, as well, the potential burdens that could result from quarantine/isolation efforts to contain a threat. The constitutional rights of isolated or quarantined individuals, with respect to their freedom of movement and their freedom of assembly, are restricted. In situations such as that of Robert Daniels, who was confined in a jail ward rather than a hospital following his nonadherence to his prescribed medication regimen for tuberculosis, the "solitary confinement" additionally resulted in mental health issues (Wagner, 2007).

In other situations, such a large-scale quarantine effort in response to a bioterrorist attack or the inadvertent isolation of healthy persons with those that have been affected by the illness in question could bring about the unintended consequence of even wider transmission of the illness, additional strain on already taxed healthcare workers and services, and a deleterious impact on the economy (Barbera, et al., 2001). The use of law enforcement personnel to enforce the quarantine/isolation order could also result in violence, such as occurred in 1893 in Muncie, Indiana following the attempted enforcement by patrolling armed guards of a quarantine order to halt the transmission of smallpox (Eidson, 1990).

A mandated vaccination program in response to a bioterrorist threat may also impose significant burdens. Mandated vaccinations, particularly of unapproved vaccines, could result in numerous adverse consequences. First, recipients of the vaccine could suffer ill effects. As an example, prior to the Gulf War, the United States Department of Defense mandated administration to troops of the investigational drug pyridostigmine bromide and the investigational vaccine botulinum toxoid to be used to attenuate the effects of an attack by the nerve gas soman and *Clostridium botulinum*, respectively (Annas, 1998, 2003b). The Department of Defense had argued successfully to the federal Food and Drug Administration that informed consent to the administration of these investigational pharmaceuticals should be waived to protect the integrity of the military mission from the possibility that soldiers would decline the vaccine and drug. In fact, the administration of the pyridostigmine bromide resulted in troops' increased vulnerability because the nerve gas that had been prepared by the Iraqis to be used in an attack against them was not soman, but sarin, and pyridostigmine bromide actually increases the effects of sarin (Annas, 2003b).

Other rights may be similarly discounted. Freedom of religion is guaranteed by the United States Constitution, and the United States has long recognized the right of individuals to decide what is to be done to their bodies and to refuse the administration of medications and the performance of medical procedures on the basis of religious belief (*In re Duran*, 2001; *Schloendorff v. Society of New York Hospital*, 1914). A mandated vaccination program would obviate this right.

Overzealous cooperation of epidemiologists or other public health professionals may also lead to an abridgement of even the freedom of speech. As indicated in Chapter 1, Epidemiology and Law, freedom of speech is guaranteed by the Constitution with only very limited exceptions, such as obscenity (*Miller v. California*, 1973) and fighting words (*Chaplinsky v. New Hampshire*, 1942). Consider the following example of how this has actually occurred.

Two researchers, Wein and Liu, developed a mathematical model that demonstrated how the release of a small amount of botulinum toxin could move within 84 hours from cows to consumers, resulting in the poisoning of thousands of people and devastating economic consequences (Wein & Liu, 2005). In response to the concerns of the

US Department of Health and Human Services (HHS) about the potential reliance on the data presented for the purpose of bioterrorism (Cohen, 2005), the scientific journal that had initially accepted the manuscript for publication decided to hold the report. In response, Wein addressed the journal's decision and provided details about the study in an opinion piece published by *The New York Times* (Wein, 2005). The journal published the manuscript in question several months after the appearance of Wein's opinion piece (Wein & Liu, 2005). Stewart Simonson, the Assistant Secretary of the HHS Office of the Assistant Secretary for Preparedness and Response, noted that the action of HHS to intervene in the manuscript's publication probably drew greater attention to the paper's content than it would have otherwise received (Cohen, 2005).

MINIMIZING BURDENS; IDENTIFYING ALTERNATIVES

The foregoing examples are offered not to suggest that law enforcement personnel and epidemiologists should not use their skills in the conduct of joint investigations but rather that such activities and functions should be undertaken wisely and thoughtfully, with a clear vision of the potential for damage that could result, the pursuit of all possible efforts to *minimize the burdens* to be imposed by the proposed investigation or program, and the creative development and implementation of *suitable alternatives*.

There exists the concept in law of the least restrictive alternative. This concept stands for the proposition that, "when dealing with the restriction of a fundamental right, that restriction must be narrowly tailored in order to serve a compelling state interest, meaning that the least restrictive alternative must be employed" (Madziar, 2002, p. 78). Recognition of this concept is evident in Minnesota's efforts to protect the public from the threat of bioterrorism while minimizing the restrictions imposed on individual rights (Annas, 2003a). Unlike Florida's statute that permits the quarantine of any individual who refuses to be vaccinated, regardless of the reason (Florida Statutes § 381.00315, 2002), Minnesota's statute specifically indicates that an individual has "a fundamental right to refuse" examination, treatment, collection of specimens, and vaccination even in public health emergencies (Minnesota Statutes § 12.39, 2003).

Attempts to identify a least restrictive alternative in the context of regulating environmental tobacco smoke are also evident. The tobacco industry argued that governmental regulation of environmental tobacco smoke imposed undue burdens on individuals who smoke, resulted in the abridgment of their rights, and created a new class of persons subject to discrimination. Philip Morris, a major manufacturer of tobacco products, produced a smokers' Bill of Rights, which asserted:

As a smoker, I am entitled to certain inalienable rights, among them:

> The right to the pursuit of happiness;
> The right to choose to smoke;
> The right to enjoy a traditional American custom;
> The right to be treated courteously;
> The right to accommodation in the workplace;
> The right to accommodation in public places;
> The right to unrestricted access to commercial information about products;
> The right to purchase products without excessive taxation;
> The right to freedom from unnecessary government intrusion (Philip Morris, 1986)

A vice president of Philip Morris, Stanley S. Scott, opined:

> The question all Americans must ask themselves is: can a nation that struggled so valiantly to eliminate bias based on race, religion and sex afford to allow a fresh set of categories to encourage new forms of hostility between large groups of citizens? . . . After all, discrimination is discrimination, no matter what it is based on. (Scott, 1985)

The restrictions that were developed to regulate environmental tobacco smoke evidence an attempt to balance the rights of individuals to smoke and the need to protect those who do not from the potential ill effects of their exposure through the identification and implementation of less restrictive alternatives to a total ban on the use of tobacco products.

A review of relevant regulations imposed by various states, municipalities, and agencies reveals that restrictions on advertising, distribution, and sales are largely designed to protect minors. Limitations on public smoking have often been imposed only in enclosed areas. For example, restaurant patrons in many locales are prohibited from smoking indoors, but they are permitted to do so in outside dining areas. And, rhetoric aside, an examination of the US Constitution and judicial interpretations of its various provisions reveals no rights to smoke, to be treated courteously, or to the accommodation of behaviors that result in harm to others.

FAIRNESS

The implementation of joint epidemiology-law enforcement investigations and programs must necessarily be fair. Unfortunately, history is replete with instances in which such efforts were not only unfair but were characterized by xenophobia and racism. Recall from Chapter 5, Law, Epidemiology, and Communicable Disease, for example, that the

San Francisco Board of Health attempted in the early 20th century to quarantine only Chinese residents for bubonic plague (*Wong Wai v. Williamson*, 1900) and, in more recent years, the United States became known as the only country in the world to establish an internment camp for the quarantine of HIV-seropositive asylum seekers, all of whom were black and Haitian (*Haitian Centers Council Inc. v. Sale*, 1993). Such actions were ostensibly premised on the need to protect the public health from the possibility of contagion.

Efforts by healthcare personnel and law enforcement to reduce drug usage among pregnant women similarly reflect an unfair distribution of the associated burdens, at least in some cases. Although epidemiologic data indicate that the rates of substance use among pregnant women are generally the same regardless of socioeconomic status or race, at least some hospitals have been more eager to screen and report to law enforcement women who are black or poor (Lane, 2001; Spector & Simakis, 2001).

New Approaches to Training

Coordinated exercises in preparedness for bioterrorist attacks have revealed the relative lack of coordination and preparedness that exists between federal and state agencies and between different agencies within the same locale to address a public health emergency (Clark, 2005; DiGiovanni, Bowen, Ginsberg, & Giles, 2005). Judges, in general, lack the training that is necessary to evaluate the underlying technical basis for proposed action to be taken in the interest of national security (Kontorovich, 2004), such as the need for specific disease control and prevention measures. Legislators who attempt to maximize the protection of their constituents from disease or injury appear to lack, in some cases, even a basic understanding of the factors that may contribute to disease transmission or injury causation and mechanisms for prevention. Clearly, additional training is warranted in the public health, governmental, and law enforcement sectors.

Moulton and colleagues (2003) have delineated four core elements that must comprise any training program and any concerted effort to enhance inter- and intra-agency coordination: laws, competencies, information, and coordination. Each of these domains is considered in the following paragraphs with respect to both epidemiologists and law enforcement personnel.

TRAINING EPIDEMIOLOGISTS FOR JOINT EFFORTS

In general, most epidemiologists have relatively little knowledge of the law apart from legal issues related to their research, such as regulations that govern human subjects protection, or their specific public health functions, such as the reporting of sexually transmitted diseases or quarantine efforts. It is most likely accurate to suggest that only a minority of epidemiologists have been called as expert witnesses in either civil or criminal trials; have offered testimony in conjunction with the promulgation of legislation at local, state, or federal levels; or have responded to proposed regulatory action through the notice and comment procedure.

As scientists, epidemiologists are led to believe that their research is necessarily unbiased and value free; however, how we even frame our research questions and report our findings reflects our values and worldview. We are trained to believe that it is sufficient that we report our findings accurately; what is done with those findings is supposedly immaterial to the neutral scientist and is best left to the politicians and legislators to decipher and apply. Advocacy in support of a position that we have come to believe in through our own or others' research is strongly discouraged in the belief that the advocacy will cast a shadow of bias over research design and interpretation, leading others to doubt the validity and reliability of the reported findings. For example, Rothman and Poole (1985) have asserted that a researcher's participation in public advocacy is inappropriate; participation in the advocacy process is appropriate only if the researcher is acting in his or her role as a private citizen (Poole & Rothman, 1990). Yet history is replete with examples of the misuse and dismissal of valid epidemiologic findings and the consequent infringement of individuals' and particularized groups' liberties.

In contrast, Weed (1994) has justified an advocacy role for epidemiologists by focusing on the principle of beneficence, which, stated somewhat simplistically, centers on the obligation to do good (Beauchamp & Childress, 1994). Bankowski (1991, p. 162) has spoken about the positive role that epidemiologists as researchers can play:

> Epidemiology is a means of quantifying injustice in relation to health care, of monitoring progress towards justice, beneficence, non-maleficence, and respect for persons, as these ethical principles apply to society, and of applying its findings to the control of health problems. That those at the political level charged with safeguarding the public health often neglect or find it inconvenient, or even impractical, to apply epidemiological findings, sometimes because the more vulnerable populations or groups lack the power to assert or safeguard their rights, often because of the complexity of prioritizing resources allocation, does not invalidate epidemiology. Rather, that this happens is a reason for emphasizing the relation between ethics and human values and health policy-making, and for an ethics of public health, concerned with social justice as well as individual rights, to complement the ethics of medicine.

Gordis (1991, p. 12S) envisions the epidemiologist assuming a societal role in the policy-making process through the presentation of data and its interpretations and the development and evaluation of proposals. He acknowledges, however, that a researcher's credibility may be lessened if he or she assumes a strong advocacy position on a specific issue:

> An additional consideration is that since our data have important societal implications, if we want society to continue to support our efforts, we will have to demonstrate the value of our research for the health of the public. This can only be done if we broaden our responsibility from the research only role to that of policy-related functions. Thus, the epidemiologist must also serve as an educator. [The epidemiologist's] efforts are directed at many target populations including other scientists, legislators, policy makers, lawyers and judges, and the public. Each must be dealt with differently depending on the specific needs of that population and the objectives towards which the educational effort is directed.

Accordingly, participation in joint activities with law enforcement necessarily demands that epidemiologists develop a broader and more sophisticated understanding of the underlying legal and ethical principles against which they and others will judge their actions.

There exists in the conduct of joint law enforcement activities the potential for conflict of interest in the roles assumed by the epidemiologist. Is the epidemiologist a neutral scientist, merely providing law enforcement with requested information? At what stage of this process does the epidemiologist become an agent of law enforcement? This inquiry is particularly critical in situations in which the proposed activity is likely to result in the uneven imposition of burdens or distribution of benefits on one or more particular groups.

TRAINING LAW ENFORCEMENT PERSONNEL FOR JOINT EFFORTS

Joint investigational efforts by law enforcement and epidemiologists call for additional training of law enforcement personnel in several areas: (1) the development of a basic understanding of disease transmission and prevention, so that personnel will have adequate training to protect themselves and others from harm; (2) an understanding of when and how to coordinate their efforts with those of the scientific and public health professional communities; (3) the identification and understanding of various laws and policies that are relevant to such investigations; and (4) the development and enhancement of skills to facilitate the coordination of activities and the release of information to appropriate media personnel (Federal Bureau of Investigation &

Centers for Disease Control and Prevention, 2006). Epidemiologists and other public health personnel can be most actively involved in assisting with training in the first two domains indicated.

Other aspects of the law enforcement function may require periodic refresher courses or augmentation. For example, many law enforcement personnel receive training related to the chain of custody of evidence and preservation of evidence. However, that training may need to be augmented to address issues related to chain of custody involving, for example, food samples that may have been deliberately contaminated. Additional training may also be indicated at all levels about channels of communication in joint investigations and mechanisms to protect confidentiality and privacy of concerned individuals.

OTHER TRAINING EFFORTS

Various professional groups apart from epidemiologists, public health personnel, and law enforcement personnel, such as police, may be called upon in their professional capacities to address issues related to epidemiology and law enforcement. This includes, for example, states' attorneys general, judges, legislators, and even media personnel. There are relatively few training programs available for such groups that focus on not only the parameters of public health law and functions (Honssinger, Ianni, & Milsteen, 2005), but also train individuals to critically evaluate the underlying epidemiologic basis of proposed action in conjunction with the relevant law and ethical principles. An integrated approach is critical if we are to avoid conflicts of interest, intentional or inadvertent breaches of confidentiality and violation of privacy, waste of government resources, misuse of the media, discriminatory practices (cf. Honssinger, et al., 2005), and the creation or exacerbation of stigma (Flynn, Slovic, & Kunreuther, 2001).

References

1. Annas, G. J. (1998). Protecting soldiers from friendly fire: The consent requirement for using investigational drugs and vaccines in combat. *American Journal of Law & Medicine*, 24, 245–260.

2. Annas, G. J. (2003a). Blinded by bioterrorism: Public health and liberty in the 21st century. *Health Matrix*, 13, 33–70.

3. Annas, G. J. (2003b). Puppy love: Bioterrorism, civil rights, and public health. *Florida Law Review*, 55, 1171–1190.

4. Anonymous. (2001, March 22). Supreme Court limits hospitals' testing for drugs. *Providence Journal-Bulletin*, p. 5A.

5. Bankowski, Z. (1991). Epidemiology, ethics, and 'health for all.' *Law, Medicine & Health Care*, 19, 162–163.

6. Barbera, J., Macintyre, A., Gostin, L., Inglesby, T., O'Toole, T., DeAtley, C., et al. (2001). Large-scale quarantine following biological terrorism in the United States: Scientific examination, logistic and legal limits, and possible consequences. *Journal of the American Medical Association, 286*(21), 2711–2717.

7. Beauchamp, T. L., & Childress, J. F. (1994). *Principles of biomedical ethics*. New York: Oxford University Press.

8. Burris, S., Beletsky, L., Burleson, J., Case, P., & Lazzarini, Z. (2007). Do criminal laws influence HIV risk behavior? An empirical trial. *Arizona State Law Journal, 39*, 467–519.

9. Campo, J., Perea, M. A., de Romero, J., Cano, J., Hernando, V., & Bascones, A. (2006). Oral transmission of HIV, reality or fiction? *Oral Diseases, 12*, 219–228.

10. *Chaplinsky v. New Hampshire*, 315 U.S. 568 (1942).

11. Clark, C. (2005, October 16). County seen as especially vulnerable to pandemic. *San Diego Union-Tribune*, p. A1.

12. Cohen, J. (2005). HHS asks PNAS to pull bioterrorism paper. *Science, 308*, 1395.

13. Denniston, L. (2001, March 22). Drug test ruling backs pregnant women's privacy: High court barred program that gave results to police. *Boston Globe*. Retrieved November 12, 2008 from http://www.highbeam.com/doc/1P2-8635266.html.

14. DiGiovanni, C., Bowen, N., Ginsberg, M., & Giles, G. (2005). Quarantine stressing voluntary compliance. *Emerging Infectious Disease, 11*, 1178–1179. Retrieved August 12, 2008, from http://www/cdc/gov/ncidod/EID/vol11no11/05-0661.htm.

15. Downs, A. M., & De Vincenzi, I. (1996). Probability of heterosexual transmission of HIV, relationship to the number of unprotected sexual contacts. *Journal of AIDS, 11*, 388–395.

16. Eidson, W. (1990). Confusion, controversy, and quarantine: The Muncie smallpox epidemic of 1893. *Indiana Magazine of History, LXXXVI*, 374–398.

17. Federal Bureau of Investigation & Centers for Disease Control and Prevention. (2006). Criminal and epidemiological investigation handbook. Retrieved August 25, 2008, from http://ww2.cdc.gov/phlp/docs/CrimEpiHandbook2006.pdf.

18. Florida Statutes § 381.00315 (2002).

19. Flynn, J., Slovic, P., & Kunreuther, H. (Eds.). (2001). *Risk, media, and stigma: Understanding public challenges to modern science and technology*. London: Earthscan.

20. Gordis, L. (1991). Ethical and professional issues in the changing practice of epidemiology. *Journal of Clinical Epidemiology, 44*, 9S–13S.

21. Gostin, L. O. (2000). *Public health law: Power, duty, restraint*. Berkeley, California: University of California Press.

22. Gostin, L. O. (2003). When terrorism threatens health: How far are limitations on personal and economic liberties justified? *Florida Law Review, 55*, 1105–1170.

23. Greenberg, J. C. (2001, March 22). Drug tests banned for mom-to-be: Supreme Court says hospital's link to law enforcement to detect narcotics use violates the Constitution. *Contra Costa Times*, p. A12.

24. *Haitian Centers Council Inc. v. Sale*, 825 F. Supp. 1028, 1045 (E.D.N.Y. 1993).

25. Honssinger, C., Ianni, R., & Milsteen, J. (2005). The emerging role of state attorneys general in public health emergencies. *Journal of Law, Medicine, & Ethics, 33*, 115–118.

26. *In re Duran*, 769 A.2d 497 (Pa. Super. Ct. 2001).

27. Kass, N. (2001). An ethics framework for public health. *American Journal of Public Health, 91*(11), 1776–1782.

28.   Kontorovich, E. (2004). Liability rules for constitutional rights: The case for mass detentions. *Stanford Law Review, 55*, 755–833.

29.   Lane, C. (2001, March 22). Court rules against S.C. anti-drug tactic; Justices strike hospital's testing, at police behest, of nonconsenting pregnant women. *Washington Post*, p. A15.

30.   Lazzarini, Z., Bray, S., & Burris, S. (2002). Evaluating the impact of criminal laws on HIV risk behavior. *Journal of Law, Medicine, & Ethics, 30*, 239–252.

31.   Madziar, L. (2002). Comment, State v. Oakley: How much further will the courts go in trying to enforce child support? *Women's Rights Law Reporter, 24*, 65–82.

32.   Meikle, J. (2005, May 9). Law lets TB infect 12 others. *The Guardian*. Retrieved May 12, 2005, from http://society.guardian.co.uk/.

33.   Miller v. California, 413 U.S. 15 (1973).

34.   Minnesota Statutes § 12.39 (2003).

35.   Misrahi, J. J., Matthews, G. W., & Hoffman, R. E. (2003). Legal authorities for interventions during public health emergencies. In R. A. Goodman, M. A. Rothstein, R. E. Hoffman, W. Lopez, & G. W. Matthews (Eds.), *Law in public health practice* (pp. 195–210). New York: Oxford University Press.

36.   Moulton, A. D., Gottfried, R. N., Goodman, R. A., Murphy, A. M., & Rawson, R. D. (2003). Public health law: Preparedness practice and teaching: What is public health legal preparedness? *Journal of Law, Medicine, & Ethics, 31*, 672–682.

37.   O'Leary, N. P. (2006). Bioterrorism or avian influenza: California, The Model State Emergency Health Powers Act, and protecting civil liberties during a public health emergency. *California Western Law Review, 42*, 249–286.

38.   Philip Morris. (1986). *Great American smoker's kit*. (1986). Retrieved August 25, 2008, from http://legacy.library.ucsf.edu/tid/qim09a00/pdf.

39.   Poole, C., & Rothman, K. J. (1990). Epidemiologic science and public health policy. *Journal of Clinical Epidemiology, 43*, 1270.

40.   Posner, R. A. (2003). The truth about our liberties. In A. Etzioni & J. H. Marsh (Eds.), *Rights vs. safety after 9/11: America in the age of terrorism* (pp. 25–28). Lanham, MD: Rowman & Littlefield.

41.   Richards, E. P., & Rathbun, K. C. (1977). The legal basis for public health. In F. D. Scutchfield & C. W. Keck (Eds.), *Principles of public health practice* (pp. 42–54). Boston: Delmar Publishers.

42.   Rothman, K. J., & Poole, C. (1985). Science and policy making. *American Journal of Public Health, 75*, 340–341.

43.   Royce, R. A., Seña, A., Cates, W., & Cohen, M. S. (1997). Sexual transmission of HIV. *New England Journal of Medicine, 336*, 1072–1078.

44.   Schloendorff v. Society of New York Hospital, 105 N.E. 92 (1914), overruled on other grounds, Bing v. Thunig, 143 N.E.2d 3 (1957).

45.   Schwartz, S., & Costanzo, C. (1987). Compelling treatment in the community: Distorted doctrines and violated values. *Loyola of Los Angeles Law Review, 20*, 1329–1429.

46.   Scott, S. S. (1985, April 29). Smokers get a raw deal. *The New York Times*.

47.   Spector, H., & Simakis, A. (2001, July 22). Poor bear brunt of drug testing; Prenatal screenings jeopardize custody; Insured women rarely checked. *Plain Dealer*, p. A1.

48.   Vittinghoff, E., Douglas, J., Judon, F., McKiman, D., MacQueen, K., & Buchinder, S. P. (1999). Per-contact risk of human immunodeficiency virus transmission between sexual partners. *American Journal of Epidemiology, 150*, 306–311.

49. Wagner, D. (2007, May 30). ACLU files lawsuit against county for treatment of TB patient. *Arizona Republic*. Retrieved June 8, 2007, from http://www.azcentral.com/news/articles/0530tbguy0530.html.

50. Weed, D. L. (1994). Science, ethics guidelines, and advocacy. *Annals of Epidemiology*, 4(2), 166–171.

51. Wein, L. M. (2005, May 30). Got toxic milk? *The New York Times*, p. A15.

52. Wein, L. M., & Liu, Y. (2005). Analyzing a bioterror attack on the food supply: The case of botulinum toxin in milk. *Proceedings of the National Academy of Science, 102*, 9984–9989.

53. Wong Wai v. Williamson, 103 F.1 (N.D. Cal. 1900).

Index

Credits

Front Matter-Openers © Loren Rodgers/ShutterStock, Inc.; 1-Opener © zimmytws/ShutterStock, Inc.; 2-Opener © Andre Natel/ShutterStock, Inc.; 3-Opener © Brian A. Jackson/ShutterStock, Inc.; 4-Opener © Loren Rodgers/ShutterStock, Inc.; 5-Opener © Photos.com; 6-Opener; © Kuzma/ShutterStock, Inc.; 7-Opener © Cheryl Casey/ShutterStock, Inc.; 8-Opener © Leigh Prather/ShutterStock, Inc.; 9-Opener © kwest/ShutterStock, Inc.; End Matter-Openers © Loren Rodgers/ ShutterStock, Inc.

Unless otherwise indicated, all photographs and illustrations are under copyright of Jones and Bartlett Publishers, LLC.